Otto Poschacher

30 Years' Travels

Memoirs

Volume One

This book is dedicated to my family

Foreword

For many years I have concerned myself with the notion of writing this book. It ought to be a legacy for my children, grandchildren and other close relatives. From the beginning it was clear to me that it wouldn't be an easy task.

I had to ask myself regardless, what was the point in writing such a book? A difficult question. I could only realise a fulfilling purpose if I could at least have the quiet hope that my memoirs would also ultimately be read.

It was clear that a soulless and chronological catalogue of events would not achieve this goal, and I saw no reason for a lengthy and time consuming project if the result would go unnoticed in some discreet corners gathering dust, for me it seemed that that would be a squandering of the time and effort required to produce it. My memoirs ought to be read at least within the circles of my family.

And so I realised that there were two requirements that the book in any case had to fulfil:
Firstly a required style must be chosen, which would be considered more in keeping with the style of a novel than it would be as coldly descriptive.
Secondly: in spite of the aforementioned more novel-like nature, the events described, their persons and activities, must be in keeping with their true experiences and sentiments. I have endeavoured as far as possible to fulfil these key requirements. This was not always easy to realise, especially since during the first years of my life predominantly passive impressions and less active self-expression were able to prevail.

Thus I was careful to not simply render my experiences into written form in a dry and chronological manner, rather I endeavoured to present the accompanying feelings and to reconstruct discussions in such a way that they still held the meaning with which they had been intended, where due to the passage of time and memory these instances could not be remembered word for word.

I spent years in barracks, spent years travelling the land in service of the country, where you didn't always care for speaking the polite vocabulary of a good domestic upbringing. It would have been tantamount to a falsification of the situation's portrayal if I had attempted to change this speech into a politer form. It would have made the style and message alien.

So I can say in summary: The experiences took place as described, the dialogue retains, though it perhaps uses different words, the same meaning as the original. The persons were real and living, or live to a great extent still. In the book there are neither invented experiences nor fabricated persons. These are genuine memoirs in every regard.

Why do I end them with my 30th year, and the return home after the end of war? Well, in the time afterwards, my children and grandchildren intervened in the memories themselves - a civic life began, personal and professional without any great dramatic changes and no longer pertinent enough to produce an exciting story.

One thing I would like to add: These memoirs should also constitute an enrichment to the existing, substantial history of the Poschacher family. It is scarcely believable that such in-depth biographies are present on so many members of this Austrian family group.

Family research had a large part in encouraging me in the composition of this book.

I would like to use the foreword of this book to express my special thanks to Franz Poschacher, in St. Peter-Freienstein in Styria. He sacrificed many hours bringing me closer to the history of our family, provided me with documents which I would have never come into the possession of without his selfless help. I consider it self-evident and as a small diminishment of my debt that I dedicate a copy of my memoirs to him as thanks for all his efforts.

In conclusion I would also like to beseech the reader to kindly turn a blind eye to the mistakes and sometimes handwritten corrections. I could not enlist a qualified editor, as is available to every novelist before publication, the costs for that would have been too high in consideration of the few copies to be made.

And so may the book make its way through these few pairs of interested hands, in the hope that the accounts are interesting enough to persevere to the end.

Ennepetal, Christmas 1982

Otto Poschacher

If you travel north from Zell am See in the direction of Saalfelden, only a few kilometers behind Zell am See there lies the little old market town of Maishofen on the road to the right. A place which has barely changed for centuries and only learnt something of modernity with the waves of holiday-makers that came at the beginning of the 60's.

On the edge of the town here, where the collections of little houses and homesteads merge with the open fields, there stands an old farm house. It is the house I was born in and the house of my mother's parents. As one of the oldest farmhouses of Pinzgau it is under historic conservation. Unfortunately the residence has been occupied by strangers for years and the care of the property leaves much to be desired.

Over sixty years had to go past before I, soon an old man myself, could cross the threshold of that house again with my brother Hans.

Many old memories were woken with this visit to the house of my birth and the plan arose to write down the most important sections of my life chronologically.

My mother had four sisters and one brother. I can't remember much of my grandparents but they must have been very kind and good-natured people. Although the grandparents were kept very busy as farming folk, their daughters would still bring them a few illegitimate children into the household. Three of these children were brought up in this house, amongst them was also my brother Hans.
When my mother brought me into the world as well, 6 years after my brother Hans, the good nature and hospitality of my grandparents was probably exhausted. There was no more room

for me in the house and so paid foster parents had to be found for the little mite.

These foster parents were found in the Exenberger family, in Kössen in north Tyrol. Under which circumstances my mother decided on the Exenbergers I don't know. What is notable is that the Exenbergers were also farm workers and were already in advanced years as I was taken into their care. It could be that a good acquaintance with my grandparents in Maishofen played a role in the situation.

My first lucid childhood memories were formed in the Exenberger house. Kössen today is a significant market town on the border between North Tyrol and Bavaria with an absolutely enormous influx of tourists.

Back then, a good sixty years ago, the place was still very small and the town centre wasn't made up of shops, workshops and tourist resorts like today, rather farmhouses in the old Tyrolean style. Back then there were three guesthouses, whereas today there are fourteen that well serve the many holidaymakers.

The Exenberger residence stood in the middle of the town, with the entrance directly in front of the church square. On the house there was a stable arranged and also a large barn with a threshing floor, from which you had a direct exit into the surrounding fields. On the other side of the square opposite the entrance of the house stood a large, beautiful guest house. Back then the building seemed huge in its proportions and from out of the Exenberger's house window I could see the amply decorated gable up into the distantly protruding roof ridge, up to the sparrows who were always chirping loudly and holding their associated squabbles. Yet more farmhouses stood in a semi-circle around the church and the guest house so that the two buildings were completely closed in, with the exception of the access road from the South.

The place of worship was surrounded entirely by a high wall which even enclosed the graveyard.

I must have been around three years old back then. Soldiers were billeted in the barn. Austrian Kaiserjäger who were off duty here. From out of the house window I watched their drills in the marketplace excitedly.

A particularly large, bearded soldier with many laces and bobbles on his uniform clearly didn't like the rest. Whenever he let his thundering voice roar out over the square, the others began to run about wildly in all directions terrified of him. In general they ran about a lot and performed all sorts of contortions which I couldn't make sense of. It was really pointless how often men changed direction while running, they clearly didn't know where they were going, they turned around in circles and kept falling over. They evidently weren't as old as I'd thought. So much of their caper and carrying on was completely incomprehensible to me.

One event from this has particularly stuck in my memory.

One day I was again marvelling at their manoeuvres from out of the window. They stood in three rows in the square directly in front of me. The great big beard marched up and down in front of them and bellowed at once as loud as he could. Suddenly in terror the entire first row fell down onto their stomachs, they lay there and didn't move, as if they were dead. The second row was still standing however, they didn't fall over, they clearly weren't as scared. I waited excitedly to see if they wouldn't still fall down after all, but no, they stood still, as still as a mouse. A cheeky sparrow hopped along the front towards a huge cowpat and pecked around on the ground nearby to it. I just saw this cowpat that lay there on the square in front of the men.

Again came the loud roaring of the man with the beard. This time the second row trembled as well, but they didn't fall over completely, rather they just knelt down. And then, I watched with shock as one of the men knelt in the middle of the thick, fat cowpat. Where his knee shoved the excrement to the side it shimmered a light green inside. And again the roaring, but the third row weren't too bothered, they just lifted up their weapons and aimed at our house. The rifles all had little round holes at the front, with which they often aimed at our house, but nothing ever came out of the little black hole. Then the kneeling and lying soldiers were allowed to stand up again. With that the fat, squelching half cowpat fell from the knee of one man, but otherwise nothing happened. They walked off all of a sudden and into our barn behind the house. So that was the story of the cowpat. I've never forgotten that image for as long as I've lived. In later years I also understood the conduct of the men which had seemed so meaningless to me at the time. I had to take part in this sort of thing myself later, but even when I was older this activity had never seemed particularly useful to me.

The soldiers stayed in our barn for a long time. Many went, but new soldiers always came to replace them. They brought me some change. Midday they would sit all around the threshing floor, each had a metal bowl out of which he spooned up his dinner. So I would get a few mouthfuls with them as well. When they shovelled their spoonfuls of polenta into my mouth, they must have surely thought of their own children, who at the same time were in some lonely mountain home spooning in their own meagre midday meal with their mother, thinking of their absent fathers.

On Sundays the church square was full of people. If I stood on the cosy wooden bench on the periphery I could see across the whole church square. The men had hats, pitch black with long curved white cock's plumes. The women wore black stiff brimmed hats ornamented with gold edging and two dark velvet ribbons that went over the back reaching almost to the hem of their skirts. The whole morning was a busy hustle and bustle. Horse drawn carriages came and went and on particular days the music marched past dressed in gaudy colours.

The way across the graveyard was always frightening for me. The graves were lined up around the church, surrounded by the high churchyard wall. Behind the church the graveyard was completed by a crypt. Here on wooden frames, cleanly stacked and numbered, lay the dead skulls of many generations. Sometimes there were hardly any teeth left, other skulls still had the full set of teeth. When we passed the crypt, I must have squeezed the hand of my foster mother or of Papa Exenberger particularly tightly. I was always happy once we had the graveyard wall behind us. The dark eye sockets of the bleached skulls gave me the creeps.

Sometimes on Sundays Papa Exenberger took me with him on a walk along the road south up towards the Tyrolean Aache. A wooden bridge with a high wooden parapet on either side and a fitted roof led across the river. On the bridge Papa lifted me up high and I could look deep down into the swiftly rushing, gurgling water. Back then it all seemed so vast, savage and formidable. Just behind the bridge at the fork of the road stood an inn. We'd make a quick stop here and if Papa Exenberger was in a particularly good mood, I'd get an Einspänner, so a single sausage. But for me it was a real treat when I was allowed to drink from his beer tankard. From the shores of the Aache, you had a fantastic view of the "Wilden Kaiser," an imposing mountain range.
So I spent my days until my fifth year in the care of the kindly Exenbergers.

All of a sudden my memories end here before starting up far away again. I have no recollection of the events in the wake of which I had to leave Kössen and these kindly foster carers. A new phase in my life began.

My time on the Osterburg estate.

One day my mother probably remembered that far away in Tyrol there lived a little boy, who actually belonged to her.

Mother had remarried in the meantime, named herself "Malzer" now and lived with her husband in Groß-Sierning near St.Pölten in Lower Austria. Somehow they had little Otto bundled off from Kössen to Groß-Sierning.

My stepfather Malzer was employed here on the Osterburg farm as a milker. The farm was named after some castle ruins nearby, the aforementioned Osterburg. At the time I was there the ruins still had rooms that could have been considered liveable in a meagre sort of way, and sometimes there were prisoners from the Stein prison institute who were housed there, they were made to work in the fields in Osterburg.

I don't know how I got to Osterburg but I can still feel today, almost physically, the deep homesickness that tormented me back then. My mother, my stepfather, my surroundings, everything was alien to me. A short distance from Osterburg the street was crossed by a small stream. I often stood on the lower parapets, looked down at the calmly streaming water, and asked myself whether that water flowed on to Kössen too. Back then I had no idea how far away from there I was.

I hung around the castle ruins a lot in those times. The old masonry seemed both grisly and mysterious at the same time. The steep, towering walls frightened me but still pulled me in like a magnet. The way to the castle seemed like a long way to me then, in reality it was only around 100 meters. When the sun went down and darkness set in, hordes of bats flew from the ruins, that too was both eerie and exciting simultaneously.

For my sensibilities the Osterburg property was huge. Swathes of women and men were permanently employed there. With its stables, barns, tool sheds and servant rooms it enclosed a large rectangle within which there was a pigeon coop and a well. Our dwelling consisted of just one big room that had to serve as a living room, a kitchen and a bedroom all at once. Playtime opportunities in these surroundings were of course manifold, yet I never felt a sense of wellbeing at Osterburg, that great homesickness for Kössen, for my Exenberger parents always stayed with me.

Malzer had a very violent temper and very little self control. Myself, my mother, my brother Hans and even the poor livestock were often reminded of this. A war wound from the First World War may well have contributed to it. Malzer had been shot in the head and the bullet had never been removed. Every day, my stepfather had to take the fresh milk from the estate up to the dairy in Groß-Sierning with a horse drawn carriage. During such a journey there was a particularly nasty incident. I was sitting next to Malzer on the coach box, holding myself desperately tight as always because I was petrified of Malzer's unpredictable driving and I was in a constant state of terror when I had to travel with him. We were a way past the ruins when Malzer strayed from the street with the carriage, the horse panicked and the wagon and the heavy milk cans tipped over. Luckily, the full milk cans were much heavier and so fell quicker than we did. One of those milk cans could have hit me. Since both my mother and Malzer were kept busy on the estate I had a lot of free time and could prowl around the property and surrounding area to my heart's content. One day Malzer travelled with me to St.Pölten. There I was given some Lederhosen on the assumption that leather was the best and most sturdy material for me. But my stepfather hadn't reckoned with my acumen in executing more complicated and gymnastic movements. In front of the estate a small shed had been built that had a tiled roof which went all the way down to the ground on one side. For the inauguration of my new Lederhosen I saw this roof as the perfect slide. But this brilliant notion made for better theory than practice. In some places this roof had such sharp edges that even the new Lederhosen weren't prepared for them. The bottom was ripped open, and spending hours covering the wounded area with my hand didn't help either, disaster quickly caught up with me. I got a good thrashing then, something which was given out lavishly in Osterburg.

At around the same time both my brother and myself came out in a rash. We were taken to the hospital in St.Pölten. While a hospital visit isn't generally a pleasant affair, those days were a great time for me. I had my own white, comfortable bed, a small cupboard for my few possessions, I thought it was great lying there and I didn't feel homesick at all. Every morning we were brought downstairs into the cellar, stripped naked, sat on a wooden shelf and dabbed from head to toe with a brown mixture. After this procedure we looked like Negroes, of whose existence I at that time still had no idea. After being successfully dabbed down we were wrapped in sheets and brought back to bed.

The rash healed, I was healthy again and one day Malzer brought me back to Osterburg. It was early evening when we returned. I had to go straight to bed, but I couldn't sleep for excitement. I missed the hospital, the white bed and the nice cupboard. With Malzer again, I could see the stove and the table directly from my bed. Behind the stove stood a water tank on which there was a zinc bowl which mother always used to wash the dishes. And so I was lying in bed when a furious argument broke out between mother and Malzer. I don't know what it was about, I just know that I was very anxious about it and was hiding ever deeper beneath the covers with my heart pounding. After those pleasant days in the hospital I found everything back home to be horrible. The room in which we dwelt, the bed, none of it as nice as it had been in the hospital and then this violent squabble which absolutely terrified me. With the Exenbergers I had never experienced an argument before. All of this commotion was no doubt due to me wetting the bed at night and then the next day immediately began with a fight.

At Osterburg I had to go to school for the first time in Groß-Sierning. I can remember neither the first day of school nor the school itself, but I can remember very well the evening classes with Malzer which I had afterward. Sadly I only have bad memories of Malzer from this time. His violent temper was constant and consumed me with panic whenever I had to be alone in a room with him. In the afternoons when the stables didn't need him as a milker he took the time to plough reading and arithmetic into me. Then Malzer would sit opposite me at the table, a small cane in his hand. I barely dared to look up, my heart hammered in my throat, letters and cane blurred together into a hostile monster. The cane which abruptly struck at my fingers wasn't even the worst, the baleful presence of Malzer alone was an incessant terror.

At this time another brother of mine, Walter, was born. His life was very short however, and he died not long after birth.

It was a small funeral procession that travelled from the estate to the graveyard in Sierning. Malzer at the head of it, a small white wooden coffin in his arm, behind them my mother, my brother Hans and myself.

After every darkest night there comes the dawn, and just as suddenly the menacing Osterburg vanished from my life. Some vague memories remained of a time that left behind more darkness than happiness. But even these months are a part of my life, and are an integral part of the whole, a branch in the wide reaching boughs of the varied memories I have.

Again there was a beginning and preparation for a change into a distant and ambiguous unknown. My consciousness awoke again as I stood at the station with my mother in St.Johann in Tyrol. I have no recollections of the parting in Osterburg, of Malzer, of my brother Hans, no memories of the journey itself, nothing apart from suddenly standing at the train station in a town next to my mother. Up until this moment in time my memories have had a few gaps that simply couldn't be filled in.

The station in St Johann however is a point after which the rest of my life has remained almost completely intact in memory. Even if I sometimes cannot remember some details, the big picture is from this point on always whole. My memoirs can now continue without forgotten details and without forgotten intervals of time.

I don't know if I was aware of it already at the station, but what is not to be overlooked is that St. Johann is in Tyrol, not far away from Kössen, the source of my homesickness and those lovely old people whom I had locked so tightly in my heart.

In Kössen lots of things had changed in the meantime. The Exenbergers had sold their farm and settled down nearby in

Niederachen. Sadly they hadn't reckoned with the instable conditions of these first years after the war. There was inflation, the entirety of their cash, seen as providing a carefree old age, was lost overnight.

It must have been a serious blow for the old people, to lose the wealth of an entire life's work overnight and to suddenly stand there totally impoverished in their old age. Papa Exenberger was forced, in his elderly days, after decades of work as an independent farmer to earn his bread as a day labourer. For him there was neither a pension, nor any other kind of assistance. Under these circumstances the Exenbergers were still very happy to raise me, provided there was a little money to pay for board.

It was completely different circumstances which I now came upon in Kössen. At the time of my arrival Papa Exenberger was working as a manual labourer for the river control of the Tyrolean Aache. Every day he had a long distance to cover to get to his work in the wide-ranging wetlands of the Aache. We lived in the house of a dress-maker. The dwelling was very small, and contained only a bedroom, kitchen and a storage chamber. A creaking wooden stair lead up to us in the upper floor.

A very frugal but nevertheless wonderful time began for me. Although my meals were meagre, my clothes more than humble, I again had the father to whom I felt an infinite trust and a deep affection. Even Mama Exenberger was, although a little stricter, of a profoundly good nature.

But though the times were also hard, the meals sparse, the whole lifestyle more than simple, I was happy and didn't care much for the overall miseries of the day.

It was a time of real famine, particularly for the people in the cities. In the country opportunities to get foodstuffs were a little better. Back then Mama Exenberger often went across the countryside and, if school permitted it, I would be allowed to accompany her. I scuttered around after her, over stock and stone up to the remote farms of the vale. Mama had a small wicker basket on her arm, half filled with straw chaff, careful packaging for the eggs that she hoped to get hold of. On her back she wore an old greasy rucksack for flour, eventually butter and whatever else there was to squirrel away. As Mama was known everywhere as a former farmer, she could always rely on the sympathy of the well disposed farmer's wives.

During this time we hoarded anything that was vaguely edible. Whether it was fresh nettle leaves for the soup, or wild caraway seeds from the meadows of the Alps for seasoning, everything was carefully taken home. I picked every attainable kind of bloom of dead nettle. I laid them out to dry on the floor. When dried they barely grew any more, but they could be taken to the chemist, and you would get a few kreutzer for them. For the most part we ate polenta, a staple made from cornmeal.

The winter in Kössen was always very long, snowy and bitterly cold. It often snowed so much that the wooden fences couldn't be seen from either side of the street. In spring, when the sun shone during the day and the nights were bitterly cold the snowy fields were frozen so hard that we could go over them on sleds.

In Kössen I now continued my school attendance which I'd begun in Groß-Sierning. I had a lot of trouble with earache at this time. In our school class on one wall there stood a large green tiled stove with a wide wooden bench around it. If the pain became particularly unbearable, I was allowed to leave my school chair and sit down on the stove bench. Then I lay my ear on the warm tiles and I felt it gave me relief. Whether it was the right cure for my ears I don't know, the treatment was pleasant and our teacher didn't know any better.

I believe that at that time I had already developed a very good talent as a storyteller. Our religion teacher, also a curate at the parish church, made us familiar with the old and new testaments. When he had finished his talk, I had to go to him at the front. Then he would sit me down on top of his desk, because I was still so small and everyone needed to see me, and I would have to retell the stories. I did so with great pride and a pious expression. Unfortunately I can't say much about my strengths in other subjects, as there are no written reports to be found any more.

Sundays were always lovely. Then I would go to the church very proudly holding Papa Exenberger by the hand. Exenberger had his dark suit on, in which he seemed very formal to me, particularly because he was very big and had a considerable appearance. In a good mood as he always was, he stuck a red carnation in his button hole and we marched off. When we got to Kössen I went into the church. Papa stayed with the many other men outside in the church square. They stood there then in many groups and caught up on all the news. They surely knew the priest's sermon by heart and when the clock struck for the holy sacrament they took their hats off outside and stopped speaking for a few minutes. The women however were all in the church. Once the first women left the church the men started up for the surrounding inns.

I swelled with more than a little pride when I was allowed to accompany Papa into the inn and was allowed to slurp at the foamy contents of his beer mug.

As the winter slowly came to an end, as the March sun became warmer and began to melt the remaining snowfields,

Palm Sunday approached. This Sunday shortly before Easter was a particular celebration for us children. Palm fronds as big as branches were cut, decorated with colourful paper and sometimes even with apples and nuts hung on them. These colourful formations were then proudly brought to the church. They were erected in front of the altar and the priest would sprinkle everything with holy water, our faces too sometimes. Afterwards the fronds would be given a place of honour in the lounges of the farmhouses until they withered and had to be taken away. They were often a decoration for many weeks.

In that year I took a (for my understanding at least) particularly beautiful, large and colourfully decorated palm frond to church. After the blessing I walked back home proudly. Many churchgoers could now wonder at me and my wonderfully coloured figure appropriately.

When I was on my way home across the Aache bridge, a stupid idea pulled me down to the shore. I marvelled for a while at the rushing water, the waves that were hopping from stone to stone, the little whirlpools that were constantly spinning in their circles. Then I put my so beautifully decorated palm frond into the water and was pleased at how it wasn't able to tear the branch from my firmly clutching hands. I was so immersed in this deed that I only heard all of the angry cries from the bridge too late. Good Lord! The parapet was awash with women wildly gesticulating and cursing, while the men who were there were behaving a little less agitatedly. I was suddenly very afraid. I hurriedly pulled my palm frond out of the water and ran far away across the countryside. After a while, as the people were leaving the bridge, I quickly ran the rest of the way home under my little legs.

But Mama Exenberger had already long been informed of my sacrilegious deed. I got a good scolding, since in my excitement I'd completely forgotten that my palm frond was holy and it was a sin to simply stick it in the Aache.

With the spring approaching, the frogs in a nearby pond came to life. There was a vast number in the small stretch of water. One day I had the brave idea to catch some of these croakers and put them in the soup pot. I swiftly got to work with a classmate from school. We made a trap out of willow rods and old scraps of cloth and the rest wasn't all that difficult. I don't know today where I got the courage from to kill the frogs, cut off their hind legs, skin them and make them ready for Mama Exenberger's soup pot. But I still remember that I did it. The soup didn't taste bad although I wouldn't eat it today let alone would I manage to repeat all of the preparation I just described.

The summer slowly came into the countryside. The daily trek to school became pleasant. After so many successive rain-free days the water level of the Aache became so low that in numerous places we could wade through the shallow waters. We threw flat stones over the reflective surface and counted the jumps that they made. We roamed through the fields and took all kinds of detours in order to take full enjoyment of our freedom.

Maria, the Exenberger's daughter, had married and lived close nearby in a little old house in the upper floor. A long straight wooden stairway led the outer wall up to her residence. Her husband was a trained cobbler and had his own workshop in the house. On weekends I was allowed to clean the workshop and got my supper for it.

I had another important side business too though. Near the bridge at a fork in the street there stood an old village inn with a farm attached. In the wide ranging pastures during summer I would often tend to the cows for the owner. In the evening when I brought the livestock back to the stable, I'd get a hot sausage and a bread roll as a reward. This sausage was the highest of all delicacies that could be imagined. I wolfed it down immediately at a huge wooden table in the large kitchen. Maybe I still like eating sausages so much today because of this time. After all the taste of this sausage is tied to the memory of my first paid work.

At one time during the summer Papa Exenberger was employed in a farm far away helping with the harvest. He stayed the night with these farmers and didn't come home for a long time. One afternoon after school had finished, the yearning for my father overcame me in such a way that I didn't go home, rather my legs moved in the direction of the farm. I knew the way, I often went that way with Mama Exenberger finding food, but mother couldn't have known that I'd be overcome with yearning for Papa and would follow the same route to get to him. It was a long treck of at least a few hours.

It was early evening when I reached the farmhouse. In the main room many men and women were sitting around a huge table and eating their supper. No doubt everyone at the table was astonished. For Papa in particular it was probably no small surprise. But I don't think that a bad word passed his lips, as his affection for me was no smaller than mine for him. But what should he do? Mother knew nothing of my running away, there was no telephone, so he took me by the hand and on that same evening we went the way back to Kössen. Very early on the next day I had barely fallen asleep before Papa had to go all that way back again to his workplace.

It was a beautiful summer, in this year nineteen hundred and twenty four. The holidays had started, and there was a lot of time to enjoy.

In these weeks I often went with my school friends to a nearby meadow in the Alps. You could get there in half an hour, an ancient alpine dairy maid worked there for the whole summer. We had it in for this old bag. On the one hand we were afraid of her, on the other hand that fear was still not so great that we couldn't have our fun with her. We approached the way up, cautious of the meadow, we mostly saw her in front of the huts working somewhere. She washed the milk buckets in the well or chopped firewood, during which she'd speak to herself constantly. The sun shone on her straggly, greasy hair, her clothes were tattered and dirty, her skin wrinkled and grey and you couldn't tell whether she ever washed herself at all. Hidden behind trees, we watched her work for a while and snickered at her and her entire appearance.

After we had watched her for a while, we cautiously stalked nearer, but always behind the cover of trees. When we had gotten close enough unnoticed, we dashed suddenly out to the open space just before the well and shouted at the top of our lungs "...old witch! Old witch!" and then at the same time tore off as fast as we could. Before we reached the wood we jeered her again and disappeared behind the trees. A furious caterwauling echoed after us, but after our feat we sauntered back to the valley cheerfully.

Those holidays were so beautiful, but sadly they couldn't last forever. As I was living a carefree existence, a storm was brewing overhead.

A summer day like the rest! It was nearly evening. I was sitting on the stair in front of our house and carving a stick of wood with a pocketknife. A large man approached me and asked, "Do the Exenbergers live here?" When I replied in the affirmative he inquired further, "So, you're Otti?" With that he climbed the stairs into the house. I didn't follow the stranger, how could I even know what this visit would mean for me.

After a while Maria, who had just been visiting Mama, came out of the door. She had been crying. She stroked me lovingly over my hair as she passed, but said nothing, rather she left quickly.

I remained sitting down in the doorway until Mama Exenberger called me. As I entered the kitchen, the stranger was sitting at the table and watching me with curiosity. Papa Exenberger stood at the window, his back was turned to me, and he didn't move.

"This is your father!" these words, suddenly spoken by Mama, hit me like I'd been punched. "Things will be good with him, better than here with us," she continued, words that seemed so very far away for me. I looked at Papa Exenberger distraught, but he still stood at the window and didn't look at me. But it couldn't be, I went up to him, took his hand and looked at him desperately. He squeezed my hand tightly, but he couldn't speak. In a few minutes my whole world had been turned upside down. Even Mama had moist eyes, she was busying herself at the stove, making coffee for this stranger....who's now supposed to be my father.

A lot of things were probably said to me that day, but all the kind words couldn't relieve my pain, the earth had been taken from beneath my feet.

The stranger, whom I suddenly had to call "father," stayed in the village inn overnight. On the next day he went with me to Kössen, I was supposed to get some new clothes for the long journey.

As we were crossing the bridge over the Aache, he asked me, "Well lad, what's this river called?" I answered shyly and in the best vocabulary of which I was capable... "This river is named the Aache," to which I got the answer, "Here lad, ye don't need to talk that pompous with me sure..."

In Kössen we went to the only store there was in the town at the time and I got a sailor suit. No doubt under different circumstances the strangeness of it all would have been immeasurable, but at that moment it was all the same to me. Father still looked at my shoes disparagingly, they were a couple of sizes too big for me, he shook his head, but nothing could be done about it at the time. Back then shoes still had to be finished by a cobbler and that could only be done over a few days. So I got a few little things like a new shirt and stockings, and with that the shopping was ended and we went back home.

Back with the Exenbergers again, Mama was standing in the hall in front of a big wooden chest and looking out the few possessions that I had. When I saw this I started to howl and cry again. Even Maria was crying while Mama was helping to gather up my modest equipment.

I was able to sleep in Kössen for one more night. But on the next day I was finally to take my leave. A small consolation was that Papa Exenberger was going to accompany us for some of the way. We went in the direction of the Bavarian border which ran a few kilometers north-east of Kössen.

Father didn't want to go the long way around St. Johann in Tyrol, Zell am See and Bischofshofen, instead he wanted to take me across the Bavarian border directly to Salzburg, but this border crossing wasn't legal.

And so we strolled across the large, forested mountain ridges, through meadows and fields towards Bavaria. We already had the border behind us and were coming out of the woods into an open meadow, in the middle of which there stood one of the many barns scattered around. As we approached the barn, a border patrol officer suddenly came out and our crooked border crossing was finished. He wasn't unfriendly but he was assertive when he made us go back. The venture was over. That day we had to go back to Kössen. To my great pleasure, but sadly only for the one evening and one night.

The next day brought many tears and our last goodbye. I went with father in a horse and cart off to St. Johann, the nearest train station. A particular source of grief was that Papa Exenberger wasn't there for my leaving. He had had to get up very early in the morning and go and help out at a farm far away. Perhaps he had wanted to go part of the way with us again.

Soon Kössen vanished from view and all my sadness couldn't help me anymore. I had to start a new life again, without Kössen and the loving, kindly old Exenbergers. An overnight journey took us by train over Zell am See, Bischofshofen and Salzburg. Onward in the direction of Linz until Attnang-Puchheim. Here we had to change over to a slow train that took us on a half hour long journey to Holzleithen am Hausruck.

Here the journey by train came to an end. Now it was just a tight half hour walk to Hausruckedt, my new home to which I walked with father.

Shy, tired, deeply saddened and racked with home sickness I trotted along after my father. We went along between the tracks of a railway. After half an hour, on the right hand side the houses of Hausruckedt appeared along the forest edge. A long row, each house like the others, a miner's settlement on the edge of the Hausruck forest. We arrived at my new home. My father ran an inn here. As we reached the house my new mother was standing in front of the door, she was young and very pretty... The third woman whom I was to now call my "mother." Kössen lay far behind me, I would never see Papa and Mama Exenberger again although after many years I saw Maria, their daughter, once more.

The years in Hausruckedt.

Autumn 1924 - Autumn 1926

And so I arrived safely in my new home. I couldn't cope with all of the new impressions which besieged me in those first few days. Even just a few days after my arrival, all of the aunts from Hausruckedt, Holzleithen and Bruckmühl came around to visit. I was examined and passed around for everyone to inspect. The assessment wasn't universally positive. For my age I was still a little gaunt, on the whole still quite small, somewhat pale and very shy. But this wee lad was slotted into a pair of shoes that were big and crude enough to last him until he finished school. It was real, solid, Tyrolean craftsmanship. For my new mother that seemed to be going a bit too far though, so one day after my arrival I went to Herr Brettbacher the cobbler, who had his workshop in a little house at the edge of the town. Since the holidays were soon finished and I had to register to start school in Bruckmühl, there wasn't much time to lose.

As I arrived in Hausruckedt the son of mother's sister, Schorsch, was spending his holidays with my new parents. I would have had a playmate in him for the first few days, but Schorsch was lying in bed with swaddled feet. Behind the house there was a large, walled ash-pit. Kitchen scraps, but also red hot ashes from the big stove were thrown in there. The ashes would glow all day and a shroud of smoke would rise from the pit constantly. While playing with other boys, Schorsch went over the rim of the wall, slipped, and the end result was burned feet. After a few days, Schorsch was collected by his father and taken back home.

As well as mother and father, we also had father's father, my new grandfather. He was already over 80 years old and had his pipe in his mouth all day. You couldn't picture grandfather without his pipe. He was very good-natured, but he could neither read nor write. If post ever came for him, which happened only rarely, mother had to read everything aloud to him.

Both father and grandfather were very keen hunters only that grandfather was no longer as active as he'd been before, he more often just told tales of his hunting.

The whole of Hausruckedt was a mining settlement. The houses stood in a long stretching row, but they all looked the same and the layout of the rooms was all the same. The whole settlement was built by the mining industry and the houses were rented out.

Each house had two apartments. The only front door in the middle led straight into a large kitchen which was shared between both of the apartments. To the left and right of the kitchen on each side there was a rather large living room and then the solitary bedrooms thereafter. There was neither a cellar, nor a bath, nor a toilet in the house. To satisfy these urges there were little separate outhouses built out of simple wooden planks, airy and cool, particularly in winter. There was a shared bakery and a large shared well around the middle of the row of houses.

This well was constantly mobbed and was a shared meeting place for the women to have a chat, for the men that was our inn. But the water from the well was always running water and it tasted very good.

We on the other hand had a somewhat longer double house in the settlement for ourselves. For rooms there was a pub lounge, a side room, the bar, a kitchen, a tiny little bedroom for grandfather, the parent's room and within that room there was my bed in a little alcove. Behind our house there was the storage room, a little wooden building which was a much loved playroom for the many mice that we had in spite of our cat Peter. Next to the storage room we were also the only household to have our own well. Then there was also the ash pit, that wily wooden hoosie and then two more wooden sheds for the pigs and chickens. There was also a bigger, roomier wooden shed too.

Subsequent to our rooms in the house there was a little cooperative with a storeroom. The large loft wasn't fully converted, only a wooden shack formed the servant girl's bedroom. In the summer it was swelteringly hot in the loft and the wasp nests - their round, grey sacks, hung in spades from the rafters.

The road went past in front of the house and on the other side of the street was our pub garden. It was cool in summer and well shaded by a row of old chestnut trees. A picket fence surrounded the garden and a long wooden bowling alley was connected to it. If there were customers in the garden, the parents had to always cross the street to serve them. On Sundays in summer when it was very busy a good few kilometers had to be run back and forth altogether from the bar, through the pub lounge, across the street, into the garden and back. On top of this the ground in the beer garden was covered with rough gravel which didn't make those journeys any more comfortable.

Our beer cellar was particularly nice and snug. It was behind the house in an open mine shaft. The entrance was kept closed with a sturdy wooden lattice. A narrow track led around 200 meters into the mountain to a wider opening where our beer kegs were. A little transport wagon with a motor called "the dog" served to move the beer kegs back and forth. You couldn't imagine a better storage place for beer. Water dripped steadily from all the walls and it was always a constant, and in my father's opinion perfect, temperature for the beer.

Just behind the house a slope went up, there were a few plum trees here and a little further where the slope flattened out again there was a vegetable garden. After that there was the forest which spanned many kilometers.

Soon time had softened most of my homesickness and I timidly made my first acquaintances with other boys and girls. My new shoes had been finished but were only kept for going to school, my father thought that the old ones were good enough for mucking about in. I had already made best friends with the cobbler's son. One day, as we were exploring my new surroundings further we came to a large open clay court. On it there stood a sports hall. Built from wooden planks, painted with tar, it made a very gloomy impression. We went through the open door and were astonished by what we saw inside.

I had never seen all the kinds of gymnastic equipment that was there. I didn't know my horse from my parallel bars, my climbing frame from my high bar, it was all Greek to me. A wooden crate was full of magnesium. With it you could paint your hands and face, we figured that out very quickly. So we made our hands nice and white, powdered our faces heartily and played joyfully like kings of winter as we surveyed one another's snowy appearance. But we came to yet another idea that would have more severe repercussions. We started to use the magnesium to paint all of the gymnastic equipment and we did so thoroughly. We thought it all looked much more sprightly now, not so dismal and monotone any more.
Since we were so engrossed in our work we didn't notice that we had had another group of children watching us for a good while.

The group ran out of the hall shouting at us and threatening us as they headed in the direction of the town.

Well now we got scared and we began to wonder if there would be consequences to our actions.
In our artistic zeal this idea hadn't occurred to us before.

And so we led a somewhat panicked campaign to clean everything down again. The cobbler's progeny crept to the edge of the forest in order to escape the site of our feat unseen. But I wasn't able to hide like that. I had to go straight through the settlement back to our house. From the cursing of some of the women and from how they were shaking their fists at me it was clear, that tales of my misdemeanour had already made their way around the town.

Arriving shortly before our house, just in front of the pub garden the coal train that travels from Wolfsegg to Holzleithen stopped, it always brought the miners back from the early shift at midday. At that moment I saw my father with his still blackened face and his miner's lamp in his hand stepping off of the train. He had barely gotten one foot on the ground before he was surrounded by the children that had seen us in the sports hall.

Oh dear! A bitter afternoon followed afterward. One strike from father's gigantic hand was enough to just about set the seat of my trousers on fire. But father and mother were clearly surprised that they could expect such high jinks from this shy boy who supposedly couldn't count to three. It wasn't a good impression that I'd made.

The holidays came to an end. Now I had to get up at six in the morning and go to school in Bruckmühl. Mother was still sleeping then, while father was long on his way to the pit. Our servant girl heated my milk for me, smeared butter on my bread

and sent me on my way to school.
I had my new shoes on and was more than a little proud of them.

The way to school was long. First it went down towards the valley past a few scattered houses, a butcher, a grocer, then on between the meadows to a collection of some farmhouses. Then ever gently downward on a path to a little farming village. Here the somewhat wider street coming in from Holzleithen flowed into a quite narrow route which went past many fruit trees and past a graveyard to Bruckmühl.

But we didn't always take this general route to school. Particularly in the summer we went over across the pastures of a beautiful brook along a shortcut to Bruckmühl. The farmers didn't like that mind you, but since their own sons would take that path, they couldn't chase us off for it either.

At the school I managed to get along with things without too much trouble. So the school in Kössen couldn't have been all that bad. While in Kössen there were two classes, in Bruckmühl there were four. I liked going to school, I actually felt more at ease there than I did at home. We had a teacher who was very fond of me. I remember one lunch break she darned my uniform together again, when I had torn it during some scuffle.

I was able to continue my talent for storytelling here which I'd picked up in Kössen. Our religion teacher, a Franciscan priest, still young and very tall was very well liked by us. He made a very imposing impression with his long brown robe and the white cord around his body, doubled over and still long enough to reach down almost to the floor. In both summer and winter he wore sandals, in summer without and in winter with thick, hand knit socks.

This priest could convey the stories from the holy book in a very dramatic, indeed almost thrilling manner. Whenever he spoke there was only absolute silence and we hung onto his every word. With his arms crossed, both hands buried deep in the folds of his robes, he always went up and down between the rows. I had to repeat his tales afterward, though I no longer needed to sit on his desk.

Sometimes when the father was lecturing us, a lizard would crawl out of one of his sleeves, creep up the arm of his robe, and with a hurried movement would disappear again like a bolt of lightning into his wide cuff.

We had a break time at lunch, since we also had lessons in the afternoon, and so I would often go to visit Aunt Luise. She lived on the edge of Bruckmühl. Her house stood on a steep slope and a long, creaking wooden stairway led up towards her entrance. Around her house she had a large fruit garden and in autumn in the house she always had a long row of plates laid out on which she had different kinds of finely cut fruit laid out to dry. She baked these into the most wonderful fruit bread in winter. I would have loved to steal some but she really didn't like that. One lunchtime I was there when she left the kitchen for a moment, I used the opportunity to stuff my pockets full to the brim. But I didn't have the time to fix the gaps I'd left on the plates before she came back into the kitchen. I wanted to leave as quick as I could, but all of a sudden she grabbed me by my legs, lifted me up and slowly let me slide down again. This forced all of the dried fruits and slices of apple back out of my pockets. Everything rolled out onto the floor. She didn't say a word, but my face burned red and I left her house in a hurry. A week later my mother knew of my misdemeanour as well and then I really got something to complain about.

Father was, much to the annoyance of mother, a very ardent hunter. Just like grandfather who was no longer so able to yield to this passion now though, because he was over eighty. Mother always said that all the hours which father spent hunting could be better spent around the house. But with father it went in one ear and out the other.

Often still in the pitch darkness of night he would make his way to his hunting ground. For months he would sit there without a shot being fired. Then mother's patience would run out and there would be a big family row, but that didn't bother father much. If it ever got too uncomfortable for him he would stick his massive hand into a hundred box of cigarettes, stick around thirty of them into his pocket and head off into the woods. When he came back hours later most of his rage, though perhaps not mother's, had been smoked away.

Grandfather didn't involve himself in any of that. He would sit in front of the house on a wooden bench, puff on his pipe, chat with all of the passers by and be content. Grandfather was a very peculiar person.

We had ants in the kitchen sideboard almost the whole year round. They would be taken in with the sugar and then couldn't be driven out again. Mother always had to wipe the pests out of her coffee cups before using them. Grandfather never bothered. The tiny ants that swam in his cup didn't bother him in the slightest. What effect could these tiny beasts have on his guts anyway?

Grandfather shot the last bearded vulture in Kobernauserwald and he was always boasting about it. When he spoke with father about hunting, then they always did it better back in his day and of course they shot better then too.

A hunt for the old gentlemen was held one day in late autumn. It was a hunt for small game. Sadly this hunt ended in embarrassment for grandfather. They didn't shoot down any game at all, not even a hare. Grandfather came back defeated and wouldn't come out to the lounge for days because he couldn't handle the customers' teasing.

Winter slowly came into the countryside. Hausruckedt was a particular snow trap in my time. You could expect the first snow any time after All Saints Day. For the most part this first snow was very abundant already. Now the sledges would be taken out and the skis, where present, would be made ready. Whoever had skis was really someone special, I didn't have any. But in front of the entrance to our beer cellar there was an old must keg whose iron fastenings were coming apart and whose staves were easy to crack off. Two of these keg fastenings ought to be a good pair of skis for me. One end was cut down a bit, a few leather straps were used to fasten my shoes to them and then the whole marvel was complete. Ski poles were quickly found, and baskets for them weren't needed.

With this primitive equipment my first adventures in the Alps began. Of course I couldn't cope with steep slopes yet, especially since the tips weren't bent up enough. The result of the first few days was more of a forward somersault, but I was very actively involved with the ski sports of the Alps. A year later I received a pair of skis made from ash, made straight from the wheelwright and I was more than a little proud of these, and using them gave me a totally new feeling when skiing.

Of course the winter also brought many hours where I was stuck inside the house. I spent most of this time in the kitchen. We didn't have a living room where I could finish my homework undisturbed or pursue any other hobby.

After the lounge the kitchen was the busiest room in the whole house. What wasn't all done in here! People would cook for themselves and eat here, people would prepare meals for the customers here, grandfather would sit around here when the bad weather had imprisoned him inside, people would wash here, would iron and every act of personal care would take place here in the kitchen. If mother or father wanted to take a bath in the big wooden washtub I had to leave the kitchen and find a corner in the lounge for a while. The German shepherd Rex and the black cat Peter lay in the kitchen. Mother would busy herself there at the stove and the servant girl would run back and forth. Father came in, took the meals out to the customers and brought the dirty dishes back. A tiny corner at the window was left over for me.

I would do my homework here, which nobody took the time to supervise, which certainly didn't bother me. I would passionately finish my watercolour paintings here. Since father was a hunter, my motifs were mostly deer that were just stepping out of the forest into the sunny meadow, there were hares and pheasants and all kinds of small game too. Hansl Brettbacher would often sit near me and we would draw and paint together. We had three double-glazed windows in the kitchen. One of them was often closed over winter, we trapped ants between the panes, which we let go again in the spring. Back then we didn't even have any electric lights. Every day we had to fill up the carbide lamps again, of course they didn't produce a particularly bright light and as they were burning a somewhat pungent, curious smell arose which was difficult to describe.

Our German Shepherd Rex was an exceedingly alert and intelligent animal. If mother needed meat, she wrote her needs on a note, put the piece of paper in a large bag and Rex would already be sitting at attention. With the bag held tightly in his mouth, he would go around five hundred meters down towards the valley to the butcher. Rex would only let the butcher take the bag in order to fill it with the goods that had been ordered. He would bring the bag back obediently, more than a little proud of his work. Woe to the stranger who tried to take the bag from him while he was on his way. And what a feat of willpower for the dog, to resist the smell of meat from the bag.

It was shortly before Christmas. The holidays had begun and snow had been falling for days. It already lay a meter high in the garden and all of the roads were deeply snowed in. Along the entire settlement there lay just a well trodden down track a half meter thick. Mother was missing a few important groceries which weren't to be found in our little cooperative. So I wanted to go to Bruckmühl and get them for her. Mother had concerns due to the heavy snowfall and the strong winds which had already blown snowdrifts across the settlement for the whole day.

The store in Bruckmühl belonged to a Jewish family and we were very valued there as good customers. When I got to Bruckmühl I bought the items which mother had written down for me neatly and finely. I was about to tie up the rucksack again, when Herr Berger came to me with a little package. I wasn't supposed to open it until I got home, then give it to mother. Incidentally this Jewish family were taken to a concentration camp during the Second World War, where all of them perished without exception, good people who fell victim to an insanity.

The storm had grown considerably stronger as I left the store and made my way back. Long snowdrifts came against me on the road. They brought the cold snow up to my throat and made it difficult to breathe. In many places meter high snow cornices were blocking the street. No wagons, no sledges were to be seen far and wide. People stayed in their houses and prepared themselves for the holidays. More and more the storm came against me, it blew fine ice crystals into my face, and tried to blow me off my feet. From time to time I turned my back against the wind in order to take a rest.

I stumbled onward like this, my eyes half closed, my mouth pursed tight, my hands stuffed under my armpits. Despite my woollen gloves my fingers were stiff with the cold. The wind penetrated every pore of my clothing. I had my woollen hat pulled down as far as my neck, I pushed my chin into the woollen collar of my jacket. I went through the little farming town. The storm wasn't as strong between the houses but it blasted me furiously again once I had the last houses behind me. Now I reached a long, raised, open space. Almost nothing more could be seen of the course of the road here. The wind was blasting me from the side now and was making my ears numb. More and more often I had to take a rest and slowly my heart sank, especially since there was nobody to be seen far and wide. I was still around two kilometers from Hausruckedt now, but the road only went upwards now and I kept getting more tired.

It had also become later in the afternoon in the meantime. In normal weather vision would have surely remained good for another hour, but in this snowstorm darkness was setting in early.

Suddenly a large dark shadow appeared in front of me, which was quickly coming towards me. Finally a human being I thought, and my trepidation immediately awoke a new zeal to stay strong for the last leg of the journey.

Once I met the figure, I recognised father, who came up to me with Rex strained in front of the sledge. Now all urgency had passed of course and I sat on the sledge for the last leg home. While on the one hand I was happy that father had come to meet me, on the other hand I was sad that I hadn't been allowed to make the adventure all the way back home myself, it would have much pleased my vanity. In the package that the shopkeeper had given me there were wooden building blocks, colourfully painted, which in a couple of days time would be lying on the Christmas table next to me.

We always ate our lunch late at our place, since we had to wait for father to come home from his early shift. I wasn't a picky lad, so I ate pretty much everything apart from fatty meat and roast mutton. Mother was an outstanding cook and most things tasted delicious for me. But father had no understanding for me not liking the taste of these few things. He thought that whatever was on the table had to be eaten. And the more father would insist on it, the more those morsels would get literally stuck in my throat. I would chew despairingly for a few minutes until even mother had a sympathetic face, but father would remain unyielding.
But if father looked away for just a second, I'd quickly spit my food out into my hand and stuff the half eaten meat paste into my trouser pocket. Afterwards I'd head out to our wooden outhouse and dispose of the evidence. And so there you had the reason behind my constantly greasy trouser pockets, I emptied them in the toilet after dinner.

On the whole, life together with mother and father wasn't bad. There would rarely be any domestic arguments but, as in a thousand other marriages, they did of course happen.

If mother had had a quarrel with father after all, then you could see from her eyes that she'd been crying and she'd not want the customers to see her like that and so a strange problem would arise. After an argument mother would only stay in the kitchen. If it was late in the evening and there wasn't anything more to do in the kitchen she would of course want to go to bed. Father would then have to finish up with the customers.

Now the only way to the bedroom was through the lounge and that's where mother didn't want to go through. In this case my help was needed. I would go through the lounge and into our bedroom, mother would slip through the bar out to the yard. She went round the house, in order to not be seen she carefully crept past the entrance to the restaurant and up to the bedroom. In the meantime I had opened the window from the inside and mother would sneak into her own bedroom like a thief.

Mother wasn't very strict with me in general. If I'd done something, she wouldn't always tell father, since she didn't always agree with how severe he was herself. Mother's punishment was that she wouldn't speak with me for days and that was the worst punishment of them all for me. In order to make peace with her I'd tidy up all the drawers in the kitchen and the bar, haul wood and water into the kitchen without having been asked to. This diligence of mine sometimes helped to reconcile her sooner.

But around this time there was even more unexpected fuss for me.

Once again, my biological mother had the surprising intention to take me into her care. As I discovered in later years, my father had made constant payments to my mother, including during the time when I was in Kössen, only mother had regularly neglected to forward this money on to my foster parents. After my father had taken me, these payments from him were of course brought to an end.

So now the dispute over my custody went off, over money. My mother wanted to have me again so that my father was obligated to make payments again. I had to travel several times with my father to the county town in Vöcklabruck. I was asked in court again and again whether I wanted to stay with father or mother. I always started wailing straight away and made it clear that under no circumstances did I want to be separated from my father. Each of these court appearances was such an awful upset for me since I was never sure that I wouldn't have to go back to Malzer again.

For a whole year these debates about staying with my father raged on. Until one day the court came to the conclusive decision that I was allowed to stay with my father. When we were in the Vöcklabruck courts about this for the last time, father had to exit the courtroom for a short while and I was insistently asked as to who I wanted to have custody of me again in his absence. My tears were the deciding factor. I was allowed to stay with father. After the trial we went into an inn and I got a Doppelspänner-Wiener and a Kaiser roll.

The winter passed, the meadows grew yellow with thousands of cowslips. The spring rolled into the countryside and it became a time of games in the woods and the meadows. Each day we were happy even just going on our way to school. Even on the roadways we could fool around everywhere, no cars were on them just a horse and cart or a cyclist from time to time. If we ever saw an aeroplane in the sky the whole town ran out to see it.

The spring was followed by a swelteringly hot summer. We played cops and robbers in the surrounding forests, we cut swords and shields from wood and had heated battles with the lads from Holzleithen. Our imaginations were inspired by the pictures from the packets of Kathreiners-Malzkaffee. We hunted after wasp nests on the ground on the edge of the woods. We filled empty bottles with carbide and a little bit of water, corked the bottles well and buried them next to the nests in the soil. With a loud bang the nests went up in the air. The startled animals buzzed around in a blind fury. But we cleared off as quickly as our legs would carry us.

One Sunday we were again involved in this exciting adventure. The sun was burning down from the sky. On the edge of the forest it hummed and buzzed with wasps, bees, bumblebees and robber flies. We had sought out a particularly large wasp's nest for our blasting operations. We carefully buried the bottle almost as deep as its neck, all the while bothered by the insects which were growing ever more agitated.
After the ensuing bang we scarpered like lighting in all directions. Or rather I wanted to. But I was stopped by a very thorny bramble branch. With my good Sunday trousers on I remained stuck in the undergrowth and fell over. Now I wasn't able to get out in time before the first wasps attacked me. I lashed out wildly, but that only made them even angrier. I ran over stock and stone as though my life depended on it, the wasps chased after me hungry for vengeance.

When I finally got far enough away from them and found safety, I had three stings in my cheeks and one in my hand. The stings on my face hurt the most. I got flabby cheeks like a hamster with his mouth stuffed for winter. When I got home looking like this grandfather could hardly breathe for laughing, mother yelled at me for my torn Sunday trousers, father went as if to hit me, but after seeing the injuries I'd already gotten he decided to let me off. I had had enough of wasp hunting for the next few weeks.

We had rats in our pig stall, the cheekiest kind of rats. You would have barely put the pigswill in the trough before they ran out of their holes and joined in with the meal, before you'd even left the stall. Every so often this circus grew to be too much for grandfather. Then he'd let the pigs out of the stall into a little grid, take a chair from the pub garden, take his shotgun from the gun cabinet and take up residence in the pen.

There was an ear-deafening bang as he fired a shot in the little stall. Afterwards, the remnants of a rat would be spread all over the wall of the pen and we had peace for a while. And so on occasion grandfather was still able to indulge in his passion for hunting.

In the early summer, still before the school holidays, the parish fair took place in Bruckmühl. Next to Christmas, it was the highlight of the year for us children. I had the afternoon free on Sundays then and I charged off so that I wouldn't miss a single precious minute.

That year Uncle Lois, the brother of my new mother, had just come to visit. Later in the afternoon I was supposed to accompany him to the train in Holzleithen and so mother thought that I could do without the parish fair this once. But I cried and threw a great tantrum. In the end I was allowed to go to Bruckmühl, on the condition that I had to return at a specific time later in the afternoon in order to accompany my uncle to the station.

I ran off with fifty groschen for two rounds on the carousel and one serving of Turkish delight held tightly in my fist. I ran the whole way so that I wouldn't waste a single precious second. I reached Bruckmühl completely out of breath.

Well you certainly can't judge a parish fair from 50 years ago by today's standards.

Apart from a few stands with the usual funfair junk, the "dicken Berta" missing most of her bottom half, the "billigen Jakob," the carousel and the man with the Turkish delight, there wasn't much around. The sums of money that we were able to wrangle from our parents for these amusements were also correspondingly modest.

I squeezed around through the festively dressed farmers and their wives, the farmhands and the girls, went round on the carousel twice and contentedly slurped down the Turkish delight.

All the other attractions were outwith my financial capabilities. So I went round for the twentieth, the thirtieth time, wiped my nose with the back of my hand and found no end to the wonder I saw.

I was especially taken in by one old woman's stand, she was fat and chubby cheeked and was offering her treasures for sale in a loud voice.

There were colourful wax flowers, little straw hats with feathers in the most garish colours, scarves and gingerbread hearts. There were handkerchiefs and sugared pretzels, a row of large glasses were filled with candy treats. But what I was admiring most of all was a bundle of long candy canes in the most vivid colours. I had never seen candy canes that size before. I shyly asked the old lady how much they cost, but sadly they were outwith the limits of what little I had left. My hand desperately clasped the last lonely groschen in my trouser pocket. I kept coming back to this stand, to this wonder of the big candy canes. They pulled me in like a magnet.

The afternoon flew past. I didn't hear the warning toll of the clock tower, I forgot the world around me and all of my mother's warnings to return home in time. The Turkish delight had long been guzzled, I was still a little ill from the carousel, but apart from that I was in seventh heaven.

The evening came, the paths between the stands slowly emptied. The children had long since returned home, the men had moved into the two inns with their wives.

But I was still strolling from stand to stand. And again and again I ended up with the woman with the oh so big, so gorgeous candy canes.
Even when the old lady began to pack away her treasures into the paper cartons she'd brought with her, I couldn't pull myself away.

"Well little boy? No doubt you're eyeing those candy canes aren't you?" I couldn't lie, my covetous looks were answer enough.

"Well listen here you little rascal," her bony hand grabbed my jacket sleeve, "if you help me to pack everything away, and if you help me after that and push the cart down to the station, then I'll give you the longest and loveliest candy cane that I have!"

She didn't need to tell me twice. Now I wouldn't just be gazing at these treasures, no, I would be able to hold one in my hand and that was bliss in the supreme.

It was growing dark already as I got cracking with the old lady and we went down the bumpy road towards the station. The train station was a good 45 minutes away by foot, and in the opposite direction from my parent's house.

It was pitch dark when I arrived at the station with the old woman. All of the lanterns were burning already at the station and the few travellers were probably gazing at the little whippersnapper strained in front of the cart at so late an hour.

The old woman rummaged around in her messy leather bag for a while and, for sure, brought out the loveliest and most gorgeous candy cane I'd seen.

The old lady had kept her word and I covetously stretched my hand out for the treasure.

"Well then little one, you nip off home now, no doubt you'll get a hot backside for this, I hope the candy will somewhat sweeten the thrashing you'll be getting."

I barely had the promised reward in my little fist before I tore off. How my mother was going to marvel at this gorgeous candy cane.

Of course, the closer I got home, the less convinced I became that mother's anger would be so easy to placate. Fear was rising in me the closer I got back and was making my heart pound.
When I arrived home after a breathless run, I avoided the front entrance, mindful of my father's powerful hand, I wanted to creep through the bar and into the kitchen and deal with mother first. An awful racket came towards me from out of the lounge, a fight was clearly underway.
My plan to go in through the kitchen unseen collapsed like a house of cards. I hadn't counted on the innkeeper, who just so happened to be my father.

Sadly I ran straight into father's arms. He was already in a contentious mood now because of the scrap that was going on between his customers. He didn't say a word for now rather he quickly gave me a clap around the ears as in passing, but a clap around the ears that was a real bruiser. A thousand stars danced in front of my eyes, the candy cane leapt from my hand and flew between the beer glasses and since father was busy at the bar I didn't have the opportunity to seek it back out of there again.

I immediately fled into the kitchen first. Mother was standing there in front of a bowl of water and cooling the swollen black eye she'd gotten from one of the customer's elbows as she'd tried to mediate in the scuffle. When I saw that, I sped off as fast as I could again, wangled my way past the chaos in the lounge and crept into bed without any supper. I howled all of my anguish into my pillow and was already afraid of the next day.

And so the parish fair ended as anything but happy for me. The next morning I got a proper beating from father, mother wouldn't deign to look at me. What annoyed me most of all was that over the next few days father chewed up the delicious candy cane piece by piece. Oh well, he always liked sweets.

I quickly got over father's clap around the ears and the hiding I got from him the day after, much worse was that mother wouldn't speak a word to me for days. That was the cruellest punishment.

At the time of the parish fair in Bruckmühl there was a sports festival in the town for the worker's sports clubs around Hausruckedt. Hausruckedt was the only place in the vicinity that had a sports hall, if somewhat primitive. After the athletes' performance we always concluded with a festive celebration in our restaurant. Things went well for a few hours, but once the beer consumption had exceeded a certain level, the great athletic camaraderie was over and things degenerated into a big fight where the sparks were flying, in this case the sparks were beer mugs, chairs, ashtrays, and generally anything we had in the room that wasn't bolted down. There were a few customers like Aunt Olga's husband who rarely came to visit, but who were always available for a good fight.

After some time, once father had managed to clear out the ruffians, which he wasn't exactly squeamish about doing either, the fight was continued on the street and along the settlement. Slats were ripped up from the fence around the beer garden and were cheerfully used to pummel each another.

After a fight like this, my parents always went to Ried im Innkreis afterward. They had loads of lids for the beer mugs in their luggage along with the remains of broken mugs in all different sizes. They would always get these turned into new glass mugs again in a specialist store.
At our place all the regulars had their own beer mugs made from porcelain or glass with beautiful hunting motifs and a monogram, and each of them had a lid. Some of the mugs even had porcelain number tags. Those were father's beer mugs, otherwise the customers brought their own mugs which father just kept for them in constant safekeeping.

The miners were very jolly, song-loving people and the majority of the time things were also very jovial in our inn, especially when the local men from Hausruckedt were there. Amongst them were also a number of men who came from Czechoslovakia. They were particularly prone to singing and merriness. The women only accompanied their husbands very rarely, they had enough to do with their households and their on average very numerous children.

A trader with a hawker tray came once every year. He'd been coming for years, was well known to my parents and was allowed to sleep on the bench in the lounge for a night. It was a lot of fun when he was there. He had a lot of news to tell, we had more customers in the evening and the man came at his own expense.

One Sunday, in my second year of school at Bruckmühl, I was presented to Communion. After the end of the festivities, we stood in front of the church in sailor suits, knee long trousers, black woollen stockings and ankle high shoes, standing in front of that huge wooden box draped with black for a group photograph.

I had been sent to the church alone. My parents weren't fond of going to church. The Franciscan priest didn't drink beer at our place and so father didn't feel he was obliged to go to theirs.

Nevertheless I was well liked by our religion teacher and so the honour was granted to me to be trimmed into an altar boy. The priest was insightful enough to only have me take part in this service on a Sunday in light of the distance I had to travel from Hausruckedt. When father learned of the dignity of my new position he just said mockingly, "You'll soon be a priest eh."

The training to become an altar boy didn't last long but I still had to learn a lot for it. I was really impressed with the red and white gown we wore when we came out to Mass and I really felt like I was almost like a priest. We always performed the service in pairs. I had to memorise the whole mass process. It was important to ring the altar bell at just the right time so that I didn't spill the water into the communion cup before the wine, and that I brought the censer to the priest at the right moment. I felt that the handing over of the wine was absolutely the high point of the service. Then I would climb up the two long red altar steps with the tray and both silver plated jugs, my eyes directed to the floor chastely, conscious of my dignity. First I filled wine into the opposing cup while the priest held it very still, but when

I came with the water he'd hurriedly pull the cup upwards, who'd want to water down the valuable wine? During the sacristy there was the wafer, the bread of the Mass, in a tin can, but the wine was kept in the vicarage just to be safe.

In our house one day I discovered an old bicycle hidden under a pile of junk in the attic corner. It couldn't have been used for years.

I wouldn't give mother any peace now. She had to get father to fix the bike for me. He took a rather dim view of the job. But when mother wanted him to do something nice for me for once she could be persistent too.

In a foul mood and holding a grudge against me, father began working on the bike. I wanted to watch him while he repaired it at first, but he frightened me away soon enough with the fierce looks he was giving me and the blasphemous swearing when things didn't work. Soon nearly all of the bike was in the bin. The rubber tubes had to be patched, the valve sterns had to be replaced and the handlebars would face in every direction apart from straight forward. But once air was finally staying in the tyres (after gratuitous cursing) and once both wheels were turning (if still somewhat stubbornly), father set the vehicle in front of the door, washed his hands, took his gun from the cupboard and went away into the woods to let off some steam.

I should also point out that by this time I had already gained some experience riding a bike with my friend Hansl Brettbacher's bicycle, and so I wasn't a complete novice anymore.

And so I took the bike that had been repaired with so much fatherly rage and proudly cycled around the settlement like a king in his castle. Even the bell worked, I rang it as I went, I wanted everyone in the town to see me, lots of folk looked at me in wonder. A little whippersnapper as I was I couldn't reach the pedals from the saddle, and so I cycled as all small boys do, with one leg through the framework, standing on the pedals with my upper body bent over, shaped like a question mark. I pedalled like heck, so I thought at least, at least forwards, the bends were still causing me trouble.

I had already pedalled up and down the town a few times and thought I was ready to head out a little further. I wanted to cycle a good part of the way to Bruckmühl.

The street from our beer garden went steep straight down and I wasn't brave enough to cycle that way. So I turned sharply while braking tightly. But the back wheel didn't like this and tried to head off to the side. I didn't exactly look heroic skidding downhill. I squinted to the settlement constantly, but thank God nobody saw me.

I pedalled faster once I reached a straight path. The road was mine alone, no cart was coming. I came to the scattered farmhouses and cycled past them briskly and spiritedly.

The track became steeper once I had the farmhouses behind me. I didn't want to stop now though, especially since some girls from my school class were coming towards me. My ride into the valley quickly got faster and faster. I hurtled past the wide-eyed girls like the wind, I got cocky and proud but I got afraid as well, I couldn't control my speed anymore. You can't control the brakes as well standing on the pedals as you can sitting in the saddle.

I approached a long stretching right hand bend after which the slope took a while to level out. As I was tearing towards the bend my eyes were transfixed on the left curbside, here the slope declined slightly and went over a meadow. Since I couldn't brake while in freewheel I braked the front wheel as best as I could.

Now I was really beginning to struggle, I was carried off of the curve at great speed, flying down the little incline towards the meadow. A wooden post suddenly obstructed the path of my front wheel. The entire back end of the bicycle reared itself up and I flew in a high arc into the meadow. I landed in lushly growing hemlocks. My head was quite dottled. I felt over all of my reachable body parts but it seemed everything was healthy and unbroken. I got myself up, but the sight of my proud bicycle turned my stomach.

My marvel lay there in all her misery. Totally bent, the spokes of the front wheel standing wildly in the air, the wheel itself buckled completely, the handlebars wrecked. Another ride was unthinkable. Miserable, close to tears, I took the bent remains just behind the handlebars on my weakened shoulder and pulled it along the way, the back wheel still turning. The girls were still standing in the distance and were doubled over with laughter.

My journey back with the remnants of what had only minutes ago been called a "bicycle" was worse than miserable. Everyone grinned unashamedly as they passed me. The way back was almost constantly uphill until I reached home. I often had to stop and gather my strength again even though all I really wanted to do was crawl into the nearest hole and hide.

Mother was appalled when she saw me coming home like this, even grandfather shook his head sympathetically and held back the mockery he usually had on the tip of his tongue.
Once father came home from hunting and saw the wreckage, in a fury he took hold of all the remains and threw them back into the attic, stuffing it in a corner. In the next years no more was said of

bicycles.

We slaughtered livestock twice a year. I hated those days like no other during the time I was in Hausruckedt. They were full of chaos and like that from morning till evening. When I saw father whetting the long knife, I would feel sick in view of what awaited me in the next hours. I hated this butchery, I could happily smoke out a wasp's nest but there was no blood in that after all.

This year the slaughter was to be particularly gruesome. Even in the pig pen there was an unholy racket. The pig we'd picked just wouldn't go to the gallows. Father had it by both ears and was pulling it out of the stall. The pig was bracing itself against him with all of its strength and came out with a murderous scream that chilled you to the bone.

But as much as the pig fought back, father was as strong as a bear. He hauled her up to the well, seized her suddenly under her belly and threw her onto a long wooden trough that had fallen over.

Mother and grandfather had to hold the flailing animal down tightly, I stood trembling nearby, a metal bowl and a wooden mixing spoon in my hands.

As soon as father slit the pig's throat with the knife I was supposed to hold the bowl underneath and catch all of the blood, stirring it as it streamed out.

This time, father seemed to miss with his first stab and only a little blood came out. The pig suddenly made a frenzied roll to the side, fell off of the trough and made a run for it, squealing at the top of her voice. Terrified of her approaching death she flew around the corner of the house and through the open door directly into the cooperative. Father stormed after her cursing loudly, mother and grandfather followed screaming and shouting.

There was an unholy racket and shouting in the cooperative, which was very small and furthermore was cluttered with rice, grains, sugar and who knows what else in sacks. The sales lady, father, mother and grandfather screamed and shouted, the pig squealed at the top of her lungs and knocked over whatever was in her way.

Mother tried to calm the sales woman down, father cursed that mother and grandfather hadn't held the pig down tightly enough. When amongst other things the pig knocked over the sack of rice with her rollicking about, she slipped on the grains scattered across the floor and plopped down on her backside. Father took advantage of this moment. He threw himself at the animal with all his strength, took a hold of its ears with one hand, with his other hand he grabbed its tail and dragged it out of the shop.

Amidst all the shouting and cursing the pig was finally brought back to the trough.
Father sliced her again, I was stirring in the bowl like crazy. The rising vapour from the warm blood made me sick to my stomach. I nearly fainted in anguish. But the more blood that flowed, the calmer the pig became.
Once she was dead, father bathed her in boiling water in the trough and then all of us shaved her clean together.

Then came all of the dissection, the elaborate sausage-making. For days the kitchen was consumed with such a ruckus that I didn't know where to go. And everyone was flustered and grumbling over the smallest detail. I was always overjoyed once these days were over and normal life returned. The freshly cooked black pudding didn't taste bad but if I thought on my role stirring the blood my stomach turned.

In our class there was a nice blond girl, the daughter of Holzleithen's railway coordinator. I've forgotten her name, but it's not that important to the story anyway. She was my first great love. I dreamed of her, I tried everything to get her attention. I strove to be close to her. I suddenly grew vain and took great care of my appearance. During breaktimes I sought to be close to her and wanted her to see me as well. I often asked mother if there wasn't anything she needed from Holzleithen that I could get for her. I'd return home sad if I didn't see the girl when I went there. Our schoolmates soon realised my interest in her and started to tease me and the girl. That didn't bother me much, but my love interest was of a different opinion and she started to avoid me. Yet the flames of my love simmered on.

But suddenly this romance was ended. This girl had a brother at our school who was two years ahead. My youthful longing for his sister surely came to his notice too, thanks to the constant innuendo of our peers.

This lad had something against me. He clearly wasn't comfortable with the idea of me as a brother-in-law. In any case, for a few days he waylaid me on the way to school a short distance before Bruckmühl. He made me understand his dislike of me in a very forceful way. Since he was older, bigger and much stronger than me, my defence of my beloved was quite pitiful. He went alongside me, said nothing, gave me a quick right hook a quick left hook, a headbutt, a kick on the back side and shoved me into the ditch.

After he had carried out this treatment for a few days and had really softened me up, he thought surely now my yearning for his sister would be somewhat cooled and he left me alone again. After such rough treatment of course, the buds of romance didn't come into bloom. The fire was put out just as quickly as it had ignited. I regarded her with contempt from now on and went my own way richer from the experience.

One day I went with mother to Wels where her parents and the majority of her siblings lived.

They had been thinking about me again. They had decided to provide me with a more upscale education. Of course in Bruckmühl that wasn't possible. Again I would be leaving home and sent on as an emigrant.

Mother's parents lived in Wels, her brother Lois who I had stood up during his visit to Hausruckedt, (why did he have to come on the day of the parish fair anyway?) There was also Uncle Franz, he was married and had a son, Toni, who was around a year older than me. Auntie Kathi lived there as well in the parent's house with her oddball husband Max, but shortly after this visit she left him. Yet another sister whose name I've forgotten. These were mother's relatives in Wels, it wasn't all of them, others lived scattered around Austria, but I'll come to that later.

Our visit was mainly meant for Uncle Franz. He was a railwayman by trade and lived in a beautiful villa in a back road near to the coast of the river Enns.

I don't know what was all negotiated about me, but Uncle Franz wasn't unkind to me and neither was his somewhat sturdy wife. In any case mother was in agreement with him. I would live with them from autumn and study at the Volksschule for a year and cross over to a higher school later.

After the deal had been done we visited the grandparents and then travelled back home. I looked on the new change of location with very mixed feelings at first, but since there were still a few months to go yet I forgot these concerns again for now and got on with daily life.

— . —

A little down the way from our settlement there lived a hermit,.. or at least we called him that... in his tiny little house on a levelled spot of a former coal yard. The man looked somewhat feral with a wild, straggly beard and ragged clothes. He bothered nobody, but didn't seek anyone's company either.

I don't know how I came to know this man. His age was difficult to guess, his tiny residence consisted of only the one room. There was a time when I came around to visit him in his hut very often. That was with good reason. The man had travelled across the world widely in his youth, he could tell fantastically exciting stories and in me he had an attentive listener. Different from the other people in the settlement. They avoided him, they didn't have anything in common with him nor he with them. Even though he looked very run down he was in fact very well read and educated. He had a number of books from Africa and South America with wonderful drawings of the landscape and the wildlife.

Mother didn't like it when I visited this man in his house, she was afraid that I would take back all kinds of pests from his place. What else was there to get? At that time there were fleas in every family, even in the so called more civilised circles. Cockroaches were in every house that had a brick oven. I don't think you can keep bugs out of the house, then there were clothing lice and head lice, they were even more problematic.

And so I took the books back home with me and I couldn't read the exciting stories and expeditions often enough. With adventurous excitement I gobbled up all of the stories of the countries and the people along with the strange wildlife. When I showed the pictures to mother she gave the book a really foul look and said that all of the brown spots adorning some of the pages came from squished lice and bugs. I found that very exaggerated and completely without any basis of proof.

I didn't let mother's scathing comments spoil my enjoyment of the books. Until then I had no idea of what wonderful landscapes existed outwith my local area and what adventures you could experience.

But one day, the man had disappeared from the settlement. His shack was empty, the few possessions cleared out, which sadly included his books as well. Nobody knew where the man had gone, but I had lost something close to a friend.

− . −

The summer came with great weather. After school we went through the meadows towards the stream. On the way we stole the unripe summer apples from the trees and made ourselves comfortable at a wide pond. The magnificent old alder trees gave us the excellent protection from prying eyes that we needed.
Here where the water was almost completely still and was warmed by the burning sun we took off all of our clothes and got up to all kinds of mischief.

On one such day there were three of us, all boys from Hausruckedt, we were at loggerheads with the lads from the town again. As always we were having a real blast in the water. We splashed each other from top to bottom, skimmed stones over the waves, caught leeches that we tried to stick on each other's bellies and searched for little crabs under the rocks at the shore.

Suddenly, over the meadow, we saw a farmer running towards us with his cane swinging alongside him. He must have seen us as we were stealing apples or the lads from the town had tattled on us.

We tore out of the water like a bolt of lightning, we didn't have time to put our clothes on. We bundled them under our arms and sped off across the meadows towards Hausruckedt, naked as the day we were born.

The farmer clearly didn't want to get his feet wet, so he stayed on his side of the stream, threatened us and shouted the coarsest swear words after us. At a safe distance, we got into a row and mooned him with our bare bottoms. Protected behind a hedgerow we calmly put our clothes on and strolled back to the settlement. But we cautiously avoided the little farming village that lay on our way to school for the next few days.

— . —

Summer had reached its peak. The second big school holiday since my stay with the parents began. Along with it came my leaving the school in Bruckmühl itself as well. But first there were the long holidays. There were weeks of more freedom and games in the fields and forests.

One time I was allowed to go hunting with father early in the morning. Full of excitement I trotted after him quietly, I knew that you had to not make a noise, not talk and move around cautiously. I must have done these things well because father had nothing to criticise.

I sat next to father on a hunters perch as still as a mouse, it was unbelievably exciting although on the whole not much happened and I was already really disappointed with the long amount of time spent waiting. Then father gave me a sign and whispered to me.. "Do you see them coming out there?" He pointed in the direction but, despite my best efforts, I saw nothing....I looked and still saw nothing.... it seemed that being a hunter wasn't so simple after all, father's impatience was clear to see, it's difficult for an experienced hunter to recognise that unpracticed eyes need longer to detect things which, thanks to the years of sharpened senses he had acquired, seemed obvious to him. Father often had men from the mineworks as guests hunting with him, often it didn't work out any better with them. He had to correct some of their missed shots with a quick shot himself in order to keep the guest's supposed "hunter's luck." It wasn't easy for father to leave things to other people, but he had to consider business in his approach here as well.

I may not have taken on my father's passion for hunting, but at least I inherited his love of nature. As far back as I can remember an especially close, loving relationship with nature was always an important factor. I always loved to wander through the forests and open fields alertly and observantly. I would have only too happily chosen a profession that went along with these interests.

Unfortunately in the years where my choice of profession took place it was exceedingly difficult to find the job you wanted and with that I mean to find a position as an apprentice in that profession. It was the time of a great economic crisis and you could thank God if you were able to find an apprenticeship position at all. As well as that, the parents took a much greater, more decisive influence on their children's profession back then.

My ideal would have been to become a teacher. My misfortune was that this profession was one of the worst paid of my time. Even the prestige of the role wasn't all that great either. Since there was also a long and more expensive education bound up with this wish, I wasn't able to go to my parents with this idea. "You'll be well paid if you get a good trade," father said constantly.

The summer holidays came to an end. We wrote the year as one-thousand-nine-hundred-and-twenty-six. I was now eleven and a half years old and a new change of location, a new phase of my life would be bound up with it.

– . –

The years in Wels.

September 1926-April 1930

    We prepared for my relocation to Wels. I enjoyed the last
beautiful days in Hausruckedt. I thought of the new changes with
a bit of trepidation. It wasn't just getting used to new people, no,
it was always a complete change of arrangements in every sense.
The surroundings, sleeping, eating, daily routine everything
changed and I had to get used to it all anew. It was already the
fourth big relocation that I had had to deal with.

    I said my final adieu to Hausruckedt a day before the start
of school, said goodbye to my friends, aunts, to grandfather and
father and went with mother on the way to the station. Bitter
tears rolled down my cheeks as I stood at the train window and
saw Hausruckedt, Bruckmühl and all the familiar little towns
disappear behind the plumes of smoke of the puffing locomotive.
But relentlessly, every second I was pulled further away from the
places of my happy childhood.

    Wels was a significant trading city in Upper Austria. Back
then Wels had around sixteen thousand residents, a few
Volksschule, two Bürgerschule for boys and girls and a
Gymnasium. Even from the plains, lying around Welser-Heide,
the mountain tops of the eastern Alps towered up barely forty
kilometers away to the South.

    Uncle Franz, my new paid host and head of the household
was hardly ever there. As a railwayman and train driver he had
irregular shift patterns and slept a lot during the day. If he was
off work, he spent every free minute in his allotment at the

northern end of the town. I mostly dealt with the aunt, she was an affable person and you could get on with her easily.

Life in the town was fundamentally different from in Hausruckedt. There were large surroundings with lots of nature back there, forests, fields and meadows in the immediate vicinity of the house. Here I was surrounded by houses, feeling cramped from the city but with lots of bustle. The big shops, the display windows, the constant lively traffic, all new sensations that helped me a lot in getting over the first pains of leaving.

The school here had somewhat higher expectations than the one in Bruckmühl. But in a few months I had filled in all the gaps in my knowledge and after that I found my feet easily. I was left to my own devices to complete my homework like I had been in Hausruckedt. Uncle had no time to help and auntie couldn't. Toni, the son, went to the Gymnasium and already had enough on his plate. Both of us lads had a tiny room to ourselves and had to share the one bed inside. The house was very peaceful in a park-like ground, was enclosed by a high wall and stood in the shadow of old, mighty trees.

From the garden you came to a narrow street and from there down an embankment to the Traun, a clear but very cold river. Across from the Enns stretched a long chain of hills that only had a few trees scattered across them. The city stretched out in all other directions.

There is little to report from this first year of school in Wels. The way to school wasn't far and was too short to have any little adventures. Pranks that took place were confined to the school, the children quickly dispersed as soon as they left the class. The long trek to school, giving rise to so many shared experiences, that didn't exist here anymore.

Free time was more often used up playing in the house than on adventures in the great outdoors. The free, wide open strolling around like I had in Hausruckedt didn't exist here.

The altar boy duties I had begun in Bruckmühl I now continued here. In fact I continued it at home. Toni had a heap of mass related articles which were used as toys. We built an altar in the living room and began to read entire masses for which we even had a tiny mass box. These games had such an effect on me that a few times I thought it could be worthwhile to become a priest. You have all kinds of fantasies when you're young, they come and go like the clouds in the sky.

With the end of the school year my further education was decided on, and it certainly wasn't as I had pictured. I brought my report card back home and I very much thought it was a good one. My aunt and uncle had a different view. They thought that because I had a two in German that I wouldn't be able to cope with studying at the Gymnasium. And mother, who came from Hausruckedt in order to take me home for the holidays, was also convinced by this view. In addition my uncle Franz said that his house was a little too small for two boys and my mother would be better finding somewhere else for me.

We went to mother's father, grandmother had died in the meantime and the family council met there again in order to decide my fate.

Auntie Kathi was the lead speaker in the matter. She also thought that the Gymnasium would be too taxing for me since I came from such a remote school as Bruckmühl and there were surely many gaps in my basic knowledge. She also believed that a two in the important subject of German was too low for a better education. The Bürgerschule was clearly the best choice for someone of my knowledge, then I could become a salesman or a good tradesman. That was the foremost view of my grandfather as well, who didn't think much of the Gymnasium. And so my further education was decided by this council in Wels, my father was given no role in the matter whatsoever. It could have been the case as well that mother and her relatives were thinking about the financial side of the matter in particular. I was not my mother's biological child after all, and so also not fully deserving of support. Father could assert himself with mother in many things, but when it came to money mother's word was final.

With this the matter was closed: I would go to the Bürgerschule and study as a salesman afterward. My timid objections, as far as I had made any anyway, weren't taken into consideration. Even on the last point, on accommodation, the council was unanimous. Auntie Kathi offered to take me under her wing. After all the issues had been decided I went back to Hausruckedt with mother.

In Hausruckedt not much had changed in my absence. Another room had been converted in the attic where I was able to set up my place to sleep. I quickly reconnected with my old school friends and so the holidays went on very pleasantly.

In the meantime we had become the only household in the settlement to have a radio and with that we'd also achieved a greater measure of prestige. It was a very extensive apparatus which blessed us with the joy of music. Three heavy components furnished us with the magical sound and with a whole new sense of life. The receiver was here too, spaciously installed in a brown wooden box, the sound was produced by an enormous metal trumpet and the whole thing was run from a host of batteries which were neatly ordered into a wooden box of the same colour.

The rainy days I spent most often with my friend in the Brettbacher house. Hansl had very nice parents. His father was a skilled cobbler and in the house all day as a result. We sat in the living room then and painted and drew whatever our fantasies produced. When the sun shone we were out in the woods as quick as we could. It was a time when the chanterel mushrooms could be found in droves and mother was always overjoyed with the bit of change they gave us at mealtimes.

If father was home I saw to it that I was as out of reach as possible. If he didn't see me he didn't miss me. But if I was in his field of view he thought he had to make me useful. And his tasks were mostly tied up with something awkward. It was so difficult to do something to his standard as well that I was always afraid of making myself useful under his supervision. Father always said as well that I could become an innkeeper like he was, the idea terrified me.

I had much more fun helping mother. She was calm and balanced and if you didn't understand it all at first she had the patience to explain things in more detail. I could talk about a lot of things with her which I wouldn't have been able to talk about with my father. Grandfather was always friendly with me but he didn't have many interests besides his pipe and couldn't deal much with any problems I had. Though father was strict and sometimes a little violently tempered as well, he was still an exceedingly peaceful person in comparison to Aunt Olga's husband, Casapicolo. Aunt Olga was father's youngest sister but she was also very unhappily married. Olga's husband was a paragon of aggressiveness, brutality and cynicism. He wasn't afraid to lift his hand to Olga either. She often came to us, was distraught, cried a lot and we all felt sorry for her. But nobody could help her, after all, who would want to start a fight with her husband? She herself was very kind and helpful. Father never liked having Olga's husband as a guest at ours. His presence always brought unrest into the bar, particularly when he had drunk too much. He was feared as a troublemaker just as much as he was as a vicious brawler.

All too soon the holidays came to an end.
I was considered old enough now to make the journey to Wels without my mother accompanying me. The tied up bundle with my few possessions in my hand, I left Hausruckedt to make my first visit to Auntie Kathi.

-   .   -

Auntie Kathi was a person who broke the mould. Difficult to describe and also often difficult to deal with. Her instructions were not allowed to be questioned and certainly not to be ignored. Her severity was not unfair but relentless. To try to convince her, to persuade her away from a demand by talking was pointless.

School, learning and work were at the forefront, free time at the back end of priorities. Where with my parents there would have existed a small chance to protest against an instruction, with Auntie Kathi this was absolutely impossible. What little remnants of rebellious spirit I had would be broken here in Wels. I had no physical punishment to fear but the price was total subjugation.

Auntie Kathi had separated from her husband. In later years she lived together with him again for a short time. He was a shadow of a man, with his spirit broken, already laughably subservient.

Alongside my aunt the household was also comprised of her father and Uncle Lois. I had a small room with a bed, a chair and a one-doored wardrobe for myself. Uncle Lois worked on setting up a beer wholesalers in the barn with his own soda water generator. In a little stable annexe stood "Max," Uncle Lois's small cart horse. Grandfather's property also comprised of an inn, it was on the same plot of land but it was leased out.

Now to the school. It stood in the middle of the town square. It was an old, imposing building, with wonderfully ornamented facades, unfortunately very aged. Very high school rooms, a wide, well-trodden wooden stepway to the two upper floors. In each classroom there was a huge, iron, pot-bellied stove for heating. The rest of the furniture was of the oldest kind with combined writing and bench desks, no better than they were in the remote country schools. The furniture was really nothing to write home about for the time but I took that as self-evident back then.

The schoolhouse stood boxed in between other business premises and didn't have a back yard. This means there was no playground either, and so you can imagine what it was like inside during break times. We had the town sports hall for P.E, which was used by all the school and sports teams. I was to spend three years in this school and my knowledge, or so it was expected anyhow, should grow fruitfully in all directions. Auntie Kathi would see to that.

I had only been in Wels a few weeks before my aunt decided that I was too little occupied and an additional lesson in music was deemed necessary to supplement my education. As a fitting instrument the "zither" was chosen. My parents were informed and I was sent to the local newspaper, the "Welser-Volksboten" to put an advertisement in. A zither was found in a pawn shop.

Several people replied to the advertisement and presented themselves as the best music teachers in their field. They were all willing, for a ridiculous fee of course, to turn me into the perfect musician.

An old matron who appealed to me the least was entrusted with my artistic education. She must have knocked all of her competition out of the field with her ludicrously pitiful salary.

From now on I took the wooden zither box, which was almost bigger than I was, once a week after school and shuffled across through the town to this madam who was supposed to teach me the correct way of handling the instrument. My destination was a shabby old house on the southern edge of the town. A well worn wooden stairway led up into the attic room. I was welcomed in front of the front door with the many voiced twittering of numerous canaries.

The old woman was really quite crotchety, but she could play the zither, she showed that to me straight away, I was supposed to gain an idea from this of what I'd be able to achieve if I put in the effort and good will with her. Well we'll see about that.

And so the lesson began with her neatly and tidily writing the notes for the day's lesson on an empty sheet of music in ink. Then she took a salt shaker filled with fine bird sand and gently sprinkled her work. This sand was a substitute for blotting paper, as I soon discovered. After a short time the sand was wiped off and was probably reused for the birds. It was no doubt due to this frugal economisation that it was possible for her to knock her rivals out of the field so cheaply. After these preparations were carefully carried out, to my joy, a half hour had already passed.

My first lessons were, like all beginnings, difficult and didn't even appeal to the canaries. Insulted, they spontaneously abandoned their song, offended by so much musical illiteracy.

When the hour was over, I was allowed to take the original hand finished lesson into my possession and reuse it as a practice template. Auntie Kathi was happy that I came into the possession of music so cheaply, it was yet another expenditure saved, how she settled all of these expenses with my parents I've no idea. If she'd been given a set rate she would have made a good profit. My musical progress seemed to advance only little in the first weeks, but if I had thought that my practices would slowly get on my aunt's nerves then I had fundamentally miscalculated, I still had no idea of her persistence.

My aunt led an exact daily routine, planned to the hour and which rarely allowed for deviation. Once I had opened my eyes (the old alarm clock made a din that wouldn't let you ruminate for very long,) I got up quickly, poured water out of a stone mug into a metal washbowl, dipped three fingers in, cleaned my eyes and wiped my hair. Slipped into a shirt, stockings and trousers, in summer there weren't any other underclothes, and sat down to my breakfast. Breakfast was very lavish. A mug of coffee, that is fig coffee without beans but with a lot of milk, poured over bits of whole German bread. You could only dream of butter or jam. On Sundays there was plum puree to spread on the bread, but do you think we got butter? Dream on. For break times at school I had two lots of bread with lard dripping, that was quite lavish, children normally only came to school with bare slices of bread. We never had lunch without soup, rarely meat but very often we had pastry. Our supper in the evening could only be differentiated from breakfast in that we drank cocoa alongside it in the place of coffee substitutes. But again only dry bread was brought in.

Auntie Kathi and grandfather were content with this cuisine, only Uncle Lois often ate in the inn and in the evening he ate good sausage on bread. But always mixed meats for a schilling. If he hadn't brought his sausage with him, he pressed a schilling into my hand and I tore off like lightning to Zelger the butcher. Then I got a slice of the delicious sausage as well, I ate it on its own without bread, I'd let the deliciousness melt on my tongue. The short stop in the butcher's shop was a great pleasure. The smell of all the fresh sausages lay tingling in my nose. To just once be able to eat sausage to your heart's content was an unthinkable dream in those days. So the daily routine with meals was always the same with the exception of Sundays where there were pickled pumpkins for pudding and that was something special.

Since school lasted into the afternoon I was alone at the table for lunch. Grandfather had his nap and auntie studied the newspaper. When I was finished with my meal, auntie washed the dishes. I had my regular chores along with this. I had to fill the oven basin with fresh water, sweep the wooden floorboards and dry and put away the dishes. Once all that was done, Auntie Kathi would spend a lot of time with me for the rest of the afternoon.

I had to take everything I'd written at school and lay it out for her to nag over and I had to complete my homework under her constant supervision. She wasn't stupid and you couldn't take her for a ride at all. Once that was finished as well and the school books were neatly and tidily put into order for the next day, I grabbed the black wooden box with the zither inside. The day's practice was one hour, if it went poorly then I had to do some serious overtime. But I couldn't play badly enough that my aunt would lose patience and send me packing either. She had incredible endurance. The afternoon sun could tempt so beautifully from outside, I had to sit it out.

Once everything was finally finished, I was allowed out into the fresh air, then the day was almost over and in winter the other children had already left the street. If I was particularly unlucky then grandfather came outside with his walking stick and I had to accompany him. My rotten expression didn't bother him in the slightest. He showed me this and that, talked of Wels as it had been in years gone by, all kinds of things that didn't interest me and only he thought were important.

I was stirred by completely different things, but the old man had no idea of these. If he had spoken to me something about the wider world, of jungles with huge snakes, of bears, wolves or tigers, well then he would have had an attentive listener.

At the time I was obsessed by a youthful urge to explore. I went into the nearby fields, dug out whole ant nests, hauled them back home and observed their conduct in a wooden box with a glass cover. Of course I couldn't do this in the house but Uncle Lois' feed shed was a fantastic place for it. I discovered a mass of pond newts during a walk with grandfather in a pond. I could barely wait to get home. I begged for an empty five litre pickle jar and tore off. Now I was in the proud possession of a small aquarium. In the early morning and in the evening my first and last trip was into the feed shed. In front of the glass window there was a long wooden table on which I had my treasures. My only spectator was "Max" the horse, otherwise nobody bothered me. The feed shed and the stable were really the one room and were only separated by a wooden railing that was around one meter high.

The requirements of the Bürgerschule were considerably higher than those in the Volksschule. Most notably the homework was much more extensive and demanded much more free time. In my opinion we lads weren't much better than the children of today, but the teachers back then had canes of which they made ample use and they had the right to use corporal punishment, and so they weren't completely helpless against us. And yet still even back then we were hard nuts to crack sometimes.

But even back then it was like it is today, some teachers kept discipline without much fuss and beatings, others never kept discipline and were constantly at the end of their wits.

Headteacher Zappe for example, a giant of a man, he needed no cane and there was no shouting with him, all were only the most well behaved boys when he held a lesson. But when I think on teachers Gans and Strasser, the pair who suffered the most under us, I still have questionable pangs of conscience today.

Deputy head teacher Strasser gave us lessons in geography and biology, physics too in first and third year. Herr Gans was the youngest and taught all of us the skill of drawing in art.

Strasser was only a few years away from his pension and with his nerves was very often near the edge of a mental breakdown. He had a son, who had already gone on two expeditions with Sven Hedin, the Swedish explorer of Asia. Understandably, this son was a source of great pride.

If the sun was shining really warmly through the window, we would grow sleepy and wouldn't have the slightest desire to learn the laws of physics, then we only needed to turn the discussion towards his son. Then a leisurely hour was certain. We just had to make sure that the pretend interest didn't wane. If he noticed our dastardly intent then of course his mood turned foul. Then for the duration of his lectures he had the peace that he could only fruitlessly hope for during other lessons.

When I brought the textbooks to Strasser's house after schoolwork his daughter often asked me, "What have you been doing to papa again? He is so old already, why don't you boys leave him in peace?" I couldn't help her either.

Physics lesson with Strasser:

Strasser explains the workings of piston compressors. Standing on the platform in front of the huge blackboard he holds a demonstrative glass object in his hand which is supposed to illustrate the workings of the pistons in a simplified form. He tightly holds the entire glass body at the end of the piston rod.

"Schneider, what purpose do compressors serve?"

Schneider is a good student, so he will certainly know the answer.

"Compressors are for the compression of gases and vapours Herr Strasser."
"Good, Schneider,"
"And through what are gases compressed?"
"Well?"
"Baumgartner stop prattling, through what are these gases compressed Baumgartner?"

Unfortunately Baumgartner doesn't know the answer.

"Well who knows the answer? Through what?"

Out of some corner in the back, some indiscernible row, came the prompt answer,

"Through your arsehole Herr Strasser!"

At first the answer was followed by total silence, nobody breathed, then the ringing laughter of the entire class.

"Who was that?"

Strasser yelled in the classroom, his face swole up a dark red,

"Own up to it at once you rogue!"

Silence in the entire class,

"I have time, lots of time, thick as mince but cheeky as monkeys, what are you lot for a cowardly gang of hoodlums."

While Strasser's agitation continued to grow, he failed to notice the piston moved ever closer to the end of the device. What Strasser had not seen the class certainly didn't fail to notice. All eyes were rigidly directed at Strasser's right hand in which catastrophe slowly loomed. All of a sudden it was far enough. With a loud bang the glass cover popped off the piston, fell to the floor and shattered into a hundred pieces. At first Strasser stood flabbergasted, stared unbelievingly at the shards of glass at his feet and then screamed:

"You knew!"

His voice wobbled.

"You saw it! Oh you scoundrels, if I hang myself one day then it'll all be your fault, you'll put me in my grave!"

He goes to his desk, sits himself down on his seat and takes a red plaid handkerchief and wipes his face in a tizz, exhausted and beaten down and with a different almost weaker voice:

"Detention, detention for the whole class, until you're blue in the face. What did I do to deserve you?"

Now we almost felt sorry for him, but we wouldn't back down.

We had to sit in detention, but we didn't go blue in the face, in the end Strasser was hungry too and wanted to go home like we did.

If we had pangs of conscience with Strasser when we were too wicked with him, we knew no pity with Gans. He was young and in our opinion could still handle a good bit more and what decided it was that nobody could stand him. Seemingly he couldn't stand us either and so the dislike was thoroughly mutual.

Art teacher Gans turns up for the first lesson. He pulls out a blue notebook, goes from bench to bench and asks:

"Name?"
"Konrad Just, Sir"
"Date of birth?"...

And so it continued. Neatly and tidily he noted every answer. He gets to the third bench in the middle row. Here sits Josef Staudinger. He must have repeated a year a few times already, because he is older, bigger and considerably stronger than we are. Cheeky enough for three and a real troublemaker.
Gans stands in front of him.

"Name?"
"Sepp Staudinger,"
"I'm clearly not hearing correctly, your name again?"
"Staudinger, Sepp"

Staudinger looks at Gans quite innocently, pulling no faces. Gans grows uncomfortable.

"Oh well look at this, the boy thinks he can pull my leg!"

He goes to his desk, ostentatiously takes out his cane and walks back to Staudinger's desk.

"So for the last time: Name?"
"Staudinger,"
"Staudinger, good, and the rest?"
"Sepp,"

Gans cracks the cane on the desk in front of Staudinger.

"For the last time... Staudinger, and the rest?"
"There is no rest, just Sepp."
"Boy do you not speak proper German?"

The cane cracks at Staudinger's hands, but he pulls away quickly enough so that it only delicately tickles his fingertips.

"But I'm called Staudinger Herr Gans."
"I don't want this clown's first name I want the real one you twit!"
"Like I told you, Sepp,"
"Yes and as it stands on your birth certificate for Pete's sake!"
"I don't have a birth certificate Herr Gans!"
"Whaaaaaaaaaaat...?"

Gans puts both hands on his hips and takes a few steps back.

"My father is a free thinker Herr Gans!"
"You just wait boy, I'll knock that cheek out of you yet."

With that Gans moved on from Staudinger's desk and in neat handwriting wrote "Josef" after "Staudinger," in his book. But he still wanted to take the boy to task.

Weeks later and Gans was becoming ever more disliked among us, we had already targeted the loathed art teacher musically. When breaktime came to an end before we had art, and his arrival was due any moment, we began to sing like a choir...

"The fox stole Gans the goose away, we don't want him back, please don't give him back...,"

Once the door opened, we'd go silent, but we still hoped that he'd secretly understood enough of our song in the corridor. His red face and the furious looks that he gave us were a balm to our souls.

Of course Gans soon knew the lyrics to the song. We sang loud enough to be understood by the deaf after all.
When he came into the classroom with a bright red face, he strode to his desk, sat down, narrowed his eyes into a narrow slit, then suddenly jumped up, went to the middle row and struck Staudinger with the cane.

One day, I had my spot in the last row right up against the back wall of the classroom, I was once caught up in a circus of events totally innocently.

We were painting maple leaves we had brought with us on big drawing pads and for once we were actually quite engrossed while doing it.

Gans sat at his desk and corrected the schoolbooks of a different class.

Suddenly we heard a loud meowing from one of the desk rows. Snickering set in. The teacher struck his desk energetically with his cane and shouted:

"Quiet!"

Silence for a while, then again the ...meowing.., Gans sprang up, without forgetting his cane, stood in the first row listening intently.

It seemed to him that the yeowling was coming from my side of the room, he couldn't make out the exact location. Nothing moved, Gans went back to his desk, sat down.... and it started again already..., like a bolt of lightning Gans shot up, went to the middle of the room, the cane jiggling in his hand. Since nothing moved, he went back to his desk, coiled and ready to jump at the next moment.

Only the maple leaves rustled, we were all very occupied.

The teacher sat down again.

He held the class tensely in his eye, but could only discern diligent artists. He bent down over his books again when again a new meowling was heard.

Like a bolt of lightning, his face distorted with fury Gans stormed past the desks towards me. He grabbed me by the chest, nearly pulled me out of my blazer and pinned me up against the wall,

"What's that supposed to be you twit!" he screamed at me.
"It wasn't me!" I screamed back.
"It was you, you rascal, you wait I'll sort you,"

He wanted to cane my fingers with his free hand, as I foresaw this I nimbly stuffed my hands deep into my trouser pockets. He pushed me higher up the wall and bellowed:

"You mischievous ruffian, admit you did it!"
"I swear it wasn't me! It wasn't me," I yelled as loud as I could.
"Herr Gans!" Staudinger's voice interrupted us.
"Herr Gans I know who it was, it was the cat."

And in actual fact, a black cat suddenly jumped forward through the middle row and raced to the door.

As white as a sheet with rage, Gans let me fall back down into my seat, hurried to his desk, gathered his books together and hastily left the classroom with his face bright red.

Unbeknownst to us even, Staudinger had taken the cat in with him and had kept a hold of it under his desk. Every time he had pinched her fur, she had begun her lamentable meowing.

The class continued in an unholy racket until breaktime and Staudinger was celebrated as a hero as a result.

Every second year a big funfair took place in Wels. It lasted a week and began on Saturday with a big carnival procession through the city. Folk bands in great number in their decorated uniforms, the brass bands with their flags and the gaudy traditional costumes attracted many spectators. At this fair, known in all of Austria, there were also breeding-animal shows and country tool exhibitions on.

In the vast area, even without an entry ticket we children were always able to find a bolthole through which we could reach the festival grounds.

My aunt let me leave the house a little earlier during that week. We even had one afternoon off school.

Of course my pocket money was always too meagre for these days. Extra money for special occasions was only given in modest amounts.

The festival also had a big carnival with all the bits and pieces. Our favourite things this year were metal frogs. They only cost a few groschen, they came in all kinds of colours and "croaked" really nicely. If you squeezed the two metal platelets together, the metal frog opened its mouth and made a croaking tone.

A few days later:
Biology lesson with Strasser. The metal frogs that we'd bought at the fair the day before were to come into action.

Staudinger, who else, had a brilliant idea.
If you put the frogs inside our woollen stockings and just behind your knee, then bent your knee, both platelets of the frog would be pressed together and it would croak.

Strasser was lecturing us about our domestic lamiaceous plants. Then the flow of his speech was broken by a many voiced

"Croak"
"Who was that?"

Nobody took responsibility. Strasser hurried to where he thought he'd heard it come from, then a new croak came from the furthest away corner.
Strasser sped to the other half of the classroom. When he ran to the front, it croaked from behind, when he was on the right it croaked on the left.

"All of you stand up at once!" his angry voice rang out. He ran along all of the rows of desks and checked all of the seats. There was nothing to be found.
"Oh you hoodlums, you good for nothings,"

He wiped the sweat from his forehead.

"You class of hooligans!" he moaned at the end of his wits.

He went back to his desk, motioned tiredly with his hand that we should sit down.
A class full of croaking rang out as we fulfilled his wish.
He looks across our rows again tired and disappointed, he sits at his desk and doesn't know how he is supposed to continue now.

All his fury is no longer enough to keep a head on the situation. He doesn't know, should he continue the lesson? Should he dismiss it?

With that he stood up, took his bag, and left the room, followed by many voiced "croaking" from every corner of the classroom.

Even back then it was no easy feat to teach a class of pubescent boys.

The winter in the year nineteen hundred and twenty seven was extremely strong. The thermometer fell as far as minus twenty seven. In the classes the pot-bellied stoves glowed, the rail switches froze and thick ice flows drifted down the Traun.

Despite the bitter cold I had to head off with my zither box. I froze like a wretched dog and cursed the aunt who herself had no pardon from this cold. Days off were not tolerated under any conditions.

On some days it was even too cold to still feel an inclination to go skiing across the Traun.

-   .   -

The first year at school came to an end. I thought the report card was really good, but that wasn't Auntie Kathi's opinion. She thought there was still a lot of room for improvement and promised to work harder with me the next year. I didn't let this talk dampen my spirits, packed up my few things, said adieu to Wels for a few weeks and travelled to Hausruckedt. I had to take the zither with me of course, with the stern instruction to practice diligently.

After a few days back home grandfather died very suddenly. His body was laid out in a side room for a few days. Through a little window in the coffin you could see grandfather's head and folded hands. Grandfather had a wonderful funeral. The music played all the way from Hausruckedt to Bruckmühl. The grave was completely laid out in fir green, lots of hunters stood at his grave. When the music left the graveyard they played quick marches again just behind the graveyard entrance.

It didn't feel right to me now, sleeping in grandfather's bed, but mother insisted. For the first few days I was really scared, I was always afraid that grandfather would appear to me from in the darkness. For the first days I always had the image in my head of how he was lying in the coffin, pale and with closed eyes. But grandfather had a heart and was good enough to stay in heaven.

My parents weren't as enthusiastic about my zither playing as I'd thought. They were surely used to hearing better from their various customers. My parents weren't as insistent as auntie had been with daily practice, they had other concerns. So on some holiday days my zither was left in the corner somewhere.

As the holidays came to an end, and I turned up in Wels again, Auntie Kathi was appalled at my drop in ability at zither playing. The few days until the beginning of school were spent practicing, practicing and practicing again, until I began to protest from the pain in my fingertips and no amount of nagging could convince me to keep playing. Then even she threw in the towel and left me in peace for a few days.

The beginning of the year at school brought a bitter disappointment. Herr Gans was moved to another school and Steinhuber took his place. He was supposed to teach us the fine arts from now on. There wasn't much we could make fun of the new teacher for, we couldn't fit his name in a song either. So we had to concentrate more of our efforts on good old Strasser and hope that he would cope with it. In the New Year we were taught by the head teacher Zappe a little more often as well, we dropped all horseplay with him from the start. Our classroom was changed but otherwise everything remained the same.

Over the next winter, art became my favourite subject. We learned lots of new techniques and a huge drawing folder with loose sheets of paper accompanied me to the lessons. I would have started to paint in oils as well only too happily, but this was too costly and the paints much too expensive to be paid for with my pocket money.

The winter was long, not too cold but with a lot of snow. So on some Sundays I could enjoy the few free hours on skis.

The zither lessons continued in the usual fashion, as always the elderly madam wrote the notes herself. As the practice templates grew ever longer, she needed ever more time for her preparations, time during which the practical side of education was absent. Slowly though I also came to the realisation that even ten years of education wouldn't be enough to make a virtuoso of me, and I came to terms with attaining the achievable. In the end I didn't want to be a musician anyway.

After the half term of second year, my mid-term report had a few better grades than I had had the previous year. Auntie Kathi was very happy. So happy, that she decided to double my pocket money for a month. Even grandfather gave up two schillings... Uncle Lois didn't let anything show, even from back home I heard nothing, neither praise nor reproachment and no money either.

A few weeks before the next holidays it was time for the two day long school excursion, for which we had saved our class money for so long. Dr. Jauch our German teacher was to be our guide.

We travelled with the train on the local line southwards one morning, our destination was Grünau in the foothills of the Alps in the Salzkammergut area. As we arrived at our destination, we already saw the partly snow-covered peaks of the mountains. A long walk in fantastic weather between rising hills on each side led to the Almsee. We found everything wonderful, when we were let out we jumped all over with a lust for life like young billy goats, we could have gone the journey twice without growing tired.

Behind a corner, the Almsee dipped suddenly. Surrounded by forests and mountains it had a very mysterious feel to it. The surrounding mountain slopes reflected a greenish blue in the water. At the end of the lake stood a large almost castle-like house, it was called 'Seehaus.' The house was run as a business and whoever had money could buy food and drink here.

At the flat bottom of the valley there stood several scattered wooden huts which the mountain farmers used to store hay. We had to spend the night in one of these huts, which was filled around two meters high with hay. This adventure excited us the most. We set ourselves up in the hay quite comfortably, listened half-heartedly to stern instructions about not starting any fires without express permission and supervision and then we were let loose on the neighbourhood.

What fun it was. A fantastic green shimmering mountain stream wound round the meadows in numerous curves. The water was so fresh, so fresh and boisterous were our hearts.

We waded through the ice cold water, tumbled over stock and stone and couldn't contain ourselves.

The provisions from our rucksack tasted wonderful in mutual company. As the sun disappeared, we sat by a blazing campfire, singing boisterous songs and telling robber stories.

The stars glistened over us for hours as the campfire slowly died out, the last song silenced. Still a long, excited whispering and giggling in the hay until finally peace set in and sleep embraced the many souls. The calls of the night owls couldn't be heard any more. Even though we already went back home the next day, it was still an experience which we spoke of for a long time.

One day, Auntie Kathi sent me into the attic in order to get some kind of item. I saw a wicker basket in a corner. I curiously lifted the lid in order to look inside. It was mostly just dusty old books, but in a corner lay a little black box, a plate camera as I realised, full of excitement.

The basket and its contents belonged to Uncle Hans, a brother of my aunt who lived in Vienna at the time. I had never written a letter as quickly as the one I sent to Vienna then. After many days that seemed to last forever, the answer came from uncle that I could by all means keep the camera, he didn't have time for photography anymore anyway. I was over the moon now. I possessed the first camera in my life. Nearly every day on my walk through town I stopped in front of the display window of a photography shop. I got brochures, which wasn't so easy back then and studied every line precisely. I didn't have the money I needed to buy the necessary glass plates, but I made myself up a list of all the required items in case the needed capital ever turned up.

It wasn't a complex camera, nobody would be content with such primitive technology today, it was a box camera for glass plates but who had a box camera back then?

The school year came to an end. We left our schoolbags in a corner for a few weeks and began an amusing life of mischief. I went back to Hausruckedt to spend my holidays there and to breathe country air again. My report card was very good and even impressed my parents. I used this good disposition to further my request to take up photography.

Some days later I went with my mother to Ried to make some larger purchases that she did there from time to time. I was allowed to get the most necessary things in order to start my occupation as a freelance photographer. I could hardly wait until we got back home.

I took my first pictures. Even father was a little impressed though they were anything other than masterpieces. It was indeed very mysterious what I concocted out of all of the different potions. Nobody in the whole settlement had any idea of chemistry or how it worked. And even though you often needed a lot of imagination to be able to recognise the people in my pictures, my ability was wondered at regardless. I didn't even need a darkroom for the paper photographs themselves, the paper was so insensitive to light that the photographs had to be left in the printing frame in the full sunlight for as long as half an hour. Then they would be fixed with bright light and had a blue-violet colour tone. The camera didn't give a very sharp image, but the standards weren't very high either.

Nothing had changed in Hausruckedt, and the holidays passed quickly. Only father didn't go into the mine anymore and spent the whole day at home. Mother was very relieved with this of course and could dedicate herself to the kitchen alone. The servant girl wasn't there anymore however, but for the most part father had taken on her workload too. My father being at home all day now didn't please me in particular and when the holidays came to an end I didn't find it difficult to leave either. So I hit the road again off to Wels in order to take on my last year at school.

Of course the frequently recurring question as I began this last school year was what I was going to do afterward. We had already agreed that I would have to complete an apprenticeship as a salesman, but sadly positions as an apprentice were very thin on the ground.

There was an apprenticeship place on offer with the Meindl company's branch in Wels. If I was going to be a salesman, this company chain really appealed to me. It was a very swish, clean business. It always smelled very nicely of coffee and sausages, the sales assistants had wonderful uniforms, for those times it was really a bloody good store.

The rush of applicants was so huge that the selection exams had to be spread out across many days. We got questionnaires for which, as far as I could make out, the answers had no relationship to our future education. I can't remember any of the questions specifically, I only know that when I had to find some correlation with a fox in one question, I didn't have the correct answer to hand. I fell out of the race in the first round, we were all very disappointed, of course only one of us could be the lucky one.

At school everything ran its usual course. We didn't have any change of teachers and we went on as normal. Poor Strasser had to deal with the entire burden of our cheek and adolescent restlessness almost by himself. He can't have seen anything anymore apart from the day he'd be able to collect his pension and leave the school behind him.

Our school stood in the middle of the town square and on Wednesdays the weekly market took place there. On those days we always had all of the windows open during the breaks and we looked at the hustle and bustle below us.

Down there the chickens were clucking in the coops, the geese were gabbling and the piglets were squealing. The farmers were shouting over each other in order to sell their products. We crowded the window panes and spat heartily into the goings-on below us. After ever spit we disappeared for a few moments and waited for the eventual reaction. But most of our spit just fell by the wayside or wasn't so much as noticed in the hubbub.

On one such market day we had physics with Strasser. It was about the function and utility of telescopes. Strasser had brought an impressive telescope with him out of the teaching materials room. It went from hand to hand and despite Strasser's energetic protests we began to view the activity in the town square through the telescope. Soon there was an intense skirmish, everyone wanted to take a look through the instrument at once and whoever had it at that moment, didn't want to give it up again so quickly. Amongst all of the pushing and shoving, the telescope finally fell out of someone's hand, plummeted into the deep, ricocheted off a ledge over the ground floor and flew in an arc into the middle of a market woman's egg stand. An awful clamour began. In the town square the farmer's wife screamed, Strasser shouted in the classroom.
The town policeman came in, the head teacher was sent for, but what could really be done? We collected in order to replace the

farmer's wife's eggs, the school had to pay the costs for the repair of the telescope and with that the situation was brought to a close.

During the month of March there was a confirmation ceremony in Wels. I was also one of the candidates for confirmation, for weeks we had been prepared in training sessions by Dr. Lang. As these confirmations had to be undertaken by bishops, of which there were not many, these celebrations took up a lot of time.

Auntie Kathi said that on this day I could eat whatever I liked for supper. Well then, I wanted to have a schnitzel that was so big, that every side of it hung off the plate. Potato salad along with that and pickled pumpkin slices for desert.

But you needed a godparent for the confirmation ceremony too. For years mother had always spoken about how a rich farmer from Zell am Pettenfürst would be my godfather. That meant that I could at least expect a golden watch, as this was tradition.
But the much touted godfather must have gotten cold feet, as suddenly there was no more talk of it. As apparently no substitute could be found either, the honour was tied up with expense after all, my father had to take on the role by necessity. Well that wasn't very nice for me. Uncle Lois could have also played the wealthy bachelor, but he didn't want to give up so much as a schilling.

Father couldn't be persuaded to leave Hausruckedt and take me to the church in Wels. So mother had to take over this role. So there were all kinds of difficulties until this was all sorted out.

Father really didn't like coming to Wels. He didn't like mother's relatives, and they didn't like him. My hopes for a golden watch collapsed like a house of cards of course. But mother took me into a clothes shop in Wels. There I got a blue suit with long trousers and even a shirt with a tie. When I saw myself in the mirror, I thought I looked very grown up.

The big celebratory meal took place in Auntie Kathi's kitchen living room after the church visit.
Just as I'd asked for, I wanted a schnitzel so large that it hung over all of the edges of the plate. That was what I'd been promised and I had a right to it.

The table was already laid out after our return from church. I noticed that in front of my seat there was no dinner plate, rather just a little sugar dish, as is used in Austria for the sugar cubes. I thought this must be a mistake and so I fetched a bigger plate for myself. After a short time, as we sat down for our supper, at my spot there was only the tiny sugar dish again. But then auntie came with the schnitzels already, handing out the portions for everyone during which she passed over me. Lastly, I received as I'd wanted my schnitzel, it even hung over all the sides of the plate, only the dish was tiny and the schnitzel "bigger" by comparison.
I sat there flabbergasted, everyone looked at me and laughed at the top of their voices.
I started to bawl, knocking the midget schnitzel back and howling like a wounded dog. I still don't know today why I had taken this harmless joke so seriously back then. I only know that I didn't take a single bite from either the small schnitzel nor from the larger one they brought out after. I was deeply hurt. First everyone spoke nicely to me, then they all told me off, but the day was totally ruined for me now.

In the afternoon my mother went with me to Thalheim, a small town over the Traun. To celebrate the day we went to a café there and mother bought coffee and cake. After that we climbed the lookout tower from where we got a good view across Wels. And so the confirmation for which we had waited for so long, for which we had been filled with such anticipation, came to an end. That damned, tiny schnitzel ruined the whole day for me.

One day, soon after the confirmation, my religion teacher spoke to me. He asked whether I would be interested in taking on an apprenticeship position with a salesman in Enns. I should speak to my parents about this and then give him my decision. Of course they were all in favour and so I asked Dr. Lang to take him up on the offer.

Dr. Lang did more for this than you could expect of him. He went to the salesman himself and after he returned he informed me himself that I should go to Enns as quickly as possible to introduce myself.

Auntie notified my parents and a few days later my mother came to Wels again in order to accompany me to Enns. It was all a bit overhasty, but the apprenticeship positions were so rare and the candidates so numerous that you couldn't spend a long time thinking it over. The general economic situation had reached a low point which was unparalleled. The army of unemployed that populated the streets grew in number every day. The great economic crisis had seized Austria too. Anyone who still had a job, or who could get hold of one of the ever shrinking number of apprenticeship positions, could count himself lucky.

It was a warm spring day when I got on the slow train to Enns with mother. We travelled in third class and that was still wooden benches and a steam locomotive pulled us along. As we travelled through Linz I wondered at the many houses. This city was much bigger than Wels, from the city centre the Mariendom tower rose up high. We reached Enns shortly before midday. When we got off the train, I saw the city lying on a hill from a short distance, dominated by a square tower looming over and guarding the whole city.

Enns is one of the oldest cities in Austria and was established by the Romans as a border fortress. Back then the border fortification was called "Lauriacum" and was the garrison for the second Roman legion. The place was even a diocese at times.

The highest point was formed by the main or city square, dominated by the watchtower previously mentioned. Three streets went from the city square. We turned down one, named "Wienerstrasse." After a few meters on the left hand side, behind a little hotel we stood in front of an unremarkable shop. Over the top of a green painted front door there was a wide wooden sign, "Leopold Hapala, clothing and textiles" stood written in large, (for the small shop far too large) letters. To the left and right of the door were two tiny display windows, likewise with wide green painted wooden shutters. In front of the shop entrance, almost concealed by a display window, a long, metal clothes stand hung thick with overcoats with fur collars.

We stepped through a dark shop entrance into an even gloomier room. Three steps, which mother nearly tripped over due to the meagre lighting, led down to the shop floor. On the right hand side there was a long shop counter, with shelves behind this down to the mighty cellar vaults. On the left hand side along the wall hung suits, jackets and women's clothes lined up densely.

The doorbell had given acoustic warning of our entry. Our eyes, dazzled with the light of the spring day, barely coped with the semi darkness inside.

A man stepped out from a side door at the back left corner. Early fifties, somewhat heavy set, his legs a little too short for his long upper body, a full face, thin hair, he stepped towards us so, rubbing his hands together with a short bow.

"Good day, at your service dear madam, how may I serve you?"

His voice was too friendly, almost a little sycophantic and I didn't find it particularly nice. Mother introduced herself and brought up our matter of concern.

"Ah yes, so this would be the new apprentice, Dr Lang spoke very kindly of him."

Hapala scrutinised me carefully.

"It was very kind of Dr Lang," said mother,
"it's difficult nowadays to find an apprenticeship position."
"Oh, don't I know it? The shops are doing badly and it's a great expense to train up an apprentice."
"I know," answered mother, "and so we're very grateful..."

Hapala interrupted mother....,

"The young man is a little pale and weak,"

Hapala walked around me, scrutinising me from top to bottom.

"But otherwise healthy..." said mother, "and a good student, his greatest wish is to become a salesman."

Mother lied through her teeth here, I didn't know when I had ever expressed the wish to become a salesman. I was told to become one yes, but certainly had never wished for it.

Hapala led us into his office now, which was just as run down as his whole shop. A tiny room, not even five square meters. An old fashioned writing desk, a few primitive shelves and a faded divan against a wall, clearly where he took his midday nap. No window brought any natural light into the gloom. Our eyes had gotten used to the dimness in the meantime though. Since there wasn't another chair we had to take a seat on the divan.

"So then, the young man," began Hapala,
"could live with me, we'd feed him well, but in these difficult times any other wage is of course impossible. For these three years you'll have to take care of any pocket money yourself."
"I understand that absolutely," said mother hurriedly, "my husband and I are just happy for the boy to be left in good hands."
"We attest to a Christian upbringing," said Hapala with a very convincing tone, "yes and what I also wanted to say of course," he continued, "even after closing time I expect an apprentice to be enthusiastic about taking on smaller matters too."

Mother nodded in agreement, she surely thought, the more work, the less mischief the boy can get up to.

"Another important point would be, as Dr Lang surely informed you, that we are a very Christian family, I put the greatest value on visiting early mass on Sundays. Of course since the boy will be taken into my family, I must also insist that for the duration of his apprenticeship rights in the matters of his upbringing and corporal discipline be given to me."

This sentence of Hapala's made me somewhat suspicious, but mother didn't take any issue at all, she agreed with everything and also added:

"Otto," (for the first time she mentioned me by name,) "had a strict upbringing with us as well, he has a close relationship to the church, he was even an altar boy for a few years."
"Yes I've heard that,"

Hapala slowly seemed to be getting used to the idea of his new apprentice.

"I mention this all," he continued,
"so that differences don't arise later. And there's the condition of a three month probation period of course. I'm sure you know nobody wants to buy a pig in a poke, and you can't get a full appraisal in a short interview either."

Mother thought these statements very reasonable.

"Good!" Hapala stood up,
"then I would suggest we go a few houses down the street, I have my house and my grocery store there. My wife should get to know the boy as much as possible as well and, if she has nothing against it, I reckon he can start in a week."

Mother was very confident with the rest of the process of course. Not much could go wrong now. I wasn't expected to make a poor impression on the wife, especially as women were always well disposed to me.

We walked down Wienerstrasse. We stopped in front of a two storied house. Hapala said that this was his property and that I would also be living in this house.

We stepped into a shop that wasn't big either, but was at least considerably brighter and friendlier than the one further up Wienerstrasse.

Frau Hapala was around early forties, tall, slim, almost gaunt but of a very kind nature. She had absolutely no objections to me, she just asked me a few friendly questions and got into a long conversation with mother.

The interview finally ended with Hapala and mother signing the apprentice contract in the kitchen living room. Mother nearly cried with happiness.

Now so long as I survived my probation period, which mother was certain of as well, I would be well cared for and my parents didn't have to worry about me learning a profession.

When I went back towards the train station with mother, we came past a parish church.

"Let's go inside and say a Lord's Prayer," said mother. "Otto, you should be grateful for this day which has brought you so much good fortune."

I certainly wasn't so convinced of this good fortune. I didn't like the shop and I didn't particularly like the boss either. But what did "liking" things mean in a time when hundreds would have licked your fingers clean for an apprenticeship like this, or rather, for any apprenticeship? And what apprentice is particularly fond of his boss?

We travelled back to Wels. Auntie Kathi seemed delighted with the outcome of our trip. Now I had a week's time to organise everything. The zither lessons were terminated, I received a provisional school leaving certificate from the school. I was advised to attend a final exam in Wels again in the summer. I could prepare myself for these exams using the school books. I would have a respectable qualification then and in the exam they would take my particular circumstances into consideration.

Small purchases were made. I got two pairs of sleeve protectors made from black synthetic fibre, also a shirt and a pair of knickerbockers made from shirting material. The knickerbockers went as far as my ankles and could be tied together at the bottom. The store coat was made from black synthetic fibre too, but it was only meant for work on Sundays and ought to be looked after. Thus I was well kitted out for taking up my duties. Lots of things that I kept but couldn't take with me to Enns I stowed away in Auntie Kathi's attic.

The trunk wasn't big, the zither was crammed into a rucksack and I was in a very mixed mood when, on Sunday the sixth of April 1930, I got on the train to Enns.

Nobody accompanied me to the train station. I left the house where I had spent almost three years without any particular pain at leaving. Too often I had already been sent with my bundle on my travels, too often in the past years I had had to change table and bed. I never came to develop a particular sense of familiarity, was never left to find my feet with time. Saying goodbye was something I had almost become accustomed to. So saying goodbye to Wels wasn't difficult for me. I left without tears, with the closing of the door Wels was just another chapter amongst many.

The years in Enns.

7.April 1930 – 30.June 1933

I arrived in Enns around midday. It was uncomfortably cold on the day I moved in. The sun had hidden itself behind low lying clouds and a heavy wind was blowing from the West.

I was no longer as sure of myself as I grew closer to my destination. I would have happily had someone with me now, to bridge over the first few hours. I really took my time on my way to the city. I wanted to stave off my arrival, I took breaks far more often than my physical state would have needed.

I was afraid of the unknown that awaited me, of the first hours in strange surroundings, with strange people.

The streets were almost empty. The bad weather kept people stuck indoors and my own mood was beyond miserable.

The city square seemed barren and abandoned as I reached it. I turned down along Wienerstrasse. Nobody passed me, a miserable Sunday afternoon.

Since Hapala's shop was now closed, it made an even more miserable impression than it had on the day of my interview. I was used to really different shops in Wels and wistfully thought on the lovely Meindl branch where I would have studied so happily instead.

But I could only walk so slowly, the time came when I stood in front of Hapala's shop and residence. When I used the door knocker I startled at the hard, loud noise it made and would have much rather continued to pace up and down the street.

But steps were already coming closer. A dignified old lady opened the door for me. She must have been close to seventy, had almost white hair, with lively eyes and hundreds of tiny wrinkles streaking her face. But the old woman had an aura that instilled immediate trust in you.

"You are the new apprentice?" "Yes," I answered, "Then come inside, you've been expected."

She went ahead, along a gently descending corridor, through a small French door and went off to the right into a tiny antechamber.

"Now put down your things and come with me into the kitchen,"

I discarded my rucksack and put down my trunk.

"My God, you had a lot to carry, now come with me."

The kitchen was a very large room. Immediately on the right hand side next to the entrance was a huge stove, to the left a kitchen sideboard with a mounted cupboard. On the back left corner a large, scrubbed white wooden table with a corner bench around it. On the rest of the two sides of the table stood four carved wooden chairs.

Gathered around this table sat five people. Herr and Frau Hapala, two girls around five and seven years old and a young woman in her early twenties.

"God bless!"

It was surely a very timid greeting that I expressed in great embarrassment.

"Well there you are, don't be so shy we don't bite."

But Hapala's brash tone increased my bashfulness even more. Arriving during their supper was very embarrassing to me. I shook hands with my boss and with Frau Hapala and stood again hesitantly. Now it was Frau Hapala who helped me get over my embarrassment.

"This is Fräulein Marianne our saleswoman,"

I shook her hand courteously as well,

"And these are Maria and Erna our daughters, and you've already met Fräulein Anna the good cook of the house." "And this," Frau Hapala stood up and walked up to me, "This is Otto our new apprentice. I hope that you stay well behaved and that we get along well together, and so in God's name I welcome you into our household."

She went to the door, dipped her hand into the holy water font that was hanging from the wall and made a cross on my forehead, mouth and chest.

Anna the cook had fetched a plate for me in the meantime, I sat at the table, felt all of their eyes scrutinising me and mostly just wanted the ground to swallow me up.

But they only asked me a few questions, I began to eat and regained a little self confidence. There was good beef broth, roast pork and bread dumplings, it was a pleasing meal and helped me to get over the first embarrassing minutes.

Marianne the saleswoman left after supper, she lived very close by in Ennsdorf.

Hapala went upstairs with his wife for his Sunday afternoon nap. The children played board games and Anna led me to the room that would be my lodging for the next three years.

We left the main building, went over a slabbed inner courtyard which was enclosed on the first side by the house, on the left side by a good four meter wall, on the opposite and right hand side by smaller extension buildings. Along from the house there were a toolshed, a washroom, two rooms and an unused chicken coop.

We stepped through a simple grey painted wooden door into the first of the two rooms.

"Here is your kingdom," said Anna,
"I sleep in the other room, make yourself at home, in an hour you can come and drink a coffee."

"Make yourself at home," that's a nice expression I thought, but to make yourself at home in this room would need a lot of imagination.

Well, not much was out of sight in this room. The bed and a one-piece, primitive wooden cupboard stood in the right hand corner. This filled the whole breadth of the room. On the longer wall, next to the bed was a narrow shelf with a cloth curtain that served as a little nightstand, after that a chair, then an iron stand with a washbowl and a tin cup. The rest of the space was filled with shelves, around a meter wide and one and a half meters tall and were likewise closed with a curtain. This was the layout. In the room there was neither a table nor a heater.

On the side of the door a window took up the rest of the space. On the left side wall there was the door to Anna's room.

I unpacked my trunk, stowed my few things partly in the clothes cupboard, partly on the shelves, sat down and howled. Suddenly I felt incredibly abandoned. I shivered in the inhospitably cold room. But I didn't want to go into the warm kitchen, I was desperately unhappy and wanted to wallow in self pity. I felt more abandoned than a stray dog. I shivered when I thought of the next three years.

After a while the cook came, she fetched me for coffee. There was oat coffee and brioche. The boss and the boss's wife were already sitting at the table again. They surely realised that I had been crying, Hapala just grinned tellingly, but his wife squeezed me as she passed and stroked my hair. She surely had more understanding for my current condition. I had my place at the table assigned next to Anna.

Straight after the coffee I went back to my room. I didn't even want to call it a room. I was cold, but I wanted to be alone, wanted to see and hear no-one. Even back then I found the lack of a table quite unreasonable. During the cold time of year a heater would have surely been appropriate too.
The cook came through my room, she said she wanted to nap for an hour.

"Otto, you'll get used to your new surroundings soon, it's not so bad really, sleep for a couple of nights and it'll all look different."

She clearly meant well by it, and maybe she was right too.

At eight o'clock the family gathered for their evening meal. For the boss this was also the appropriate time to give me his instructions for the following day. Hapala wanted to know if I had an alarm clock, but Anna answered before I could and said that she'd take care of waking me at the right time. On the following day I was supposed to get up at half past five and be ready for the way to the shop at half past six.

As I lay tired in bed not much later, I deliberately kept myself awake to put off waking up again. I was afraid of the next day even though these fears were surely unfounded. The petroleum lamp on my nightstand was still spreading the scent of the smouldering wick, a smell that wasn't unpleasant to me.

Anna's waking call startled me out of my sleep. It was uncomfortably cold in the room. Washing with the ice cold water took me a lot of willpower and was done in a very mediocre fashion. I got dressed as quickly as possible in order to get into the warm kitchen. I didn't forget to put on my sleeve protectors, threw the duvet back and went to breakfast.

I was sitting at the table with a big jug of coffee when my boss came down from the top floor too. I went with him to the upper end of Wienerstrasse. I was instructed as to how all the doors and windows opened, from the next day I was supposed to do this myself. We went through the doorway entrance and went through a side door into a tiny room that was filled halfway to the ceiling with sawdust. We came through a particularly narrow door into the office and shop again. In the office there was a heater the inset of which was taken out and filled with layers of sawdust. Once it was filled, the heater burned for the whole day without any further maintenance.

The office door stayed open and then the warmth could spread across the shop floor as well. If it was really cold in winter you could barely cope with the heat from the office, nevertheless in the shop it would still be very cold and uncomfortable. I had to appear in the shop a half hour earlier in the colder months to set the heater up.
At seven o'clock on the dot I had to open the shop door and open the shutters of both tiny display windows and fasten them open. Then I set up a long metal rack between the entrance and the leftmost display window and depending on the time of year fetched jackets, suits or clothes, in order to hang them thickly on

the metal bar. You can imagine what these things looked like after a few weeks of being affected by the constant dust from the street.

On the first day, once the heater had been set up and the shop had been opened, Hapala set down a huge bundle of knotted cords in front of me. I was supposed to neatly untangle them and wind them into a ball. I saw no great sense in this toilsome business but what could I do? So I spent the whole day with this stupid job. I wondered why not one customer appeared for the whole day. Hour after hour went past without the doorbell once disturbing my peace and quiet. The boss sat behind in his tiny office and didn't appear once.
So I stood a whole day long in very questionable lighting and untangled all of the cords from all of the packages from the past year.

The shop was closed for an hour at twelve. I went up to the house with the boss and we had a little snack break there. The main meal always took place in the evening. Of course the goods that were set out in front of the shop had to be removed for an hour and then set out again after our break.

I was very happy once the first day was over and I was able to close the shop under the boss's supervision and control. With the exception of the one hour at midday, I had been imprisoned in this gloomy cage for eleven hours. I was really disappointed with my apprenticeship and cursed the chance happenings that had brought me to Enns.

That year we stood at the beginning of a period of great unemployment. During my apprenticeship I can remember countless days when not one customer entered the store. It was better in the second shop, even in times of need you needed some sort of groceries, the shop always went on modestly.

After I had spent a few days in the shop, the huge bundle of packaging string forgotten, I had to begin to check the rolls of material for their respective lengths. I had to measure the length and then fasten a tag with the length in meters.

After a few weeks the boss stayed away from the shop ever longer and I was left to my own devices. Particularly during times when there were barely any customers I stood in the gloomy dungeons alone and daydreamed. How differently I had imagined everything to be. A lighter, cleaner shop with nice work colleagues and a constant flow of customers with which the time passed quickly too. But here the hours took ages to pass by, I couldn't look out to the street and was almost always alone. If the boss was there he sat in his office through the back and didn't bother himself with me much.
Hapala was always in an awful mood too, due to the miserable way business was going. Even though the shop rent was surely minimal, it still had to be serviced. Of course I also had to suffer under the boss's awful mood.

Once all the rolls of material had been measured, I got to start to brush all of the suits and overcoats clean. The shoulder sections of many were already grey, partly faded through the sun, partly dirtied by the dust from the street. But since our customers were composed almost only of farmers and farmhands these items still sold, Hapala developed a particular talent for that which I'll come back to later.

The daily routine was always the same. I've already described how the day began, once I'd closed the shop door in the evening at seven o'clock, I began to sweep the dark oiled floor clean for the next day. Then I set the heater to the smallest flame and went to the main shop. I was needed there straight away to weigh out a stockpile of sugar, grains, rice and so on from large sacks into different weight portions.

At eight o'clock, all of us gathered in the big kitchen living room for our evening meal. The meal typically lasted an hour, then the saleswoman left, the children were already in bed for the most part. But around nine o'clock, Hapala and his wife regularly disappeared to their upstairs chambers as well. Once the household had disappeared, there were four pairs of shoes in the lobby, the boss, his wife and the children, which I had to polish along with my own. This job was assigned to me in order to relieve the strain on Anna, the old woman.

In the meantime Anna had tidied the kitchen and we sat for another quarter hour together at the table and read Hapala's newspaper.

It was much too uncomfortable to linger in our rooms in the evening, they were really only used for sleeping and washing, even Anna the old woman didn't have a heater, there wasn't a connecting chimney for it either.

In Hapala's house there was no bath. The toilet was situated outside of the house in the courtyard. It was a real outhouse leaned against the big courtyard wall.

On Saturdays the shops were open into the evenings like during the week, on Sundays from seven in the morning until one in the afternoon.

I had a week behind me, the first Sunday came and I had to get out of bed at five o'clock already. We all went to early mass apart from the children. Afterwards I had to go to the shop on the double in order to set up the heater before opening time. Sunday was the best day of the week for sales. The country folk came to Enns then and they were our best customers.

I was really out of my element with the customers at the beginning. The boss demanded more from me than I could handle in such a short time. When there were a lot of customers in the store I was supposed to play the trained salesman, even though I still didn't have the foggiest idea of what I was doing.

Hapala's sales technique made my hair stand on end. He lied through his teeth, knew how to gloss over the shortcomings of his goods. He good and properly swindled the poor inexperienced country workers, who had to work hard for their money. I was appalled at how the salesman's respectable pursuit of profit was defiled here through a behaviour that was almost criminal. I didn't want to be a salesman now, it was clear to me too that I would never be able to sell merchandise by such dishonest means. We didn't sell here, here we cajoled our customers to buy things with the wickedest tricks. I couldn't understand how the boss consolidated these sales methods with his Christian way of life. I'll come later to some of his methods. But one thing I knew already after the first few days, in the eyes of my boss, I would never become a good salesman.

I had to quickly learn how to read the secret display prices, which were composed of letters, and adapt them into numerical form. Every product had two assigned groups of letters. One for purchase, one for sale. No customer was capable of ascertaining the price himself. No product was labelled, as is customary today, with the price legible for the customers. This gave the boss opportunity for the most unbelievable manipulations.

"Free time" were words which had lost all validity for the duration of my apprenticeship. From six in the morning until late in the evening I was always on the move, the few hours that were left over from the day were needed for sleep.
Only the Sunday afternoon, from two to six, belonged to me. I could only do what I wanted outside during these hours. I didn't

have a key for the house, I could have easily left the house without being noticed, but I wouldn't have been able to re-enter. One single exception was the really important holidays during which all the shops were completely shut, then I was allowed to leave the house for a few hours in the mornings as well.

We got a lot of items mailed to us with the Bahnpost. When these parcels arrived I had to travel to the train station with an old hand cart, sign for the parcels and take them home. This way my good boss saved himself the cost of delivery. On the way back I always passed the Ohrenstein department store, the largest and most modern store in Enns. If the proprietor, a Jew, stood in front of the door, he shook his head at the tasks that my boss expected of people. After all they had nothing to do with my education as a salesman, to which Hapala was firmly obliged by the apprenticeship contract. My boss cursed the Jews at any opportunity, but that was maybe only business envy.

Summer slowly came into the land. I went to the river Enns in my few free hours on Sunday. It was a deep green, clean, brashly roaring mountain river. Its icy water came from the Styrian mountains.
Left and right of the Enns a vast wetlands stretched to the junction with the Danube at Mauthausen. You could go on expeditions here without being disturbed by anyone. All kinds of birds and animals could be observed here that were barely to be seen elsewhere. Lizards sunned themselves on the stones of the shore, slow worms and grass snakes hunted for beetles and mice. Frogs and salamanders cavorted in the numerous wetland ponds. Partridges, pheasants and wild rabbits lived in the undergrowth. It was a shame that the afternoons were so short, too short for my passionate, alert senses, too short for a thorough observation of all the mysterious goings-on.

There was a very large barracks facility from the old Habsburg Empire in Enns. The 4th Dragoons regiment was stationed here during my apprenticeship. The boss, always ruminating on how to get the full use out of his apprentice even better and more profitably, had a brilliant idea. Many officers lived in the barracks, their wives fetched their daily milk in our shop. It was around seven minutes from the barracks to the shop. After some reflection Hapala thought it would bring in a few extra customers if he delivered the officers' wives' milk to their homes for free. What could be more obvious than entrusting his apprentice with this task?

So I became the officers' milk deliverer. Sure enough the lazy wives approved of this convenient delivery and now it became a permanent position for me. So every evening I went off with the hand cart full of milk cans. And so I got into even more work that had nothing to do with my actual education.

The house next door to Hapala belonged to a somewhat elderly spinster of whom not much was known and who you barely saw on the street.

One day this lady lay dead in her bed. She had slipped out of her life very quietly with the help of lots of pills and without saying goodbye. I don't know how, perhaps at the instigation of existing inheritors the house was put up for auction and came into Hapala's possession.

This house was really unsightly. Narrow and low, it stood crammed in between its neighbours. The best of it was the large garden that lay behind it, which you could reach through a door-shaped opening in the washroom. A larger opening to the house next door was even made in the shop and the establishment now seemed substantially bigger.

A few weeks later a strapping grown girl, around sixteen years old, stood on the threshold. An apprentice girl had been taken on to relieve the strain on the saleswoman. Lina Geiblinger was a baker's daughter from Urfahr near Linz. She was quartered upstairs near the bedchamber of the lord and lady of the house. Thus the necessary space between male and female apprentices was also established, much to the relief of Hapala's Christian conscience. Furthermore, I was still under the supervision of the almost seventy year old cook. The old woman would have been better off in the upper floor, but try explaining that to a suspicious master of apprentices. This change had an advantage for me, in that the shoe polishing in the evening was now carried out with Lina's help. I wasn't able to offload the job of the daily milk delivery, however.

From this point on though at least I wasn't totally alone in the hardships of my apprenticeship, things are always easier to cope with company.

Every month a small sum of pocket money came from the parents. As I didn't have any opportunity to spend the money, a small sum of savings slowly came into being with which I could fulfil a few modest wishes. But up to this point I had no use for money and literally stuck it in my savings stocking.

Hapala, who was constantly brooding over how he could increase his little fortune, suddenly had a brilliant idea again. He wanted to have fresh eggs in the shop ready for his customers at all times. The eggs were to be bought directly from the farmers and for as cheap as possible.

The boss's old bicycle was hauled out of the shed and made roadworthy. A large weaved basket with two lids on each side of the handle was fastened to the bike.

And who else, of course "Otto," was to travel across the

countryside and busy himself as a bulk purchaser of eggs. Even though it had nothing to do with either clothing or manufacture, this was a task which I loved to carry out regardless. This way I could at least leave the musty, gloomy shop for a few hours and merrily cycle in the fresh air across the countryside.

I was supplied with schillings along with a notebook to neatly write down all of the purchases. It was entrusted to me to bargain capably, to not pay just any price and to make sure that I only brought fresh eggs back with me.

"Most farmers are scoundrels," said the boss,
"don't let them take you for a ride."

I assured him I'd keep my eyes open and bargain well, I knew well that I was least likely to be able to keep the last promise.

So I happily set off on the bike and set on course southwards, towards Steyr.
But I left the state road not far past Enns and cycled off on back roads between the few farms.
At the first farmer's, I filled the basket halfway with chaff. That was the best padding so that you weren't taking scrambled eggs to Enns at the end.

After visiting a few farmers I'd already filled my target and the basket was full. The price that I'd paid for them was a small amount over the limit which Hapala had given to me, but they were really big eggs which he could really make a show with. Very proud of my aptitude I very steadily started the journey back. I took my time. I knew that the boss would use my time consumption today as a basis for the future as well. I didn't want to make a mess of my time limit at the beginning already. I'd taken up a first step towards a labour unionist mentality.

Many more trips went over the countryside following this first successful egg run, not always with the same profitable results.

Up until now I've not mentioned that there was also a son, Anton, in the Hapala family. He studied in a monastic school in Seitenstetten. As he rarely came home there isn't much to say about him. Years later, when he was already in college and I was no longer in Enns, he got an infection while on a trip in Africa from which he soon thereafter died.

A message came from Auntie Kathi that I ought to come back to Wels for a day for my graduation exam. I hadn't thought about this exam for a long time and hadn't prepared for it at all either.

The exam was more of a formality. I was only asked easy questions and after three hours it was all finished.

I went back to Enns in the late afternoon. The visit with Auntie Kathi was short. I spent the whole time answering questions so I was happy when the clock announced it was time to go.

I belatedly discovered that there was a small public library in Enns as well.
The first book that I got to read was "In the Desert" by Karl May. The adventurous narrative took me captive from the first pages. Equipped with a lively imagination myself, the adventures described in them very much appealed to my longing to travel foreign countries.

Every evening I had to refill the petroleum lamp. I lay wide awake until late in the night and devoured page after page and simply couldn't come to an end. I took all of the descriptions of adventure at face value, and only much later realised that the writer wasn't reporting from his own experiences, rather from the deeds of his heroes and an inexhaustible imagination. When I woke the next day I was tired and unslept, but I already longed feverishly for the evening.

It was a restless time for Anna. She called anxiously several times every evening,

"Are you not going to sleep Otto?"

"I'm fine I'm not tired yet," I answered but I couldn't bring myself to stop reading.

Anna was afraid that I'd fall asleep and unconsciously knock the lamp from the nightstand. A fire in my room would have blocked her escape.

In the clothes shop we had some of the officers' wives from the barracks as customers. For the most part these women only wanted odds and ends because we couldn't tempt them into the store with our choice of clothing. One woman, tall, somewhat heavy set with very black hair and looking somewhat foreign visited several times and that was quite conspicuous. In addition most of the things she bought were very trivial, and she spent far too much time in the store for them. She would whisper with the boss incessantly. When this woman came in the door I was always in the way somehow. Either I had to go into the office or Hapala would send me to the house with a meaningless task.

I knew fine well that the pair of them were at the very least telling dirty jokes in my absence and they wanted to keep me out of earshot. Even though we'd only enjoyed a very scant sexual education in our last year at school I wasn't born yesterday either. If I tried, sometimes persistently, to catch some chunks of their discussions, Hapala would get hopping mad and on one occasion even kicked me up the backside quite thoroughly when I didn't disappear quickly enough. I would have loved to know what sort of foolery they were up to in my absence. But as the boss was a very Christian man, it can't have been all that bad.

With the beginning of autumn my compulsory education at the vocational college also became very demanding. The boss wasn't happy about the hours I was missing from the shop and he had to hold the fort alone. The many hours of absence in my school report indicate to me that he clearly used many opportunities to keep me away from lessons. The lessons rescued me from some hours of gloominess in our shop however, and I was very grateful for that.

I had long settled into Enns by the time the first winter came. I was well familiar with my daily duties, but the realisation had also been firmly cemented in me that I couldn't really expect a good education in the profession with Hapala. Our shop had far too much choice in individual categories but totally inadequate variety within those categories. The share of non sellers was far too large so that they blocked our shelves, which always had to be cleaned again, dusted and resorted. We had some things which led a quiet existence for the entire duration of my apprenticeship.

The late evenings (and sometimes half the nights) I still spent in the company of Kara-Ben-Nemsi and Shatterhand. I lived through all of the adventures as if they were my own and felt just as at home in the deserts of Africa, the prairies of America and the Balkans. I had rented out a new book "Wild Men of Kurdistan" and devoured the contents page after page. The clock had gone past midnight, Anna called for the thousandth time,

"Otto can't you sleep?"

The poor woman, she couldn't get any sleep and didn't have the heart to give me a good telling off.

I couldn't bring myself to extinguish the lamp, the further I got through the book the more exciting the events became. Crawled up under the duvet, I experienced the shivering cold of the night and the sweltering heat of the days which my heroes had to endure.

Tonight Hapala was no doubt racked with severe stomach ache. He had to go across the courtyard in the pitch dark to the outhouse in the yard which he never had to do otherwise, he always had his chamber pot under his bed for the small errands in the nights. After he had weakly left the outhouse again, the light from my window lured him to my bedroom like a moth. What he saw there through the window surely well surpassed his imagination. A furious tirade stormed out of the darkness of the night towards me. In shock I turned down the wick of the lamp like a bolt of lightning, but it didn't help any more. The situation that presented itself to my boss was clear.

The result was a long, continuous rationing of petroleum for the next weeks, bad for me, but days of undisturbed sleep for Anna. Taking away the light stopped my reading craze in passing, but certainly not my interest for adventure.

I read an advertisement from a company in Munich offering ski and mountain gear under the slogan "Thunderstorm-Mountain-Skis" in Hapala's newspaper. I had a brochure delivered and was delighted by all of the nice things that you could buy in it. I dived into my savings stocking and ordered myself the following equipment: A gel fuel camping stove, a cooking pot, a canteen, a tea strainer, a pocket compass and a fixed blade camping knife. I already had a rucksack.

On receipt of these things, I used the first Sunday for an expedition into the nearby forest. The snow was still lying and the thermometer was below freezing. I made a good camp. I cooked tea out of melted snow, ate a small bit of stolen salami, which replaced the smoked bear paw of my imagination, and nurtured the fantasy of being a real trapper.

Hapala shook his head as I headed off, he surely thought 'the boy is crazy,' he wasn't completely wrong.

In Enns we had a private contractor who, once a week, brought the refuse from the shops to the tip for a small fee. This was a small expense, but the boss begrudged even this and would have found a better use for the money.

"Business is bad," he moaned one day at tea time,
"You have to save every schilling in order to get through these rotten times," nodded his wife in agreement.
"Every day groceries are getting more expensive, I always have to think of new ways we can save money."
"Yes it's bad," Frau Hapala concurred dutifully,
"sales shrink more almost every day."

Us workers kept our mouths shut, we remained completely impartial on the matter.

"We could save the cost of the garbage collection for example," as he ascertained this, the boss looked at me particularly emphatically. I knew immediately what that meant.
"It wouldn't be a big saving, but in these times every schilling is important." Hapala said and what that really meant was, "from now on Otto, you can take the rubbish to the tip."

The rubbish dump was situated a half hour southward towards Steyr, near the country road. Well then, from now on then every week Otto the idiot went off with the hand cart, loaded with empty drums of herring fillets and everything you could think of that wasn't flammable or that Anna couldn't make use of in the kitchen.

It certainly wasn't a job for an apprentice in his second year, but what could I do? And so I also became a specialist handcart operator.

Sundays were the best days for sales in late autumn. Business with the greatcoats began then. With and without fur collars, plain or chequered, normal or thickly stuffed, they hung in long rows on a rod in front of the store. Then the farmers and farmhands stood in front of the treasures and wondered at them. We had little to offer the women in comparison.

On these Sundays the boss was in full swing. His oratory talent was astonishing and of an irresistible persuasiveness. I would be kept busy packaging the bulky articles of clothing. There weren't any shopping bags back then yet, all of the items were laboriously packaged in paper and elaborately tied up. I really had my hands full then, I felt like a mechanical packaging machine. But by the end of my apprenticeship I could proudly claim that my packaging was the most beautiful in all of Enns. Of course the boss was the master of talking up his wares, his skilfulness, the art of his persuasiveness, his deceptive manoeuvres that he used thereby were insurpassable. We didn't have much choice between the different sizes. The boss limited himself to the standard sizes between forty eight and fifty two. The greatcoats were often similar in colour and pattern. We always had a few pieces that were well worn from the sun and dust. These items were always in a particular corner behind the shop counter on Sundays. If some honest farmworker had decided on buying a coat then Hapala, at breakneck speed, would swap the purchased item for a beat up version of the same thing. Hapala knew exactly who he could pull off this fraudulent trick with.

Making a fool out of the customers played out something like this. If some honest farmworker neared the items we had on display, the boss shot out of the shop at lightning speed towards his intended victim like a spider.

"Good morning, well? Aren't they something?"

Hapala strokes across the display with a movement of his hand.

"Here's an item that'd be particularly handsome for you, perfect in quality,"

The young man stands in front of all the splendour somewhat helplessly,

"Such an opportunity won't come again, first class products at a fantastic price." The man feels somewhat caught unaware. "Actually I wanted to wait a bit, it's not cold yet,"

Hapala shakes his head disapprovingly.

"Wait? Do you want to throw money out of the window? In a few days my stocks will be exhausted, guaranteed, what comes after will be enormously more expensive. I'm sure you don't have money to give away, you have to work hard enough for your money I'm sure."
"But I still want to wait," says the man.
"Listen, I know I'm ruining myself but you look like a nice man, I'll give you a great special offer, just wait," the boss looks at the price label, written in code, illegible to the customer, is one hundred and twenty schillings.
"This good item," begins the boss,
"costs one hundred and sixty schillings, a ridiculously low price

for this quality, with the beautiful fur collar, in every way exceptionally lined, faultlessly made. For you one hundred and forty schillings, what do you say? I'm almost giving it away."

The man is unsure, but is still undecided and timidly says,

"There are coats hanging in Ohrenstein's that cost a hundred and twenty schillings, they look good too."
"Yes, yes I know these wares and I know the company that they come from and I know their workmanship. If you really want to waste your money then in God's name go to Ohrenstein, you know the owner is a Jew, I'm sure I don't need to say any more."

The boss hangs the coat back up on the rail, shaking his head.

"But the products there don't look bad either," the man dares to protest.
"Ha, listen here, an expert wouldn't pay a hundred schillings for that garbage, but please, if you're happy to go with trash over quality then please I can't stop you, you can go to Ohrenstein and give away your hard earned schillings for garbage."
"Of course you want to have good quality," added the man,
"But twenty schillings more or less is a lot of money for me."
"As if I don't know," answered Hapala,
"listen here then young man, it'll cost me the last of my earnings and I have a wife and children to feed but I can't bear to see you being ripped off, here, one hundred and thirty schillings my final offer."

Hapala takes the item from the rack and holds it in front of the lad's face formally.

"At least come inside and try it on, well come on, trying it out costs nothing."

Somewhat hesitant, the man comes into the store. He tries on the coat which hangs far too wide on his emaciated shoulders.

"Well just as I thought," Hapala sashays around the customer, "You have the ideal figure, it couldn't fit you better."
"A little too big I think?" the customer argues timidly.
"Now listen here, do you want to buy a greatcoat or a straitjacket? You'll still be wearing this quality in twenty year's time, then you'll be fatter and it'll still fit you."
"Hmm, I don't know..."
"I'm telling you, it's not a centimeter too big or too small, in that coat you have shoulders like a prize boxer."
"Maybe I'll check in here again in a week," the man still can't make his mind up.
"In a week!" Hapala practically gasped for breath, "I can't give you this price in a week. Well then because it's you and the devils gotten into me one hundred and twenty going once, going twice."
"Well then I'll take it," the young man smiles somewhat proud, thinks he's done really good business for himself.
"Otto pack the coat quickly so that I don't have to look at my disgrace anymore."

While the customer grasps for his wallet the boss, like lightning, swaps the coat for a somewhat weathered article of the same size.

"Might I interest you in something else? I have good quality trousers," the boss is only just saying it, he knows fine that there's nothing more to do with this customer and his interest in the man ceases immediately. Hapala goes into his office, the sale is in the bag.

Of course Hapala hadn't made a loss in the deal, one hundred and twenty schillings was the regular sale price. The one who'd been duped was the poor farm worker who was carrying a coat that had been exposed to the sun and the dust for a week in the false belief he'd gotten a really good deal.

Such sales practices went completely against my principles. I had very different ideas of my profession and hated the boss's methods in the extreme.

I was now in my second year as an apprentice and was allowed to set out the little display windows on my own as I saw fit. This was a job that I carried out with greatest enthusiasm and with which Hapala himself was happy. Unfortunately the opportunities for the layout were very limited, I didn't have any promotional items available and the selection of clothes was also so one-sided that I had trouble laying out the display window differently each time. Larger items like suits I couldn't put on display at all due to how small the display window was. I looked on the windows of our competitor Ohrenstein with envy. He had an entire window front and they even had lots of display mannequins there.

At this time the whole economy dropped ever more down into the doldrums. Unemployment rose at an alarming rate, whole groups of beggars travelled the countryside, much to the annoyance of the farmers. Even miners from the Hausruck area were let go. In Schneegattern a town not far from Hausruckedt there was a very well known miner's band. In the worst times of joblessness this band broke up and went in three and four man groups across the country begging and playing music. It was a very bad time and everyone counted himself fortunate if he had bread and work.

I hated the Sundays in winter because then I had to get up so early in order to not miss morning Mass. When I crawled out from under the covers shortly after five, the wash water in the tin cup was often frozen and I had to remove a thin layer of ice first. Of course the soap barely took to the ice cold water too so that everything ended up more or less with a meagre sort of cat-lick. Getting into the cold clothes was just as uncomfortable. It was only comfortably warm once I got to the kitchen where in the meantime Anna had already been busying herself for a half hour. When I got to church it was still pitch dark all around. Normally a number of women already stood in the front court in the snow and blathered a bit before the beginning of mass. I wondered then at the light brown pattern that they left behind in the snow once they'd gone. I soon uncovered the mystery. Back then they had no trousers on even in the coldest winter and when they felt a necessity to free themselves of greater or lesser quantities of fluids, they spread their legs a little and relieved themselves of their burdens without stopping their conversation as they did it. Only the brown patterns in the snow betrayed their businesses. And so back then the women made themselves more comfortable than the men.

It was around this time I became aware of the RUSTIN company in a newspaper advertisement. They were based in Berlin and were offering courses for independent study. According to the advertisement with some diligence and perseverance you could make up the grades for your Matura. I was immediately very enthusiastic, I wrote to Berlin and had the corresponding brochure delivered.

Suddenly Karl May was forgotten and I dove into independent study in my few free hours. When I got good reports back from the first assignments I'd sent in I was convinced I'd reach the goal I wished for within a few years. Frau Hapala seemed very pleased with my enthusiasm, Herr Hapala doubted that I would stick it out. The parents that I informed about it didn't react at all. But I was very enthusiastic and started to swot and used every free hour for my studies. It would have surely been good if someone had given me words of encouragement for it.

A sugar factory was built not far from Enns and had been bustling with activity for months. The farmers of the area had gotten involved early on and laid out large fields of sugar beets. At harvest time in early autumn many farmhands from Yugoslavia came to help with the harvest. On Sundays a modest number of these Yugoslavian helpers could also be counted amongst our customers. They were tight with their money, they mostly bought trivial things. A regular purchase was men's socks. They didn't take them with them though, no, they took off their old, sweaty, stinking socks which were comprised almost only of holes in the shop and put the new ones on straight after. They did this with a frankly astounding casualness. It didn't enter the boss's mind to try to put a stop to this scandal, no, it could have cost him a schilling's profit. After that I had the task of disposing of the hardly savoury remnants of the former stockings. What I had to put up with.

Business suffered under the economic decline more every day. Days often went by where we didn't come across a single customer. Even in the grocery department turnover dropped down to a minimum. Very early I realised that after my apprenticeship ended I couldn't stay with Hapala for long. He had to keep me on for three months afterward, then a new apprentice would no doubt take my place.
Still I didn't worry about it too much. I'd finished my vocational college in the meantime with a very good leaving certificate too.

I almost forgot a story that took place a few months before.

Back then there were all kinds of snakes in the wetlands around Enns. Mainly grass snakes and Aesculapian snakes. I found a grass snake with fantastic markings sunning itself on the sun warmed embankment one Sunday afternoon. I was on one of my adventurous travels along with all my trapper gear including rucksack and camping knife that I had been spurned on to by Karl May's imagination.

It was one of my more spontaneous ideas to catch the grass snake and share my dwelling with it. I cut myself a small stick so that at the end of the branch a fork remained, around four centimeters long. I held the snake down just behind the head with the fork, picking her up took a lot of willpower but I grabbed her bravely at the neck and induced the furiously squirming animal into my rucksack, which I hurriedly tied. I felt like a great animal trapper in the bush all of a sudden and was very proud of my achievement.

I ended my excursion early. It was worth it to safely take the dangerous captive animal into my room. When I arrived at Hapala's there was only the calm of a Sunday afternoon. The boss and his wife were busying themselves, or relaxing in the bed chamber. Anna the cook was sitting in the living room and darning the holes in her black woollen stockings. Lina the apprentice girl and the children were nowhere to be seen. These circumstances suited my plan well. First of all I shoved my rucksack with the loot into my wardrobe. Then I grabbed an empty margarine crate out of the shop. In the shed I found the part of an old window pane I needed. A makeshift terrarium was now complete.

I had to work everything in secret as it was obvious to me that Hapala would have sent me packing with my grass snake. I padded the floor of the crate with some grass, prayed that Anna didn't come running in and jockeyed the animal from the rucksack to the crate which was easier said than done. But all went well. I weighed down the glass with the twenty fourth volume of Karl May, shoved the small menagerie in the shelf and pulled the curtain over it carefully, hiding my secret from Anna's eyes. It rustled very suspiciously behind the curtain, but the cook was a little hard of hearing and would no doubt notice nothing.

Then I went into the kitchen to unwind after this excitement. I thought of how I could get hold of some frogs the following Sunday, but since I already knew that snakes could live for several months without food, this worry wasn't too pressing. As we all sat together at the table for supper a little later, my thoughts were still with the grass snake. It bothered me a little that I had to keep everything such a secret, on the other hand it made things more exciting too.

Once I knew Anna was in bed, I fished the crate out of the shelf, placed it in front of my bed and could observe my reptile in peace. The snake still couldn't come to terms with its captivity and darted its tongue in and out desperately against the glass cover. I found it all terribly exciting and could barely sleep.

The following Monday passed without incident, only that for the whole day my thoughts were less with the shop and more with the snake, and I yearningly waited for evening. But the day came to an end eventually and, full of impatience, I locked up the shop.

I immediately went to my room to see the snake. I pulled the curtain aside. The snake was still in the crate, but she was lying coiled up in a corner and wasn't moving. She didn't lift her head to me and I didn't like this listlessness at all. I pulled the crate out of the shelf, lifted the glass lid up and blew hard onto the reptile. With that she shot up like a bolt of lightning, I barely had time to pull my face back to safety. So she was still alive and kicking! Then I heard Anna suddenly coming across the yard, she clearly wanted to go to her room. I quickly lay the glass cover back on top and shoved the crate back into the shelf, as soon as I pulled the curtain back the cook entered my room. The good woman had no idea what sort of neighbours she lived with, I was lucky that she didn't think anything of my hasty movements as well. How could she have known what I was struggling with anyway. Anna grabbed something trivial from her room, came back straight away and said:

"Come along Otto, we're eating soon."

The evening meal was the main meal of the day and took up a considerable amount of time. Today it was the same. After the meal, Hapala immediately set out the tasks for the next day. On this evening, when I was in a hurry to get back to my room, he oddly enough had surprisingly numerous requests on his mind and kept me in a longer discussion on them. Since the cook had also popped into her room for a moment I had to wait on her return either way, then she would be occupied in the kitchen for at least an hour and I could carry on with my reptile study in peace, or so I thought, but again as so often, I had counted my chickens before they'd hatched.

The rest of us besides Anna were still sitting together at the table when a loud agitated screaming penetrated the kitchen from across the yard. Everyone jumped up from the table and ran to the yard in order to see the reason for the excitement. Then our good Anna came rushing up to our boss breathless, she was in such a tizz she couldn't speak at first, pointing with her outstretched hand towards her room.

"Herr Hapala," her voice nearly failed her,
"There's a snake in my room, a huge, slithering creature!"

With that they all screamed at once, only the boss acted with courage and ran into Anna's room and I, with a fair amount of jitters, followed him.

What we saw must have been a thoroughly huge shock for Anna. Here she slithered, my damned grass snake at her full length over the floorboards of Anna's room just up to her bedside.

I knew that I'd lost the snake now, and I made the best out of the matter by showing myself off as a crafty animal catcher again. I grabbed a broomstick from the washroom and while the children ran to the yard screaming loudly and Anna and the boss's wife went to a safe distance, I shooed the snake to the yard. Once I'd gotten over a feeling of disgust coming on I grabbed the snake by the neck and threw her in a long arc over the encircling wall into the neighbour's garden. I basked in the awe which this courageous deed generated amongst everyone present. There was a long palaver about how the snake got into Anna's room. Nothing seemed to throw light upon the whole fuss, until sadly as he was leaving Anna's room the boss saw quite a lot of broken glass in front of my shelf. He pulled the curtain aside and saw the crate and the whole series of events was immediately obvious to him. There was a real good scolding for me which had a real effect and ended my dreams of a little snake farm.

I had unfortunately forgotten, as Anna had appeared unexpectedly, to weigh down the glass lid with Karl May's twenty fourth volume again. And so the snake was able to push the lid from the crate and escape. Sadly instead of going into a corner of my room she went on her way through the open door to Anna. The cook was furious with me for days and I couldn't persuade her of the animal's harmlessness. So this adventure ended ingloriously and quickly and I had to turn my lively imagination to other things.

Even the Sundays in the shop slowly became very quiet. Even the farmers held back with their purchases and the boss's mood grew worse from week to week. And I was the first outlet for his ill temper. I got a share of some knocks and was thoroughly scolded for every triviality. If the Sundays were too quiet, the boss would pace around the shop like a captive tiger, immediately stepping into the street when someone had barely gotten close to our items on display. He thought he could encourage people to buy things by force, but people who were genuinely interested were scared off with his overzealousness. After that I was ecstatic once midday neared and closing the shop opened up the free Sunday afternoon.

For many years I was annoyed at the way in which Hapala used me for all sorts of jobs that had nothing to do with my professional education. Today I see things a little differently. It was an awfully hard time for the boss too and at least I had spent the years with him well and ate well and the value of that I would learn later.

It was on one of these quiet Sunday mornings when suddenly muffled drum roll penetrated through to us in the gloomy store. I went with the boss onto the street and here we saw them for the first time, tightly in step with each other they marched so, Hitler's SA and SS. They marched along the main street with no singing, no shouting of propaganda, the column passed by in an almost eerie silence. I had never seen anything like it and the withdrawn display made something of an impression on me. Certainly you read things in the newspapers about Hitler in Germany, but back then I had other interests and politics was the last thing I squandered my thoughts on. It would have perhaps been better if had done so, but I only realised this years later. The name Hitler meant so little to me back then, I couldn't have yet known how much this man would influence my coming years.

In the following months we saw these brown and black columns marching through our towns quite frequently. Always more people gathered on the streets when they went past and the columns became ever longer and every day more was spoken of them.

And so the months went by. The last winter in Enns with all its discomforts in my cold room went past too. I used every free hour to bury myself in RUSTIN's textbooks and slowly I realised, how long and hard the way to a Matura qualification was when you can only busy yourself with the learning materials for at most two hours a day and were totally left to fend for yourself alone.
But for the time being I was still untiring in my hard work and every good mark in my correction books spurred me on to persevere further. All of the study expenses I paid from out of my meagre pocket money, I received no subsidies from anyone.

On the seventh of April nineteen hundred and thirty my apprenticeship came to an end. I was presented with the certificate and was sent to the trader's cooperative with it. I got a big, beautiful duty stamp imprinted onto the paper there and was now officially registered as a sales employee too. The official who put the stamp on my certificate was surprised that my boss had used the cheapest paper for this important document.

Otherwise the day went by without any celebrations. On the evening of my release Hapala presented me with the key to the house. He did this with the thoughtful observation:

"Now master Poschacher you may".. for the first time he spoke to me formally, "leave the house in the evening, and so come and go as you please in your free time but I would be grateful as a Christian paterfamilias and furthermore as your responsible guardian if you were to make as little use of it as possible. I give the handing over of the key more of a symbolic meaning so to say."

Incidentally over the coming weeks the boss fell back into the familiar "Otto." It didn't bother me much. The only advantage that my graduation brought was that I didn't have to polish the household's shoes any more. That was now Lina's task alone. The boss didn't even want to expect me to do the weekly rubbish removal anymore. By necessity he had to pay out the few schillings for the commercial rubbish collection again.

The saleswoman had left us in the meantime as well. She married a blacksmith. It was a marriage of love with which her parents absolutely were not agreed and which for her also meant being banned from the house and disinherited by her parents.

The saleswoman's position had to be filled by the boss's wife for the most part. A new saleswoman wouldn't be employed since Fräulein Lina was already in her second year of apprenticeship herself. The boss helped out a lot too, while I was mostly left to my own devices in the dark fortress.
There were days when I didn't have a schilling in the till by the time I closed the shop and the boss's grumpy face ruined the whole evening. If as an exception I had actually made a lot of dough, Hapala would be jovial and beam at me patronisingly, but then even I was more than a little proud. But the poor days were the norm and the boss's bad mood almost a permanent condition.

A few weeks before my graduation I was with Lina in the lobby polishing shoes after dinner. Unlike their usual custom (they normally went to bed very early,) the boss and his wife were still up and talking with Anna.

Of course we got up to mischief when we were cleaning the shoes as well. Lina must have surely teased me more than usual that evening, in any case I wanted to do something violent to her. But she avoided my attack through a speedy escape through the hallways and up the stairs to her room which she was able to lock shut before I thundered on her door. I was furiously banging on the door while the boss was already advancing up the stairs snorting. I don't know how it happened, he grabbed me by the collar and, trembling with rage, positively dragged me to the stairs and pushed me in front of him step by step down to the hall and back to the lobby. He swore most furiously while he did it and couldn't calm himself at all. If he should find me in front of Lina's bedroom door again he threatened, he would throw me head over heels down the stairs and I could pack my bags immediately.

"You are in a Christian house!" the boss bellowed at me, "I'll drive these silly ideas out of your head soon enough my boy! You're not so stupid as to chase after the apprentice girl, and don't you open your gob where it's not appropriate. I'm not afraid of giving you a good clap over the ear, and you'll learn that if I ever once catch you in front of Lina's bedroom door again!"

Since the boss's speech was clear enough and Lina's room was next to the boss's bedchamber, I very wisely refrained from risking chasing her upstairs in future. Downstairs the good, pious Anna guarded over my moral conduct. The old spinster was very pious but also very good natured. On the most part due to her excellent cooking I also have very fond memories of her. She had no relatives and at almost seventy years old she had to slave away from five o'clock in the morning until late in the evening day after day in order to eke out her little existence. I always felt sorry for her when I thought of the lonely twilight of her life. What was she supposed to do when she couldn't work anymore?

A few weeks after my graduation I had to set off unexpectedly on one of the many egg tours across the countryside. The egg stocks hadn't held up to the demand and of course the boss was very proud of always having fresh country eggs. I always enjoyed these journeys. So I swung myself onto the already very battered trusty bicycle and headed off. I still recall that it was really a very warm sunny day in late spring. It was excellent to cycle over the countryside so carefree, even when the pleasure only lasted a few hours. But today I had to travel further the eggs seemed to have become scarce or the demand had increased.

It lasted a good two hours longer until I'd filled the basket and all of the eggs were well packed in chaff. So I wasn't allowed to dawdle on my journey back if I didn't want to needlessly raise the boss's ire.

So I took a shortcut on the journey back which I otherwise avoided out of fear of the bulls which lived on a meadow I'd have to cross. The great pasture was secured at the start and the finish by a large wooden fence which could be climbed over on each side without opening the fence itself.
I saw the bulls grazing peacefully a few hundred meters to the side, so I thought this time I could dare the journey. So I manoeuvred the bike and egg basket over the fence and set myself into motion towards the bottom end of the meadow. I wanted to get out of the danger zone as quickly as possible. When I threw a glance at the bulls however, I saw with shock that two bulls with their tails raised were already starting to move quickly towards me. My heart began to beat in my throat, I pedalled harder but had to make dreadfully sure to not come

away from the narrow path. That could have resulted in landing, bike, eggs and all, in the nearest cowpat.

The quicker I cycled, the quicker the two bulls got trotting and were getting alarmingly closer to me. I didn't know if there was a patron saint for egg collectors, I would have surely called on him for help.

I had to keep my eyes pointed like hell towards the narrow path, but I didn't let the two bulls out of my sight either. Their raised tails seemed particularly menacing to me, seemed to me like a sign of particular aggressiveness. How quick they could run!

I hadn't gotten halfway towards the other end of the meadow yet, I just saw how the animals were getting menacingly closer. The closer the bulls nipped at my tail, the more dangerous my cycling became. I was close to falling a few times. If only I got out of this unscathed! I saw the saving fence a few hundred meters in front of me, but I could also already hear the pounding of the animals which were closing in on me more every second.

All of a sudden, once I saw the threatening shadows of the bulls appearing at my side, my cycling skills were finally exhausted. I violently fell head over heels forward, the egg basket was fastened tight but some of the eggs themselves flew after me like white tennis balls. There I lay, closing my eyes and waiting on the killing blow. But the blow didn't come, everything remained very peaceful. I didn't hear any stomping any more, in the air a lark warbled, a gentle breeze stroked over my hair.. otherwise calm. I overcame my fear of looking the danger in the eye, opening my eyes just a little at first, slowly more and then saw both bulls standing a few meters to the side and gawping at me curiously. My heart hammered in my throat and I didn't dare to make a peep. Around me lay scattered scrambled eggs, the back wheel was still turning slowly, the front wheel was buckled. Me lying there so lifelessly no doubt became too boring for the bulls. I don't know if animals can laugh, but they can certainly smirk quite maliciously, for sure they were laughing at me, they turned their back sides to me then, swirled their tails through the air cheerfully and trotted off leisurely to their own kind.

Now that the immediate danger had passed my strength grew, I lifted my fists threateningly at the departing bulls as I lifted myself out of the omelette I was in and swore bitter revenge. In reality I was happy to be alive!

And so I gathered together whatever there was still to gather. The front wheel I made somewhat roadworthy again, blurting out very courageous threats to the animals as they pulled ever further away and made myself on my journey back very embarrassed.

I got no triumphant entrance in Enns. Only a few eggs remained whole, the boss made an awful howling over the loss, our apprentice girl and the boss's children laughed themselves half to death. Anna felt sorry for me and got a half dozen eggs to boil. The boss said in all seriousness I sure was a real dope.

My time in Enns now slowly came to an end. As predicted, after three months I had to quit my position as an employee. A new apprentice was going to take my place and thus reduce expenses. It meant leaving the old roman fort in whose walls I had learned a profession, one which I would never practice again. And so more wasted years? Back then I had no idea how many wasted years were still to follow those in Enns. I grew wiser from some life experiences, I learned really very little for my profession.

On a Friday my service came to an end. On Saturday the first of July thirty three I had packed my bundle. In my blue, already much too small confirmation suit, I departed from Enns. The boss's wife made the sign of the cross on me as I left in the same way she had done at the start, only good Anna shed a few tears. I sadly trotted off to the station, climbing on the train to Wels. Now my educative years finally came to an end. The locomotive puffed out tremendous smoke and a soot particle flew into my eye which marred my last glance back to Enns.

-   .   -

A year of poverty.

While I'd been apprenticing in Enns the parents had given the restaurant business in Hausruckedt away to father's sister Ernestine. The parents themselves took over the inn business in mother's parents' house in Wels. If someone was unhappy about this trade then it was surely my father who had to give up his beautiful hunting grounds in the Hausruck forest and along with it his home area and his siblings. On top of it came the fact that father couldn't stand his wife's relatives. Stepmother's maiden name was Eisschill and the whole Eisschill family had nothing good to say about father either.

The whole Eisschill family was completely at loggerheads with each other again. The entire clan had disintegrated into two large groups. On the one side was mother, Auntie Kathi and Uncle Louis on the opposing side were Uncle Franz, another sister and a brother. In the end the whole argument degenerated into a growing series of court trials, for years the siblings couldn't come to agreement on the distribution of their inheritance. It was an altogether peculiar family that my stepmother belonged to. A whole number of siblings finally met their end through suicide. Auntie Rosi from Kundel started it by poisoning herself. A sister from Wels drank Lysol, so also a suicide by poisoning. Hans, the brother from Vienna whose camera I found in the attic, shot himself and a brother in Villach, a butcher, hung himself, you could say they were a suicide family.
Father disliked going to Wels so much, he must have conceded to years of his wife's pressure in the end, but it can't have been easy for him.

In Wels they were clearly not that happy about my return home. The reception was cool and it seemed they blamed me for losing my position in Enns. But thousands of young men were in the same boat back then, they had barely ended their apprenticeship before they had to make space for the new apprentice because for the majority of businesses continued employment as a fully qualified employee simply wasn't sustainable. Neither the freshly graduated journeymen nor their teachers were to blame for this, it was the miserable economic situation which dominated those years. There was no prospect of me finding a job in Wels as a qualified employee either.

In this situation my stepmother no doubt came to the conclusion that it was high time that my biological mother looked after me once again. I don't believe that my father was the driving force behind it, but it was decided to get rid of me, the useless mouth to feed ought to leave the house as soon as possible. And I have to say the parents had me out of the house very hurriedly. Today a young man of my age back then would simply take up a room and enlist help partly from the state, partly from his father for his livelihood. Sadly the situation back then wasn't so simple. You were much more dependent on your parents and their concerns and all of the education that you were subject to went in a completely different direction and didn't allow for the independence which the young people possess today.

I had been in Wels for maybe fourteen days before I'd be tying up my few possessions into a bundle again. My personal possessions weren't in great number. The zither remained in Wels, it could be used in the inn after all. I had to part with my textbooks for the first time, they remained packed in the cellar. And then what else did I have? Along with my confirmation suit a few sets of underwear, knickerbockers and a woollen jacket along with a cloth overcoat.

I didn't find it difficult to part from Wels, from stepmother and father. The constant feeling of not being welcome in the house anymore weighed heavily on my mind. And if I had to go, then I'd rather it be as soon as possible.

And so I was to go back to Malzer. Around twelve years had passed since I'd left Malzer and mother as a child and had been brought to Kössen for a second time. I didn't have good memories of Malzer and I was burdened with very grim thoughts on the prospect of having to go back there.

There was no warmth as I left my stepmother, Auntie Kathi sent me on my way lecturing about all kinds of things and father wanted to accompany me on the way to my new home himself. I don't believe he did it gladly.
As I travelled off with my father in the direction of Linz, another chapter of my life had been closed again. Until now I had lived through years of eternal travelling, how would the next years take shape? Would they finally become years of peace or would the eternal wandering continue? We will see. After around an hour's travel, having already left Linz behind us a while ago, the little town of Enns appeared in the distance on a hill. I had only left it two weeks ago and so soon after I was already seeing her walls again. I saw the town go past with wistfulness in my heart. I would have gladly gotten off and continued my life inside her walls. But the train steamed with us onward, we travelled over a railbridge and crossed the border into Lower Austria.
From father's comments during the journey I gathered that mother's family had been the driving force for my eviction, but how did that fact help me? I didn't want to stay in Wels as an unwelcome guest anyway.

It was a hot day in July, we sat in third class on wooden benches and the train stopped at every station. Father had clearly chosen a local train in order to save money and so it progressed very slowly. This dawdling was totally fine by me, at least it delayed my arrival with Malzer for a few hours. We had a longer stop in St. Pölten and father bought a Zweispänner sausage and a roll for the both of us. It was the last time father spent money on me for many years. I felt that the sausage had quite a bitter aftertaste. We arrived at Neulengbach in the early afternoon and had to get off. We weren't that far away from Vienna.

Our journey's destination was Altlengbach. Malzer was living here with my mother and my brother Alfred at the time. From Neulengbach, a town with around a thousand residents, we had a three quarter hour walk on a path. The path went over a forested summit, when you reached it you could see Altlengbach lying in a wooded basin. The Autobahn goes past today, back then the little nest lay in slumber far away from any main road.

Altlengbach didn't have a fixed town centre rather it was basically composed of two rows of houses on either side of a back road that came from Laaben and went to Pressbaum. It was around thirty five kilometers to the outskirts of Vienna.

But back to father and me. The sun was burning from the sky as we marched along the dusty country road between Neulengbach and Altlengbach. I grew very afraid the closer we got to our destination.

Right at the beginning of the town there stood an old, small inn where Malzer was supposed to be living. The landlord pointed us on to a small somewhat dilapidated building next door.

Before we'd even reached the door Malzer opened it and stepped outside. I recognised him again immediately. His face still narrow and clearly defined, his receding hairline had worsened somewhat but otherwise he'd barely changed.

"Ah yes, Otto!" Malzer made a thoroughly friendly face as he greeted us. However I immediately noticed that he was prepared for our arrival. Therefore an understanding must have already been arranged by post beforehand. Maybe handing me over had even been agreed while I was still in Enns.

As we entered the tiny kitchen mother stood in front of the washing up. She was very embarrassed at the welcome, particularly in front of my father. You couldn't talk to her. While we sat at the kitchen table with Malzer, mother kept working as if nothing was happening.

Father didn't stay long, you could see he was keen to leave the house again as quickly as possible. The whole thing felt like trading livestock at the market. People involved in those transactions are also in a hurry to leave again once it's complete.

Before my father left, which he brought about decidedly quickly, a few embarrassing minutes passed by. Even I couldn't shed any tears when he left, the resentment was sat too deep inside me. I could understand father wanting away from Malzer quickly, after all they had sat in court for years over my custody. All the more incomprehensible was the conduct of the folks in Wels towards me now. It was a parting from father for many years.

Now I sat here with my few possessions feeling very awkward and didn't know what to say. Father had disappeared in a puff of smoke and I sat there now and had to see how I'd deal with the current situation.

The whole dwelling consisted of just a tiny kitchen and a bedroom that wasn't very big either. My younger stepbrother Alfred came late in the afternoon, he was six years younger than me. I had great difficulty settling in and the first days were awful.

I shared Alfred's bed with him now and I was very miserable for the first while. I wished I had my cold room in Enns back which

I'd at least had all to myself. Here everything was so cramped, you stepped on each other's toes. During the first few days I soon realised that the cupboard was always bare. I could only dream of the good food from Anna's kitchen.

As soon as the day after I arrived I went with Malzer on the way to the employment office in Neulengbach. I applied for the half year's unemployment benefit I was entitled to. To begin with it wasn't much, the sums grew ever smaller as the months passed.

Soon I realised that my unemployment benefit was the only source of income for the family. Since Malzer himself had been unemployed for so long his entitlement had expired, which meant he didn't get any support anymore.
It was taken as a matter of course that I'd have to hand over all of the money. Not a schilling remained for my own personal needs. How could I oppose this anyhow when I saw that even my entire benefit claim wasn't enough for the cost of living?

I would have had so much time to continue my independent study for RUSTIN now, but I didn't have the money to buy the needed books. For the time being I had to bury my dreams of a better education.

How mother kept our heads above water with my few schillings is a mystery to me even today. Malzer had rented a field nearby and so we at least had some of our own potatoes and vegetables. Soon though we had to give the land back again because Malzer couldn't pay the rent.
The desolate lives we lived really depressed me. Most of all I would have liked to get up and run away, if only I had known where I could have gone.
Fantastic, warm summer months followed and we loafed around idly. I sought brushwood in the forest for mother's kitchen stove,

busied myself somewhat on the small field, but otherwise didn't know what to do with myself. Altlengbach had a small outdoor swimming pool that was surrounded by a high wooden fence. I stood here sometimes in front of the fence and peered through a large knothole to the merry bustling of the children and few adults.

In front of the pool I met a nice blond girl around my age. She seemed just as broke as I was, in any case she was also lacking the few groschen to buy entry to the pool.

"Are you from here?" she began a conversation one day.

"I'm not really from here, but for the moment I live here," I answered.

"I know already, you live in the inn with Malzer."

"How do you know that?"

"I've often seen you coming out of the house."

"Don't you want to swim?" I asked quite pointlessly,

"Well yeah I'd like to, but my father's got no job you know, I just don't have the money for it."

"Well there's more to life than swimming anyway, do you want to walk with me for a bit?"

"Well sure we can go for a walk if you want to, but where will we go?"

"Doesn't matter, just somewhere, we can walk along the street."

"You are the first girl that I've got to know here."

"Yeah?"

"Don't you have a boyfriend?" I asked somewhat stupidly.

"I wouldn't wander around alone if I did."

"What's your name anyway?"

"Hanni and you?"

"Otto."

"Oh, it's like that then,"

"What do you mean, 'it's like that then?'"

"Because my father's name is Otto as well, that's why."

"I don't particularly like my name," I answered.

"I think mine's quite good, don't you?"

"Yes, I think 'Hanni' is very good."

"I have to go home now though."

"Already? OK then, but we can meet again tomorrow?"

"Maybe."

"In any case I'll come to the pool in the afternoon again."

"I don't know yet, maybe I'll come too."

"Bye then!"

"Bye!"

That was the first day with Hanni, I didn't know her last name yet but what did that matter? I could always ask later.
I was very cheerful for the rest of the day, for the first time in many weeks.

I met Hanni the next day again as well, and also the day after that and something would have surely come out of it, we hit it off with each other straight away, but things developed very differently.

Over the next few days, when mother saw me walking with Hanni, she came to speak about the girl in the evening. She said that of course she was a sweet girl, and everyone in the town was fond of her, but under no circumstances should I get any closer involved with her. Her father was very ill with a disease of the lungs and Hanni wasn't healthy either, she knew this very well. The girl certainly didn't have long to live.

At first I thought mother just wanted to stop me from seeing the girl, but why should she? And why in such an awful way? All the same I grew quite afraid. That disease was a death sentence back then, or at the very least meant a continuous and serious illness. Just as well that I'd only known Hanni for a few days and nothing too serious had developed. I didn't go to the pool anymore, I avoided Hanni if I saw her in the street. I felt awfully mean and cowardly doing this, but I didn't know how I was supposed to act either.

But after a few days I found a remedy for this too. I no longer avoided her, even spoke with her, but allowed our time together to peter out imperceptibly without hurting her feelings.

Day after day, when the autumn came we went into the surrounding woods. We picked blueberries by the bucketful for hours until we wearied and our backs grew sore and then in the evening we went to sell our day's work in the better villas around Pressbaum. I was still much happier picking the berries than selling them. We were often turned away at the doors very ungraciously and we felt like beggars. But mother had tremendous perseverance, she never lost her spirits, never gave up. Later we hunted for porcino and chanterel mushrooms and again we knocked on doors to bring our wares to people. Alfred wasn't very enthusiastic about this work and Malzer avoided it only too happily as well. Only mother was indefatigable and fought to earn every groschen.

Even if it was hidden by the side of the road, no cigarette could elude Malzer, who was a heavy smoker. When I got my unemployment benefit, his first errand was to the tobacconist. He bought himself a packet of Film cigarettes, the pack for one groschen. Back then it was the cheapest cigarette and they were even called "the jobseeker's cigarette."

So I was the main breadwinner at the time and it seemed to me, the saving angel for Malzer and my arrival wasn't so unwelcome after all.

As soon as I'd arrived I'd noticed a profound change in Malzer. He'd lost a lot of his violent temper from earlier years. He was far more affable than he'd been at the time that I was with him as a small child. Even now he was still the dominant element, but mother had gained a lot of ground and could still cut through with her opinion sometimes. Mother hadn't had an easy marriage particularly in the early years. She must have loved her husband very much to be able to cope with all of the hardships he expected her to put up with.

Over the years Malzer had moved from being a milker to a head milker and finally to an administrator. So he must have been good at his job. Unfortunately though, he was a man who couldn't handle anyone having any authority over him. He quarrelled with all of his superiors. His gruff, domineering nature always swiftly got him into the best roles again. So he was never in a job long, constantly moving. And time and again he'd be lucky and slip into a good job but wasn't able to learn from his past mistakes. Mother put up with all of this with infinite patience. And she always stuck with him no matter how dumb the things he did were as well. What woman let's it all roll off her back when she's hauled with all her belongings from one place to another more than thirty times in her life?

When I had been staying with Auntie Kathi in Wels and attending the Bürgerschule, Malzer had been very close nearby, employed as an administrator at a farmhouse in Thalheim. Back then I'd no idea how close to me mother and her husband had been, it would have no doubt greatly disturbed me. I only learned about it later from my brother Hans.

One day Malzer had gotten up to some kind of escapade again and had to leave the farm on the double.
He packed the bare essentials into a trunk and hastily left the farm with mother, Hans and Alfred. He marched to Wels with the whole family and rented a room in an inn for the night.
Well now Malzer, despite his difficulties with his stomach, was a

heavy smoker throughout his life. He set his quilt in the hotel room on fire by being careless while smoking in bed. He was only just able to extinguish the smouldering fire with the help of his family, but he wasn't willing to pay for the resulting damages, and he probably wouldn't have been able to avoid these on the next morning.

So in the middle of the night, Malzer sounded the retreat. He dragged all of his loved ones out of bed again and left the scene of the crime through the back door in secret. They went to the train station in a flash, spent the rest of the night on the benches and with the first train in the early morning the entire family vanished from Wels. That was Malzer all over.

In his earlier years he'd been rough to the animals entrusted to him too. This only got better once he'd been to an agricultural course and had learned more about how to handle them correctly. One time on Osterburg he'd given a bull a savage beating with the ox whip. When, days later, he had to lead the bull out of the stall, it remembered this loving treatment from beforehand. It pressed him against the barn wall, slowly intensified its pressure ever more, so that Malzer's breath grew ever shorter. It would have surely killed off its tormentor if a few milkers hadn't come to his rescue.

When I came to Altlengbach Malzer had already been jobless for a long time. If, time after time, he'd been able to move straight away into another job before, he wasn't in a position to do so any more in this great economic crisis. Nevertheless he always had a lot of plans, plans that mostly went beyond his means and barely accomplished anything. But he still understood how to keep his head above water at least. He was and remains an eternally pugnacious spirit.

Slowly the political struggle grew ever more difficult. While I'd barely taken notice of politics up until this point, now I was also slowly confronted with the political events of the day. Malzer sympathised a lot with the National Socialists and I believe that he was already a registered member at that time. Like many he'd been a dyed-in-the-wool Social Democrat beforehand. Federal Chancellor Dollfuß had banned all parties, but their work went on underground all the more intensively. Malzer often spoke about how he was under surveillance, I noticed nothing but it could have been true. The Nazis had a lot of followers amongst the farmers back then. Since I'd recently moved there and wasn't suspicious either, Malzer thought I could quite easily bring some propaganda material to the farmers, it would have been too difficult for him and I would no doubt get a good snack with the farmers for the job as well. That made sense to me. So I packed Hitler's writings into my rucksack and made my way to the farmhouses that had been pointed out to me beforehand. The good snack had been true enough and that was very important to me.

We had to leave the dwelling in the inn because Malzer couldn't pay the rent anymore and we found shelter with a fellow party member, a Herr Hupka. He had a very nice wooden house on the other side of town and didn't ask for rent. Here we also had only two rooms like in the inn but they were decidedly somewhat friendlier than in the old building.

Amongst Malzer's acquaintances there was also a reputable older gentleman. Herr Jordan was a magnificent zither player and composed and published pieces of music. We met with him frequently and there were always musical performances then.
In Jordan's cabinet there stood two thick tomes: "The Merchant's Handbook," volumes one and two. I was very taken with these books. Jordan wanted to sell them to me for five schillings, five schillings wasn't much, but when you don't have any schillings

at all, they were really a fortune. I came up with a solution, in that I took on extra shifts in the picking and selling of blueberries until I actually got the money together. I proudly took the books into my possession. Nevertheless Malzer and mother were very displeased, they thought the money should have been used for the household. But this time I remained adamant. Of course the books were no substitute for RUSTIN's textbooks.

So the months went by, the winter came and it grew all the more boring in the little village. You couldn't earn any extra schillings picking berries now. It was a real time of need. I ran my errands to the farmers again and was able to earn myself some sort of meal that way. "Meat" had long become a foreign word to us. Mother must have been worrying the most, she had to put meals on the table every day after all, it was little enough.

In the month of February I went to get my unemployment benefit in Neulengbach for the last time. My time had run out, I'd claimed my maximum allowance. As I wandered over the hills I heard muffled rumbling in the direction of Vienna. It sounded like cannons were being fired. When I got to the employment agency there was a lot of excitement amongst the dole claimants gathered there. They said that the revolution had broken out in Vienna. The home guard and the military were bombarding the large housing estates, there were already many dead to mourn. The stories were true and for days the thunder of cannons could be heard even where we were. The revolt was finally suppressed. Even between Hausruckedt and Holzleithen, the towns of my early years, there was heavy fighting. It was an uprising of Social Democrats against the Dollfuss regime. Many young Social Democrats from Hausruckedt fled over the border to Germany. Some of them I met again later.

As spring came into the countryside our situation had visibly worsened. Now on some days even mother was really despondent. We were four mouths to feed and none of us earned so much as a schilling. Even living in rent free accommodation didn't help us anymore.

One morning all four of us set off. We went far across the countryside and visited farmhouse after farmhouse and begged for whatever we could. I would have never thought we would have been pushed so far.

In the first days I couldn't bring myself to go to the front doors of the farmhouses and to beg for alms. I waited with Alfred on the driveways until Malzer and mother came back and we went a few houses further. We packed all of the panhandled things into my rucksack.

So we knocked on door after door, often chased by the dogs and cursed by the farmers.

It took a while before I brought myself to get over my pride and to call on the farmers myself. But what won't you be driven to by need? The worst thing for me was how the farmers treated you with such contempt. In these weeks I often thought of Wels, and what father would have felt if he had seen me begging like this across the countryside.

We wandered through the villages like this at least once a week. Slowly I'd gotten over my shame, until I was once again called a "tramp" by a farmer and couldn't bring myself to beg anymore that day. The farmer brandished a pitchfork and shouted the foulest curse words after me. I wanted the earth to swallow me up, I was so ashamed but had unbridled fury in my stomach for the farmer. It was an awful time for me and I couldn't escape from it either.

There were a few farmers' wives with whom mother could get an egg, a spoon of lard or a small sack of flour each week she went past. You had to remember as well that we weren't the only ones that went begging across the countryside like this, it was a great nuisance for the farmers as well. Many of them kept their doors closed all the time or had the dog kennels so near to the front door that entry was blocked.

When lunchtime came we sat in warm weather at the edge of the field and chewed on a heel of rye bread. Then I thought on the good cooking of old Anna in Enns. I felt like crying in moments like this and I cursed God and the earth in which everything was shared out so unjustly.

There was a bad time after the Second World War as well but it was no comparison to back then. The poverty was universal after the war, there were thousands of others in the same position when you went foraging across the countryside and you mostly had something to offer yourself and more of a barter took place.

Malzer got himself ever more tangled up in politics and hoped for all kinds of improvements from Hitler. Soon even I had given myself to these dreams as well. You heard that everyone had work again in Germany, heard of the wonderful motorways being built. The political conflict became ever harder, business life ever more catastrophic, things went constantly downhill.

So the months went past without any prospect of improvement. It was a good thing that Malzer was much calmer and more approachable in his manner than he'd been before, I think I'd have gotten up and left one day. I'd considered the idea often enough. But where was I supposed to go? I would have had to keep on begging and wouldn't have had a roof over my head either. In these times there were enough people who still had it good, who lived in affluence, who had work and food. It was all the more difficult for the outsiders, and I was in that box as well. When I'd been selling my blueberries in the posh villas of Pressbaum during the past autumn, I'd seen the beautifully furnished rooms of these houses which mostly belonged to civil servants in Vienna. I dreamed of having such a beautiful house one day, but I was miles away from that.

So the weeks went past, we starved, we begged and we dreamed of a better time. But our prospects were so dismal that only despondency could seize hold of us.

On a beautiful weekend at the beginning of May, we made an excursion with the Hupka family to Schöpfl, a mountain around eight hundred meters high in the heart of the Vienna woods. We marched for almost the whole day through fantastic mixed and fir woodlands. For once it was a change from our miserable daily lives. We'd brought a snack with us of course, and we drank fresh spring water. Stopping in one of the comfortable inns was out of the question of course. But even without money we really had our fun, you become so modest in your aspirations when you know that they can't be fulfilled.

About this time I noticed that Malzer had suddenly grown restless. He was away a lot of the time and didn't come back until night-time. He whispered with Hupka a lot, a few men came to visit that I had otherwise never seen before, something was going on.

When I questioned mother about this change, she answered evasively.

"I don't know either, you know your father, he doesn't say much, but it's definitely got something to do with the party."

"Is something important going on?" I pushed her further.

"Don't ask, I don't know, and if I did I perhaps wouldn't be allowed to tell you, but honestly I really don't know," nothing could be gotten out of mother.

I gave up asking, but remained very alert in my observations. I didn't want to ask Malzer himself, he rarely gave details about things he didn't want to discuss, he would just give you a course putdown.

When I came back home in the early evening a few days later, I noticed mother had been crying. I noticed that Malzer kept talking on and on at her, but stopped when I stood nearby. Something decisive was in the air and I had a feeling that I would soon be briefed about it.
As we sat in the kitchen the day after, mother was working at the stove, Alfred wasn't there, Malzer suddenly said to me:

"Otto, do you want to come to Germany with me?"

In the moment I was so flabbergasted by this revelation that I couldn't find an answer quickly enough.

"Later tonight," Malzer went on, "a really big thing is going on, I can't tell you what will happen yet, but I can tell you that afterwards everyone taking part will have to head off to Germany. I can take you with me to Germany, even if you're not directly tangled up in the matter."
"Of course I want to come," I answered quickly, "what am I doing here anyway? But what about mother and Alfred?"
"They have to stay here for the time being, but they could definitely leave legally soon, the Austrian state would be happy to be rid of them."

While mother stood at the stove and silently wept to herself, Malzer went on.

"But you could maybe run into difficulties here if you stay."
"I absolutely want to go," I asserted, "what would I do here? I can half starve anywhere else just as well."
"Good," said Malzer, "we have to go at nightfall, we can't take anything with us, but I have to tell you as well, the whole thing is well organised but of course we could still be caught, and then of course we'd be going to prison."
"I don't care," I answered, "I'm coming with you."

Mother was completely distraught and was crying incessantly.

"Franz, that you'd do this to me," she said over and over.
"Calm down Emma, you still have Alfred, and soon you can follow us I'm absolutely sure."

Malzer hugged his Emma over and over and tried to console her. But mother couldn't be calmed. It wasn't easy for her either. But after Hupka spoke to her as well and told her that of course she could continue to live with him until she emigrated, she grew a little calmer.

There were no further preparations to be made for our departure. We couldn't take anything other than what we were wearing. I put my knickerbockers and my lodenjanker on.

Malzer impressed upon me further that if we got into any danger I was to come back to mother and Alfred and apart from that I was to play dumb as much as possible.

"That shouldn't be difficult after all," he said jokingly.

I feverishly waited for the evening. For the darkness, which was supposed to veil our departure from Altlengbach. Apart from Hupka we couldn't say goodbye to anybody.
I had lived for almost a year in Altlengbach, I didn't have the greatest memories of this time. Enns and Wels were long ago

already. Leaving the little village hidden in the Viennese woodland really wasn't difficult. Now I would finally venture out into the world. There would be adventure, everything was unknown and full of mystery. Away from the confinement of this tiny village, perhaps I would escape the poverty of the past months as well.

No matter what comes, onward, just onward out of this stifling confinement, out into the world at last!

The Great Adventure.

As darkness lay over Altlengbach on an evening at the end of May, we said our goodbyes to mother and Alfred, to Hupka and his wife.

We left the lights of the house behind us and disappeared into the darkness of the warm evening. We wandered along the street towards Pressbaum first. Shortly before the town we turned right and followed a narrow footpath into a thickly wooded area. After a few kilometers Malzer got into the ditch and gave me a signal to do the same.

"It's still a little too early," said Malzer, "we'll wait here for another quarter of an hour and then we'll go further up to a clearing in the forest, we'll meet more comrades there," it was the first time I heard Malzer use the word "comrade."

Malzer was excited himself, I could see that in him, he lit a Film which glowed cautiously in the cup of his hand. We sat like this for a while wordlessly, both no doubt thinking on the coming hours and days.

After a quarter of an hour we went onward. The narrow grassy path muffling our steps. The voices of the night slowly waking up around us. I trembled with excitement, thinking on the stories of Karl May and their exciting adventures.

On both sides of the path were thick bushes which made the night even darker. If I looked to the sky there was a thin ribbon of bright stars.

Suddenly the path opened up ahead of us. High fir trees towered up at the end and marked the boundary of a clearing that was around fifty meters wide and just as deep.

Malzer stopped moving, giving me a signal to stop too and walked cautiously to the clearing himself.

He disappeared into the darkness, I stayed back, full of agitation. I found everything awfully exciting.

After a few minutes, Malzer came back.

We then went to the clearing together. A half dozen men were sitting there under the cover of an imposing fir tree. We went to them.

I recognised a few of them as well. There was Kollmann, a teacher from Pressbaum, he was a lesser SA Leader in this area. There was de Paly, a journeyman carpenter from Altlengbach, next to him a farmworker from Laaben who I'd seen quite frequently on my bike errands, Bittermann a stocky lad likewise from Altlengbach and another two younger men whom I didn't know.

I sat down with Malzer beneath the fir tree, we barely spoke and when we did we only whispered. A few smoked, concealing the glow of their cigarettes cautiously. All of them couldn't quite hide a certain excitement.

. After around half an hour Kollmann stood up.

"It's time lads, you all know what you have to do, do it well, Heil Hitler."

"Heil Hitler," they answered in a choir.

Kollmann turned to Malzer.

"Franz, you know what you have to do, keep exactly to our arrangement and nothing can go wrong."

"It'll be all right," answered Malzer.

Silently the men disappeared into the night, we stayed behind alone in the darkness.

"Where are they going?" I wanted Malzer to tell me.

"They're setting several explosive charges on the railway," answered Malzer.

"And what are we doing?"

"We're scouting the route to the arranged meeting location, making sure it's free of any checkpoints."

"And if it isn't?"

"Ach you know, it's just a particular precaution, I'm sure our task will go ahead smoothly."

"Do you know the way?" I wanted to know.

"We already decided on that a long time ago. Why do you think I was away all those nights? Everything is well prepared."

After around another quarter of an hour, we went on our way as well.

After we had wandered further down the path for a while, we heard three hard, short explosions from the North-West.

"It's worked," was Malzer's only comment. I knew now that in some places, sections of the track had been blown into the air. Now there would be an alarm at every checkpoint in the area.

At one point the path made a sharp bend. Malzer turned southward here, at a right angle. First we went through thick bushes, then we waded through a stream that was so wide that we couldn't jump over it. Soon we arrived at an open meadow, which we didn't cross but rather whose edges we followed eastward under the cover of the scattered bushes. Far away behind us scattered gunfire could be heard.

"Now the boys will be full of beans!" said Malzer.

The railway line had been particularly guarded for months. From time to time we cautiously walked to the edge of the bushes and looked over the meadow, immersed partly in the pale light of the moon. Everything was quiet. Thin veils of mist lay over the ground and a cool wind blew against the protective edge of the forest. Night birds interrupted the silence on all sides. Cautiously we continued on our way. Our shoes were soaked through from crossing the stream and water squelched between our toes with every step.

"Another few hundred meters and we'll get to a barn," it was the first words Malzer had spoken after a long and silent march. "We have to creep up to it carefully, there could be a patrol inside, stay a bit behind me, I'll give you a signal when you can follow."

I let myself fall behind a bit, while Malzer carefully crept up to the barn which appeared now as a dark shadow.

At that moment I thought of when father had taken me from Kössen, how we had tried to cross the border illegally and a border guard had suddenly appeared out of the barn.
But these ideas were driven quickly from my mind again, I waited on Malzer's signal which I momentarily missed.
But then he stepped out from behind the barn, made a reassuring hand signal and I followed him up to the barn.

It stood in a corner that was formed from the two edges of the wood. A large amount of meadow stretched to the West and South while the northern and eastern side were fenced off with bushes and copse. A wagon track, which was barely visible due to infrequent use, led to the shack. The door was only secured with a colossal wooden beam. In the interior there was a shallow remainder of the hay from last year's harvest.

The shack was an ideal hide out. On two sides the open meadow, with a good view across it, on two sides the thick bushes were made for a speedy escape.

"Our comrades will come here, we'll spend the rest of the night in the barn."

"And then?"

"You'll learn how things will go on in the morning, but don't worry, everything is well organised," Malzer seemed very sure that everything was going to turn out well, and in the end this surety carried over to me too.

After a longer period of time the rest of the men came in pairs. They were all visibly exhausted from the business which lay behind them. You could still see the excitement on their faces.

"Well, grab a corner and try to get some sleep. You, Franz, secure the barn as arranged, you can take your boy with you, if anything suspicious approaches raise the alarm immediately," Kollmann spoke and betook himself to the others in the barn.

I took up a position alongside Malzer near a lookout post from which we could partly observe both the open meadow and also the bushes immediately in front of us. I was bleary eyed, but excitement drove all tiredness out of my eyes and limbs. But with wet feet, cold slowly crept up your whole body and heavy slaps on your arms only brought passing warmth. Slowly the stars began to fade, the early mist grew. A few hundred meters away a few deer stepped out of the bushes, made themselves secure and started to graze peacefully. That was a good sign for us, danger didn't seem to be nearby.

After a while Kollmann came to us.

"Let the boy sleep in the barn," he turned to Malzer.

"I'll stay up, I can't sleep anyway."

He didn't have to tell me twice. But of course I couldn't sleep either, even though loud snoring was coming out of a corner of the barn. I sat down, but with wet feet, missing a cover chills were running down my spine. I stood up again and constantly kept moving, that way the chill was easiest to bear. But even that night came to an end eventually.

The rising sun couldn't be seen while it was spreading a pale light across the forest, but life immediately looked different. The meadow in front of the hut was almost obscured by passing clouds of mist now. Things came to life in the barn as well. Bent creatures stretched themselves, overslept, shivering faces appeared, with hay in their hair. Kollmann and Malzer came back into the barn.

"We'll now set off in pairs in intervals of fifteen minutes. You know your meeting points, go alone where possible in urban areas," Kollmann grasped in his jacket pocket, pulling out some envelopes.
"In each of the envelopes you'll find a sum for two men, share the schillings, they're intended for the next three days. Don't behave conspicuously and don't forget the addresses of your contact points. From now on we don't know each other anymore, don't get caught, well then have a good trip, Heil Hitler."
"Heil Hitler."

Kollmann disappeared with de Paly as the first group into the forest.
So in intervals, group after group, we separated.

When I was alone with Malzer, he said:

"So Otto, now there's only the way to Vienna left, then we'll have the worst behind us. We have to keep to the South-East, march to Gaaden and then on to Mödling."
"That's a pretty long trudge though," I said.

"Well then let's go, let's see that we get hold of some breakfast somewhere, the walk will be worse on an empty stomach."

We left the barn behind us and marched eastwards across through the woods. Soon we reached a forest path that made the march easier. We got on well. The fresh morning air and the hurried pace soon made us really lively.
All of a sudden the wood receded. We came to a basin and to a better track. Soon we came to the first signposts. "5 kilometers to Kaltenleutgeben" stood there on a wooden sign in tangled writing.

"We have to manage these 5 kilometers until breakfast," Malzer stopped for a moment and lit a cigarette.

And so we stepped onwards sprightly, the sun came higher, a light, mild wind appeared. Nobody passed us on the path. At one point a farmer in his field at some distance. At the side of the road a single farmstead. The squealing of pigs, a cockerel crowed, a flock of pigeons flew over us.

"God am I hungry," my stomach was already rumbling loudly, "Do you think I'm any better?" answered Malzer.
"You have your cigarettes at least."
"You think? I just lit up my last one, hopefully there'll be a tobacconist's in the village."

When we reached a hill shortly afterward we saw Kaltenleutgeben lying a small distance away from us. The town didn't seem to be any bigger than Altlengbach.
Now we had to make sure we didn't run into the arms of a policeman or a home guard patrol. We reached the town at around nine in the morning. We immediately realised that these small villages weren't altogether safe for us. We immediately stood out as strangers, everybody knew everyone here. Luckily

there was a grocery and general store right at the entrance of the village.

"Go ahead, wait somewhere away from the end of the village, I'll get something to eat," Malzer headed towards the shop, it was a tobacconist too and that had to placate Malzer.

I continued on quietly. I didn't concern myself with the curious looks from the few farmers' wives who passed me. Nobody spoke to me, but I was certainly noted as "not a local" immediately.

A bit behind the village I came to a fork in the road. One arrow pointed to Perchtholdsdorf, one to Gaaden.
I followed the track to Gaaden. The open fields retreated back, an elongated stretch of forest moved up as far as the street. Here I stopped, I sat down on a woodpile that was stacked up a little to the side of the street and waited on Malzer.
I didn't need to wait long for him. The ringlets of smoke that rose up in front of him already showed that he had well supplied himself with cigarettes. He carried our breakfast in a brown paper bag. There was a Schusterwecker bread roll and a pair of Landjäger smoked sausage for each of us. He pulled two bottles of beer from his deep jacket pocket as well. He didn't say anything about the pile of cigarettes he'd bought. But from his cheerful face I could tell that he wouldn't have to go without this indulgence for a long time.

We sat on the woodpile, enjoying our breakfast and the sun shining warm on our bent backs. Life was showing us a thoroughly friendly face for the moment.

From a distance we suddenly heard the clattering of a motor. A motorbike with a sidecar came roaring up from the direction of Gaaden. On the bike and in the sidecar sat two men in uniform.

Malzer was up like lightning!

"Go! Get to it, restack the wood!" he hissed to me.

We sprang from the woodpile like monkeys, seized the around about three meter long spruce trunks, carried them to the street and started to pile them up again.
When the motorbike got to us it stopped briefly.

"At work so early already?" asked the man in the sidecar. They were two policemen.
"Yeah the gaffer will be here soon," Malzer answered quite naturally, I held my tongue like I was told to.
"Well then keep it up," the officer casually grasped at the peak of his cap. The bike accelerated and roared off, towards Gaaden.
"Yeah, see you," Malzer breathed out deeply,
"the shit could have hit the fan there."

No doubt I was white as a sheet as well.
The joy of our breakfast had been ruined. We broke off our snack and continued our march onwards.
We were on our guard.
A villager could have easily spoken to the police officers in regards to the two strangers who had passed through the town a short time ago. Then the officers would have quickly grown suspicious of us. So we got going.

We arrived at Gaaden after the sun had already reached the peak of her height. The hills of the Vienna woods receded and were replaced by rolling hilly countryside. Now we were already moving on the edge of the great wine producing area around Gumpoldskirchen. We bypassed Gaaden on a back road and turned ourselves north towards Mödling. Now the street was already a little busier and we felt a little safer.

We stopped off for a short rest in a little country inn.
We ate a Hungarian goulash that was so spicy that fire almost shot out of my mouth, along with a bread roll and a glass of beer.

It was very comfortable. We couldn't afford to stop for long though, there was still a long way to go and we didn't want it to get dark.

"How far do we still have to go anyway?" I asked Malzer impatiently.

I would have been only too happy to learn more about our escape route, but with Malzer it was like pulling teeth, he was more than taciturn with these questions.

"Be happy that you don't know too much, I'll tell you what you need to know in good time."
"Well yeah but I won't say a word," was my objection.
"You think so? They would soon beat the information out of you and our contacts would end up in prison and the whole escape route would be closed for those who come after."
"Well in that case...."
"You don't need to feel offended, the less you know the better for you," with that Malzer stood up, we left the inn and carried on.

The street grew ever more lively, it was obvious that a big city was close, Vienna wasn't that far away now.

In the early evening we reached the western edge of Mödling.

Malzer asked an older woman about a "Pacher metalworking shop."
It turned out that we weren't even a hundred meters away from it. That was a lucky coincidence which saved us further questions.

Between a row of old, shabby rented flats a narrow alleyway led to a back house with living quarters and workshop.
On a wooden sign above a wide double door there stood in large letters: "Johann Pacher, Locksmith and Metalworker."

We stepped through the door into a dark workshop. A young man was sweeping iron fillings with a coarse broomstick in a corner of the workshop under the fading fire of the forge. On a long workbench lay a half finished balcony railing.

"Can we speak to the gaffer?" Malzer turned to the young man. "Herr Pacher is in town somewhere, but Frau Pacher is at home, first right next to the workshop," the boy stopped his sweeping briefly as he looked us over curiously..

So we headed towards their residence. Malzer hammered the large iron door knocker.
After a short time a chubby middle-aged woman appeared.

"Good evening, I would like to speak to Herr Pacher."
"My husband is in town, he's probably sitting in the inn, he'll certainly get back late, it'd be better if you came some other time."

The wife looked us over very mistrustingly.

"It's very important," Malzer continued,
"could you maybe send a message to your husband?"
"What do you want from my husband then?" The woman looked us over mistrustingly.
"It's something that I can only discuss with him," answered Malzer.
"Oh so that's it?" her face became visibly less friendly,
"you're a party member too, well that can only be trouble!"
Malzer didn't react to this less than friendly reception.

"Sepp!" the woman shouted across the yard. To the apprentice that appeared she said:

"Find the boss, he's maybe sat in the 'Ochsen,' he ought to come home, there's a visit for him,"

she spoke and slammed the door in our faces.

"Not very friendly," I said.

"We've no business with the wife," Malzer took the woman's behaviour quite calmly.

We stood around in the courtyard for a long time until the boy came back.

"The gaffer will be here soon," he told us and disappeared into the workshop.

At any rate it lasted another quarter hour until a man, about fifty with white hair and a pitch black moustache stepped into the yard wearing blue work clothes.

"Herr Pacher?" Malzer went to the man before he could open his mouth.

"Yes, and what's going on?"

"We're to send warm greetings from your friend in Munich," said Malzer.

"Oh yes, what's his name again?"

"Floda," Malzer answered promptly.

"That's right, I remember now," he came up to us and offered his hand.

"How was the trip?" he asked turned to Malzer.

"So far so good."

"Come with me and we'll have a snack in the living room, until we continue once it gets dark," with that the gaffer led us into his house.

I asked Malzer later how he came up with the name "Floda," "We arranged it before," Malzer explained to me, "it's the Führer's first name hidden as an anagram," I didn't find it particularly imaginative.

In the meantime we sat down in the gaffer's living room.

"Marta" he called to his wife, "sort out a small snack for us, then I'll have to go to Vienna for business."

The wife hadn't grown any more friendly in the meantime. But she brought us a good meal and the gaffer poured us a glass of wine with it.

"Hopefully the rest of the journey goes well," he said then, "the amount of people giving me these warm greetings have been a little numerous over the last few days. I've got a job as well you know."
"It's obvious that your wife isn't happy with our visit either." Malzer pointed with his head to the wife who had left the room. The metalworker made a dismissive hand movement.
"Ach women, don't worry about it."

And so we set about the food and got tucked in.
The long march had made us hungry and the wine along with the meat and bread tasted superb.
After a short while Pacher stood up.

"I'm going to change my clothes, I'll be back soon, get stuck in in the meantime," with these words he left the room.
"Where will we spend tonight?" I asked Malzer.
"No idea," he answered, "from now on I'm just as wise or as dumb as Otto, I'm taking things like you are."

When Pacher appeared again he was squeezed into biker gear, dust cap and goggles in his hand.

"We can get going if you like," he urged us to leave while taking another hefty gulp from his wine glass himself.

"Martha," he shouted through the door into the next room, "I'll be back in about an hour, I'm going to visit a customer, you know already."

The gaffer led us into the yard again. In the meantime it had become pitch dark. He grabbed a motorbike and sidecar out of a shed.

While Malzer made himself comfortable in the sidecar, I was dumped on the luggage rack, which had a potato sack tied to it as makeshift padding. We raced off over a cobbled street north, towards Vienna.

Even after a short stretch, with Mödling barely behind us, my backside was in terrible pain. Despite the potato sack, it was thoroughly strained against the iron frame. I desperately clung to the driver, while Malzer bounced along far more comfortably next to me. Slowly we got closer to the outskirts of Vienna. We drove through the streets, turned right and turned left, I had no idea which district of this huge city we were in.

After driving around aimlessly Pacher suddenly stopped in a narrow back road.

"Wait for me here, I have to see if the coast is clear," he dismounted, went a short way further down the street and eventually disappeared into an entrance hallway.

Soon he came back again, swung back over the machine and roared off with us again.

As he drove onward he shouted over his shoulder to us:

"God damn it! They caught your host last night, someone must have grassed on him."

"What now?" Malzer looked at Pacher questioningly.

"Let's get out of here," and off he raced with us, all across Vienna again, quite aimlessly it seemed to me.

Pacher stopped in a small alley once more.

"Let's try our luck again," he said, dismounting and disappearing into the darkness. When he appeared again after a while he said, visibly relieved:
"Come on lads get off, it's your lucky night," we had barely complied with his request before he raced off without a word of goodbye. We seemed to be a really hot ticket for him.

A young man in a striped baker's uniform stepped up to us.

"Come with me comrades," he began, "I can give you shelter for a night."

He led the way for us, unlocked a bright green painted door and led us through a modestly furnished shop floor into his bakery. An uncomfortable warmth hit us as soon as we entered. It smelled very strongly of yeast and flour and it was a mystery to me as to what we were here for.

But the man pointed to a small free space between sacks of flour and the dough tray and said calm as you like:

"You can make yourselves comfortable here for the night, I'll bring you two blankets for cover as well, I can't do much more than that," the baker seemed to be a real comedian, his remark: "You can make yourselves comfortable here," seemed totally over the top to me in light of the circumstances.

Sadly we didn't have a choice, so in the end there was nothing else for us to do other than to make the best out of this unfortunate situation.

And so we tried to make ourselves as comfortable as possible on the bakery's hard tiled floor with the blankets as miserable cushioning. That was easier said than done. By all means I tried to follow the baker's advice and sleep for a few hours, but despite my best intentions it wasn't possible.

The whole bakery was unbearably warm. I turned from one side to the other on the hard floor in vain, I couldn't close my eyes. On top of that the horse hair blanket was constantly tickling either in my ears or my nose. Since I could neither sleep nor do anything else, I stared continuously at the bright bands of light which were crossing over the floor.

Although Malzer had initially been rolling from one side to the other, soon enough I heard an irregular snoring which was interrupted from time to time by a short period of waking.

I was dog tired, but it just wasn't possible for me to get any sleep. Suddenly, I saw a dark shadow running around the band of light. Without question a mouse, or even a rat?

I sprang up like a bolt of lightning.

"A mouse!" I shouted shocked.

Malzer got up reluctantly.

"So what?" he said, "those little pests won't bite."
"Maybe even rats!" I shouted full of disgust.
"Probably just mice, just try to sleep," Malzer couldn't be roused from his sleep.

But if I couldn't get to sleep before, it was completely out of the question now.

I sat upright, I didn't want to lie down anymore. My senses were sharpened and I constantly heard rustling in some corner.

So I spent the night in a fugue state, half asleep with exhaustion, half awake with a fear of mice, in the bakery of a Viennese suburb.

It must have been very early in the morning when the light in the bakery suddenly flared up. The baker appeared in baker's trousers, a white apron and rolled up sleeves.

"Get up comrades, I'm afraid the night is over," he shook Malzer awake, who rolled onto his other side still snoring.
"My assistant will be here in half an hour," the baker continued, "you have to be gone by then," groggily, Malzer now stretched himself awake as well.
"Where can we go so early in the morning?" Malzer asked, it was half past three in the morning after all.
"You'll have to pass the time somehow, you can't come back before later in the afternoon, then we'll see how things go."

What lovely prospects, we had imagined this trip somewhat differently.

"I'll give you both a decent snack bag, you can buy yourself something during the day as well. Get moving, even if just off to some small bar and don't act too conspicuously, the secret police are sniffing around all over the place and there are enough informants as it is," the baker gave us the two packages and brought us to the exit.
"Remember the street and house number, come back around five in the afternoon and ask for me in the store. Well take care, Heil Hitler."
"Heil Hitler, round five then," we shook the baker's hand and disappeared into the gloomy street.

After the heat of the bakery we found it very cold outside. We wandered past the houses silently with both hands deep in our trouser pockets, the package wedged under our arm. You would have thought we were on our way to work.

How were we supposed to spend the whole day without drawing any attention?
In any case we didn't want to distance ourselves from the night's accommodation. After a quarter of an hour, we came to a park. But it seemed too dangerous to put in an appearance here so early already.
So we wandered aimlessly in circles for hours. It grew warmer and then we got fed up of the running around as well.
And so we headed for the park again. A few older women were sitting scattered on the benches that had been warmed by the morning sun.
I left Malzer and we sat down on separate benches within sight of each other.
God, did that feel good. Nothing is so exhausting as walking over cobbled streets for hours. I stretched my legs out long. And soon had to fight against the missed sleep.

In order to keep myself awake I took a sausage bun from my reserves, sating my huge hunger and missing a cup of coffee or milk with it. But after that I was somewhat fresher again and the world immediately looked a little friendlier.

After a while Malzer passed me. I followed him as inconspicuously as possible, we went a little deeper into the park up to a pond.
Here we sat down on distant benches again.

There's no day longer than one where you're desperately waiting for the evening.

We left the park around midday and sated our thirst in a little dairy store for now. We wandered up and down a few streets for a bit of a change, all over and finally ended up back in the park after all where we at least found the opportunity to sit. Now a lot of the benches were already occupied and numerous people were going for a walk.

After a while, an older, stockier man took a seat next to me. He looked me over quite unashamedly and extensively, but he said nothing. I had an inexplicable, uneasy feeling, somehow the man was giving me the creeps.

I got up, going slowly along the benches, passed Malzer and the man actually followed after me. A chill went down my spine, it was clear to me the man was following me.

When I found an empty bench and he sat next to me again the whole affair became too ridiculous for me. I stood up again, acting as naturally as I could and strolled the way back. I went past Malzer again, giving him a signal by pointing my thumb behind me and continued on my way. Malzer understood for sure, but remained sitting calmly. When I looked around as inconspicuously as I could and I noticed that the man was following me again, there was no doubt for me that he was an informant.

When bushes obscured the view on a crossway, I increased my pace as fast as I could without drawing attention to myself. I turned down every junction that I came to, careful to stay hidden by bushes.

When I dared to look around again, there was no trace to be seen of my pursuer. Nevertheless I kept going until I came to the park exit. I looked behind me once more, but the man must have lost me.

I wandered through the neighbouring streets and turned back towards the park after a good hour. Many detours led me back to the pond again. But far and wide there was no Malzer to be seen.

And so I sat down on a bench again from which I had a good overview. But a good two hours had to go by before I finally saw Malzer strolling back.

"There you are, God was I worried," Malzer was visibly relieved to see me, "a snoop was definitely chasing you, but you made yourself very conspicuous with your running about," his tone was somewhat reproachful as he sat down next to me again. "Should I have waited until he began to interrogate me?" I was disappointed that Malzer had thought my reaction incorrect, I'd expected praise instead.
"Whatever," Malzer continued, "you could see your guilt from miles away. But it's worked out well again anyway. But let's get moving, you won't be lucky like that all the time."

We left the park and made our way back to the bakery.
I just hoped that we didn't have to spend another night in the rat nest.

As we reached the store a bike and sidecar was standing in front of the building again, it seemed to be already waiting for our transport onward.
The baker introduced us to a middle-aged man with a full black beard who had been waiting for us in his kitchen.

"Sepp will bring you to Grossenzersdorf," the baker explained, "you can spend tonight there."

And so we left the place where I'd already spent a sleepless night very cheerfully. But this time I had a properly padded passenger seat. Sepp drove us through the city like a madman. I wasn't accustomed to these trips, I had a delicate stomach which soon began to rebel as well.
We drove around Vienna from the South across the eastern bit, thereby crossing over the oft-praised blue Danube which seemed

very grey to me though. After that we drove onward towards the North-East. We eventually left the sea of houses behind us and raced between Aspern and Leopoldsdorf, towards Grossenzersdorf. Here we went through a district that had been hard fought over in the decisive battle against Napoleon.

Shortly before Grossenzersdorf we stopped in front of a somewhat secluded farmstead.

Sepp dismounted and went into the house. But he came back out again immediately, swung himself over the machine and roared off with us. We drove the way back to Vienna again.

"Dirty bas!" Sepp cursed, "the post is cleared out and under surveillance, I'll have to take you back. Ach feck it! God damn!"

And so we headed back again, Sepp took every bend like a berserker, mistreating his machine and leaving a wave of dust in his wake.

We didn't feel right during this trip and I thought I was going to be sick any moment. Sepp was forced to drive a little slower in the city.

So Sepp took us down all kinds of roads back to where we'd started. The baker was anything but pleased about our new appearance. It had grown evening in the meantime. The baker ushered us back into the bakery first of all and told us to wait.

"What a fucking joke," were Malzer's first words once we were alone. I didn't say words like that back then but I surely thought the same, it really was a "f*****g joke."

And so we sat down on a corner of the floor near the baker's oven and waited to see how things would turn out.

We sat for one, two, three hours, but nothing happened. We were hungry and thirsty, nobody appeared.

Finally after what seemed like an eternity had passed, the door opened and the baker turned up with two little mugs of beer and a few sandwiches.

"Well then," he said, "it seems we're cursed, there's nothing more we can do today, you'll have to sleep here for another night, there's nothing for it. I'll bring you the blankets again, but at half three in the morning you'll have to be gone again, I don't want to risk everything after all. I've had enough troubles with you as it is."

The baker had no joy with us, and we even less in his overheated bakery. I was filled with dread when I thought on the vermin we had to share our accommodation with. But first of all we stilled our thirst and the worst of our hunger. The head of the house appeared with the promised blankets, heavy horse hair blankets whose hairs had tickled my nose the past night.

"Don't put the light on," with this warning the good man left us alone.

And so we'd see how we'd get through the night with some sleep.

If only it hadn't been for the mice or maybe even rats. I had a great abhorrence of the little long tailed pests, but I was so awfully tired again as well that my eyes soon fell shut all the same and I sank into a restless sleep.
In the middle of the night I woke up and immediately stared at the strips of light crossing over the bakery floor which were magically drawing my gaze.
I saw no mice, nor any rats, but I instinctively felt that I wasn't alone in the room with Malzer. Malzer snored as calmly as you please while my senses were sharpened to the point of snapping.

I stared.. and stared always at the same strip of light and there! I wasn't wrong, a creature ran through the middle of the band of light with its long tail following behind it. No that was no mouse, that was definitely the size of a rat.

I forgot the baker's warning, sprang up, ran to the door and turned the light switch on.

But first I could see neither a mouse nor a rat, all the same I shivered with dread.

But there! A long tailed beast ran over the edge of the long wooden dough tray, eventually dropping down to the floor and disappearing behind the sacks of flour.

Now there was no chance of sleeping. I turned the light off again, sat down on the floor with my back against the wall and frantically clung myself awake.

I strained to hear every noise, struck the palm of my hand against the floor again and again in order to make a noise.

Malzer's deep breaths annoyed me, his healthy sleep while I spent the rest of the night wide awake. I sat like this until the morning dawned and the baker made us leave the building.

We stumbled around the streets of Vienna for another day, even travelled with the tram a bit. It was a boring day but even it passed eventually and in the evening we went on our way back to the bakery.

"I'm telling you," I said to Malzer, "I'm not spending another night in that bakery, it's teeming with rats!" I was filled with dread when I thought on another night in the bakery.

"I didn't notice any rats," Malzer answered.

"Yeah well you were sleeping and snoring quite loudly,"

"You could have done that too, you wouldn't see any mice if you were asleep."

"Oh you can talk, I simply can't stand those things, I'd rather sleep with snakes."

"Well that I'd like to see."

"You can believe it, I've caught snakes with my bare hands and I've eaten frog's legs, but sleeping with rats, bleargh, Jesus!"

But thank God, we were saved from a third night in the baker. A young lad around my age led us through all kinds of main roads and back roads to a new place for the night.

In the meantime it had gotten dark and sparsely scattered gas lanterns lit the way a little, we eventually stopped in front of a narrow shop door. The lad knocked on the door in a particular sequence. When it was opened a very pale, really weedy man stood in front of us. He looked up and down the alley somewhat frightened and pulled us into the little store one after the other. We'd ended up in a barber shop. It seemed we only dealt with tradesmen.

If things continue like this I thought, then we'll surely never get to Germany, where we actually wanted to go, or we ought to do the rounds with all of Vienna's tradesmen first.

"Comrades," the barber whispered terrified, as if we were surrounded by enemies, "I'm afraid I can't offer you much accommodation, but it's OK for one night."

We were already well used to this speech by now, by that point they could have surely thought of something better. The hairdresser hauled a couple of blankets to us that didn't seem the cleanest to me and left us to our fate. Nobody thought of food or drink.

While Malzer made himself comfortable in a chair two barber stools were left for me, between which I tried to find some comfort for the whole night.

Malzer bridged over his hunger with a few cigarettes, I stared at the pale crescent moon which was squinting through a half clouded pane of the display window.

"We'll surely manage," Malzer began, "to keep our grumbling stomachs in order till the morning, but after that I'll head to the nearest shop and get food."

We would have been able to take something to eat with us before, but we thought that we would have gotten something from our host. The barber was nowhere to be seen though, we surely weren't the first to have misused his barber shop as a bedroom either.

I spent half the night rearranging the chairs into every possible position. I jerked this way, jerked that way, none of it worked. In the end I did the most sensible thing and lay down on the floor. I actually fell asleep too. When I woke up in the night I felt an awful itching on my body. It itched in my neck, my sleeves, my ears and nose.

Soon I realised the mystery, the barber, the dirty slob hadn't swept his shop clean and I was rolling in the tufts of hair from his day's work. As soon as I noticed it I began to itch all over.

Now sleeping was out of the question. I had a proper fury in my guts, while Malzer snored away as calmly as you please.

I had barely closed my eyes before I was totally worn out and bleary eyed in the morning. The first rumbling trams announced the new day, but it still lasted an eternity before the agonising tossing and turning had an end.

When the door opened and the host appeared he brought us two mugs of really thin milk coffee and a slice of bread for each of us. We'd had better breakfasts before but first of all we had to get out of this shop.

"I have to keep it secret," the barber said in reference to the meagre breakfast,
"My wife can't know anything about it."
"Don't worry, comrade," Malzer consoled him.

"Once you've eaten please leave my shop immediately. I'm supposed to give you orders to be at the main entrance of the Südbahnhof train station this afternoon, you'll learn further details there,"

"Who are we to go to there?" Malzer wanted to know.

"Don't worry, the right man will find you."

We'd barely swallowed the last mouthful before we were shoved out of the door. Now we stood on the street again and had to see how we would pass the day.

But it all went better than we'd thought. First of all we filled our stomachs properly in a tiny pub. I tried Kaiserschmarrn, which was really chewy but on the other hand lay bloated in my stomach and so gave me a real feeling of being full. Malzer ate sour sausage and we both drank beer with it. Despite the early hour the green painted wooden tables were still full of cigarette butts and dinner leftovers from the past night. But in our hunger we generously overlooked that. The host was grouchy, spoke only a little and was even less curious about us and that suited us fine. The last thing we needed was questions about where we came from and where we were going.

We left the pub feeling thoroughly satisfied, betook ourselves to the next stop and travelled into the city. We looked in shop display windows and I wondered at all of the beautiful things which I hadn't known existed until now.

But the previous night weighed down on me heavily, I was exhausted and all my bones ached. When we reached a park area, we hastily sat down on a sun warmed bench and stretched our legs wide in front of us.

That felt good. We let the warm sun shine on us and dozed away tiredly. I dreamed of a soft bed for the night. The park was small and easy to see across and I left it all to Malzer to keep his eyes open for our safety.

We weren't far from the Südbahnhof and so we had time to properly laze around.

Once the sun was setting we slowly made our way to the station. We satisfied our thirst again in a kiosk, neither of us felt hungry any more.

When we arrived in front of the entrance of the Südbahnhof, I couldn't believe my eyes when I saw Kollmann standing in front of the entrance. Now we were in the right spot again then, now things could get moving again, we hoped.

Malzer received an envelope from Kollmann, but the SA Leader disappeared into the train station without speaking to him that much.

Malzer disappeared into the closest station toilet and told me to wait for him. There was a lively bustle on the platforms. I kept close to the exit and waited for Malzer's return. Surely he'd soon be able to tell me more details about the rest of our journey. When Malzer came back, he pressed a train ticket into my hand,

"In an hour we're travelling into Burgenland as far as Mattersburg," Malzer informed me frankly, "stay close to me, but as far as possible don't speak to me, there are a host of other comrades on the train, none of us know each other, you understand."

So I whiled away the time until our departure and watched the lively coming and going in the large train station. A police patrol went through the waiting rooms and across the platform. All the passengers were keenly taken note of by eye. But since so many men were coming from work and populating the station waiting for the commuter trains, we didn't draw attention in any way.

The train left the station punctually and took us southwards. We travelled in a calm, very warm evening for this time of year. We stopped in every little train station and at every stop there was a lively getting on and off.

I stood at a compartment window, the low lying sun on the
· horizon was giving the evening countryside an attractive glow
and lighting up all of the colours richly. In Wiener-Neustadt we
stopped for a little longer and changed over to another train.
When we finally arrived in Mattersburg it was already dark. Now
we were only around ten kilometers away from the Hungarian
border. We found ourselves in a very forested area. As I realised
later, we found ourselves on the eastern edge of Rosaliengebirge,
whose foothills reached as far as Ödenburg.

Ödenburg, also named Sopron, had belonged to Hungary since
the end of the First World War. Lying at the southern edge of the
Neusiedlersee the landscape flowed into wide Hungarian
lowlands without a transition.

In Mattersburg I saw Bittermann once again. I hadn't seen him
nor any of the others since that night in Altlengbach. De Paly
from the party was there again as well and of course Kollmann
who I'd already seen in the Südbahnhof in Vienna. Along with
them I also encountered another two men who I'd not met before.

We left the train station as quickly as we could and gathered in
front of the freight shed's loading ramp.

A gaunt old man was standing in front of us here in a green cloth
suit. He clearly must have been waiting for us. Barely a word was
spoken. The seven of us silently followed our new leader into the
darkness. Soon we turned off of the narrow path and went off to
the side into the woods. After the sunny day mighty clouds had
reared up now and so it was pitch dark but not cold.

We moved silently onward along a narrow woodland path that
we soon reached.

"We're going to Hungary," Malzer whispered to me, "we're
really close to the border already."

But as I soon found out, there was still another ten kilometers to go yet.

Again and again there were hold-ups which considerably delayed our march. I couldn't find out the reasons for these interruptions. We often stood still for as long as a quarter hour in silence until the whole group started moving again in single file. Since I was at the tail end with Malzer we couldn't see what was going on at the front.

The path ended suddenly, we reached a narrow street which we went along for a short bit until the shed and the woodpile of a sawmill appeared from out of the darkness. We had a longer rest in a half dilapidated shed. We settled ourselves down on a woodpile and all around us there was an eerie silence. I could only doze intermittently, the cool of the night made me shiver and the rough bedding wasn't really made for sleeping well. Along with this I was also much too excited, my senses far too sharpened, we were in the middle of a great adventure and every hour could bring us a surprise. And it really wasn't safe either. If we were arrested by Hungarian border officials we would have had to first serve a long prison sentence for crossing the border illegally, then afterward we would have been deported and handed over to the Austrian authorities, which would have consequently led to prison again.

After an hour long break in the sawmill it had become midnight in the meantime. Suddenly a man in fairly tattered clothing with a pitch black beard turned up. He spoke with our former leader for a long time, they didn't speak loudly more gesticulated.

"I think the black-haired fellow is probably supposed to take us across the border," Malzer whispered to me, "he looks like he's a Hungarian to me."

And Malzer was right. Kollmann gave us a signal to gather around him.

"This comrade here," with this he indicated the stocky, black haired lad next to him, "will take us across the border into Hungary. If you want to get there safely, trust his leadership absolutely. He will do his best to get us to our destination. Once we're in Hungary we're going straight to Budapest and to the German Embassy. If any of you should be caught and interrogated by Hungarian officials, don't tell them anything. You are German citizens and you will only give further testimony in the presence of the German Ambassador."

It was Kollmann's longest speech until that point.

At the Hungarian's signal, we set off moving in single file behind him. We immediately left the street and turned off into a trackless woodland area. We were going steep uphill and at a pace that we could barely keep up with. Nobody was allowed to lose sight of the man in front of him. It was still really dark, we crossed through a valley and then thick vegetation. The branches constantly snapped back into your face. Nobody was allowed to smoke and we weren't supposed to speak. We were moving right on the border and the utmost caution was absolutely necessary. We moved along the edge of a marsh, soon dipping into the woods again, soon we went uphill, then soon downhill. When the sky was beginning to darken a little, we suddenly left the woods behind us and stood in front of a vast orchard. A street suddenly appeared and an ancient, shabby house. The shutters without colour, the plaster crumbling away almost all over it looked more like an abandoned robber's cave.
The Hungarian went straight up to the house. Knocked several times on the door. It didn't last long before an old, grey bearded man in dark trousers and a dirty, baggy grey shirt opened the

door. The man didn't say a word, he just made a clear hand movement inviting us to enter. Only once we were through the door did we realise that we were in an inn. In front of us there lay a very primitive dining area with a row of wooden tables and benches which were just as simple. On the tables there just stood big shakers for salt, pepper and paprika. Aha! I thought, now you're in Hungary, as I could only associate paprika with Hungary.

From the host's behaviour I could tell that he was prepared for our arrival.

I must have been right because he appeared with hot goulash soup, white bread and red wine unexpectedly promptly considering the time.

The prospect of getting a hot meal in our stomachs raised everyone's morale immediately. But the soup was so spicy that I thought I was going to burn my throat. It would have been really nice if it had been a little less spicy, but it was a hellish ordeal as it was. Even the others had their difficulties with it, the smokers had the least problems.

After the consumption of this spicy affair we still had time and made ourselves somewhat comfortable on the benches.

Before I closed my eyes for a short doze, I thought on how far Hitler's arm already reached and how many collaborators stood ready and waiting for him, even in foreign countries. In what way was the old forest innkeeper to be compensated for his relocation services? It certainly wasn't safe for him. He could of course have been of Austrian descent as well, from the time when Hungary was still incorporated into the old monarchy.

I couldn't have slept long before I was shaken awake:

"Come on Otto, let's go," it was Malzer who gave me a little nudge which woke me up immediately.

We left the dining room and stepped into a morning of low lying swirls of mist.

We left the street again, and climbed up a long steep slope. The ground was covered thick with ferns, we made arduous progress and soon our stockings and trouser legs were soaked through with the morning dew.

We had been underway for around an hour, had gone around in a long arc, had passed over a mountain ridge and now we were going steeply downhill again. We stumbled more than we walked and some of us fell on our backsides.

Suddenly the woods receded. Some distance away we saw there lay the small Hungarian town of Ödenburg.

We marched in pairs on a wide road towards the town. It seemed to be market day in Ödenburg. The streets were lively, horses and carts were underway with vegetables, young pigs and poultry. There was cackling and grunting from in the wagon, the women gossiped and the men puffed away on long pipes, nobody bothered themselves with us.

We met up again together at the town train station. We each had a train ticket to Budapest pressed into our hands, the Hungarian leader had disappeared. Kollmann gave each of us a small sum of money in Hungarian currency.

Now things were really looking up for us. Once we were in the country the rest of our journey didn't seem to raise any more big problems. We didn't see any policemen, nor any other men in uniform and we soon felt very safe.

We still had time until the train's departure. We visited a small tavern, ate heartily and drank red wine. The wine seemed very tangy to me, but that's just the way things were, but what the hell I drank wine and felt very manly.

We spent the rest of the time until the train's departure as inconspicuously as possible, we didn't want to tempt fate after all.

Later in the day the train took us across Györ and Tatabanya to Budapest. The journey passed without incident.

At every station on the train there was absolute bedlam. The farming folk got on the train along with chickens, geese, even piglets and there was a great mixture of all kinds of smells. We found everything very amusing and adventurous, a very particular experience.

The route was very peculiar. First it went into the lowland plains to the East, then we soon turned north again almost as far as the Czech border. Then we turned off to the East again, through a very wooded area and finally we travelled sharply southward towards Budapest. Near Budapest the hills grew almost like small mountains. We had reached the Hungarian highlands.

We were in a very jovial mood when we arrived in Budapest in the evening. We had the most difficult part of our adventurous journey behind us after all. We were overwhelmed by the beauty of this wonderful city. Here we met the Danube again which we had left in Vienna.

Immediately after arriving we went on our way to the German embassy.

Here we were taken into a large room, supplied with lockers and mattresses. There was coffee, butter and bread. Thus provided for we were left to our own devices until the following day.

"Well Otto," said Malzer contentedly,
"Now hardly anything can go wrong."
"Yeah we're out of Austria for now," I answered, "when will we see it again?"
"Do you regret it a little already?"
"Not really, I just mean, it could be years before we can go back."

"I don't think so," Malzer said, "and even if so, things will definitely be better for us in Germany anyway."
"Let's hope for the best," I replied, pulling the duvet over my ears, ready for my first proper sleep in days, I was dead tired.

Nothing happened at the beginning of the next morning. We were able to wash ourselves in an adjoining room, we got a huge pot of coffee, ample white bread and butter.
Then we loafed around for hours. We weren't allowed to leave the embassy. Finally around midday a small white-haired embassy official appeared and gave something along the lines of the following as an explanation:

"Gentlemen, within the premises of this embassy you find yourselves under extraterritorial jurisdiction, ergo in absolute safety. The embassy is prepared to take you as safely as possible to Germany. To avoid diplomatic complications it is necessary to change your identities. You will deposit any identity papers that you may have taken with you here. Do not worry, these documents will be handed out to you again in Germany. The embassy will issue you with temporary passports. This passport will have a cover name which you should please commit to memory very carefully. In your own interest I recommend that you practice the signature thoroughly and also that you memorise your new place of birth. It is possible that you will be questioned on the details of the passport by Hungarian agencies and ordered to carry out handwriting samples as well as give other verbal evidence. In any case explain that you are refugees of German origin from Siebenbürgen. We will ensure a quick departure across Czechoslovakia to Germany. Everything else you will learn from the relevant men in the building. I wish you all a good homecoming to our great, mutual Fatherland, Heil Hitler!"

"Heil Hitler," we answered and were happy to finally know where we stood.

A great, jovial mood gripped us all. Now nothing more could go wrong. Passport photographs were taken of us, then there was a sturdy pea soup from the embassy kitchen, it tasted good, like no meal had beforehand.

We could barely wait to get our passports in order to be able to see the fantastic city shortly before departure. When would we have the opportunity to see Budapest again?

We were put into separate rooms in the afternoon, our passports were issued. But before it was ready we had to sit at a table, get a piece of paper and then we had to write out our new names a dozen times. Only once the embassy official was convinced that you could do a halfway capable job of it were you allowed to add your new signature to the document. I was given the name Otto Schnaller, born the 13.1.15 in Klausenburg in Siebenbürgen.

Once we had our passports in our hands in the late afternoon, Malzer slapped me on my back:

"Well Otto, what do you think? I knew it would all work out."
"Hopefully the rest works out too," I said.
"Why wouldn't it you pessimist? Hitler will take care of it," was Malzer's comment.

Indeed, even back then Hitler's power seemed to reach far across the borders, if only I'd realised back then that even at that time much was achieved through crooked, illegal means and there were no moral scruples standing in the way.

Provided with our precious German passports we were also now able to leave the embassy for a stroll through town. Budapest lies fantastically bedded in the wooded highlands. The roads wide,

clean and filled with fantastic, vibrant life. Imposing state buildings lined the streets. We ambled towards the Danube and marvelled at the fantastic chain bridge. We were also able to make a stop in one of the many comfortable inns, having been provided with a modest sum of money by the embassy.
Almost fifty years have passed since that time, details of the city have slipped my mind, I only know that it had an overwhelming impression on me back then.

The next morning we made our first trip to the Czechoslovakian consulate. We applied for a transit visa which we received the same day. The magic word for this promptness was a good tip for the consul employees which they accepted as the most obvious matter of course. Of course they advised us of this circumstance in the embassy beforehand.

There was another midday meal in the embassy, after that we were issued train tickets from Budapest to Munich via Prague, our joy was indescribable.
We gathered in the evening at the station. In a small restaurant, I ordered another Hungarian dish that I would have been better without. It was so spicy that it was impossible for me to eat even a single bite, even Malzer couldn't cope with the spicy sausage. As a group of eight we finally left Budapest. It was already night when we reached the border station with Czechoslovakia. First two Hungarian border officials came who found our papers in order, the Czech officials who appeared after them were obviously of a different opinion. They flicked back and forth through the passports, shaking their heads and fetching the Hungarians to certify them. They asked us our reasons for our journey, finally they took the passports and left the compartment. They soon came back with another official who repeated the detailed examination and also spoke good German. Finally he gave us our passports back and said..., "Well gentlemen, we

know the crooked game, but what the hell? Your papers are valid, so have a good trip," with that our border crossing was done and all obstacles were out of the way. We steamed through the dark night towards Germany.

The Lost Years

1934-1937

It was a sunny morning at the beginning of June in nineteen-hundred-and-thirty-four.

At Furth im Walde we arrived in Germany, as we crossed the Czechoslovakian border for the second time.

Finally in Germany. We had dreamed of this hour for months, now the dream had become reality. We travelled onward towards Munich.

"Munich" itself was a magic word for us. And naively we thought we wanted to stay in Munich.

I already saw myself as a salesman in a fine store. Malzer dreamed of a well paid administrative position on a large estate near the city.

But only too soon we would realise that dreams don't always come true.

We reached Munich at midday. I wondered at the huge station, was fascinated by the hectic hustle and bustle that already dominated it back then. But there wasn't much time to gather impressions. A small truck was already standing in front of the station, we clambered onto it, sat down on the wooden benches, the sheets at the side were let down and, sat in the dark, we left our surroundings.

When the truck stopped and the sheets were pulled up we were in the forecourt of the Munich Franciscan barracks. We had reached our first destination in Germany.

The Franciscan barracks was a transit camp for Austrian refugees. Many a dream of freedom and employment found a sudden end here. The first sobering-up was brought on by a medical inspection which was carried out in a wholly militaristic style.

Two doctors in SA Uniforms saw to our first bitter disappointment, saw to the realisation that freedom and action would now no longer only be decided according to our own wishes.

Now the further course of my life was decided by the two gentlemen behind a brown heated wooden table.

My front and back were inspected, I had to bare my teeth and stick out my tongue. I was felt, weighed and measured and a file was made up about me.
For many years I was obstructed from a means into a civilian profession by the final result: "fit for service." I had dreamed of Germany so I could begin a more human life, I didn't dream of spending years in drills and stinking barracks.
But now a file had been drawn up about me, I was rotad in, I myself had given away my freedom to make my own decisions. I became just a cog in a big machine, and in the future, any tiny grain of sand which got into this machine would cause me pain as well. But there was no going back now. My modest objection that I had expected to be integrated into my profession was dismissed with the irrefutable observation: On top was the welfare of Germany, right at the bottom were all personal desires. With this observation my lost years began, years in which I was shoved here and there like a pawn on a chessboard.

First of all I took hold of that renowned tin bowl from which for years I would be forced to eat the bitter soup that I'd made for myself.

If it tasted tolerable to me at the beginning, then from year to year it would become less digestible, from year to year weighed heavier in my stomach.

Here in the barracks I heard for the first time of the establishment of an Austrian Legion, consisting of Austrian refugees that were able-bodied and at an age for military service. It was said that this Legion would soon march into Austria and send the government there packing.
What was certain, was that those of us who were fit for service weren't free to go into a civil occupation, instead we were stuffed into SA uniforms and quartered in the barracks.

There were no further orders for us. We lay around in the rooms, peddled all kinds of rumours concerning the near future and loafed around bored.

Malzer was classified as partly fit, he knew how to emphasise his injury from the First World War correspondingly and he had hope of being freed for a civilian job soon.

Almost every hour, more comrades from every corner of Austria arrived in the barracks. We wondered at how many men were leaving their homeland.
As soon as the next day, still dressed in civilian clothes, we were loaded onto the truck again. We left Munich in a southern direction, our destination was the small town of Bad-Aibling, to the west of Rosenheim.

When we arrived at our destination the Opel-Blitz we were riding in drove us into the grounds of an old brewery. We were loaded off here and were led into a large hall in which around forty to fifty beds were set up as bunk beds.

The majority of the comrades who were present were already clothed in the brown SA uniforms. A lively bustle reigned. Loud commands echoed across to us from a nearby meadow, whole groups were marching in step with each other all over the yard, while the individual superiors outdid themselves in the volume of their commands.

We were allocated a row of empty beds and were left in peace for the rest of the day.

Apart from Kollmann I met all of those that I had left Altlengbach with again. A few had already arrived earlier and were already stuck in full uniform.

Since we'd already gotten hold of a day's ration of field provisions before leaving Munich, we had nothing more to expect for today.

And so we ambled around the old brewery for the rest of the day, took a look at all of the premises available from the canteen to the washroom to the kitchen. Since we'd not been assigned a military rank, nobody bothered themselves with us either.

The next morning the shrill tone of a whistle startled us awake. But the signal wasn't meant for us, we weren't planned into the whole operation yet. Around nine o'clock we got breakfast and after that we new arrivals were led to the medical barracks.

It was actually laughable, but there really was another medical inspection already. I would name it more of an examination today. But I wasn't nameless anymore now. A file had accompanied me since Munich and all of the information which the gentlemen needed to ascertain was already recorded therein. In future this FILE which accompanied you was more important than you yourself, you were a nobody without it, a nothing. Without the FILE there was no clothing, no food, you didn't exist.

So I got undressed again in the anteroom of the medical barracks, standing around naked for a good while and freezing despite the day's heat. You felt so helpless without clothes, you cast off a part of your own self with it, you were suddenly a stranger to yourself. When my name was called I had to think whether or not that was me, but the orderly was already shoving me through the door.

I almost only saw the huge spectacles when the abrupt voice already rang out at me, "Bend over!" so I bent over, "mouth open!" upright again I tore my mouth open, bared my teeth again, allowed everything that was required of me to happen. Unfortunately I still wasn't any bigger after the second measurement. I was allowed to get dressed again after the inspection was done with me. The observations from Munich were chopped off, and a second important signature went on my FILE which thereby gained ever more significance. At any time in the future my superiors could help themselves to it, to my benefit or detriment, only I myself never set eyes on it.

The outfitters lay directly next to the medical barracks. Measurements were converted into clothing sizes here, the precision was dependent on the supply available. But I had a common size of course, everything at least half fit and when I left the room I could barely see over the pile of clothes in my arms. The colour was matched to the brown that was in fashion back then, the underwear was an exception to that of course, but perhaps brown underwear wouldn't have been bad either. Us new arrivals gathered in the drill square with our clothes heaped in front of us. Here we were assigned to our pre-established units.

I went to Scharführer Koller, a young but very wiry man from Inn im Innkreis. A new bed was assigned to me, while I was separated from Malzer who was assigned to a different squad and also changed his sleeping quarters.

First of all this meant refilling my straw mattress, sorting out my locker and building my first straw bed for the night which was also a failure, in any case the Scharführer closed both his eyes as he went past, as if it deeply pained him.

For our superiors that seemed enough for the first day. We gathered in front of our accommodation, chatted about our future and discussed the new situation, which definitely didn't seem so rosy to us anymore. But we were still young, looking for adventure, our food concerns had been resolved, we saw no reason to give ourselves up to sad thoughts yet. And above all we saw everything as being just a short interlude, we were convinced we'd have it all behind us in a year's time at most. So we went on slowly, and before the bugler could blow the last post, most of us were already lying on our straw mattresses and thinking our own thoughts. Malzer still went along the beds through our sleeping quarters scrounging cigarettes. We still hadn't received any tobacco products and that was some bitter medicine for him.

A shrill whistle tore me from sleep.

"Get up, everyone assemble for morning exercise! Rise and shine! Move, move!"

A piercing voice startled us out of our straw mattresses at six o'clock in the morning. You didn't have time to rub your eyes, let alone roll over again.

"Move men, assemble in sports clothing!"

I slide down off my top bunk at the exact same time as Haas, the man below me, was rolling out of his bed as well. With full force I landed on the small of his back, he gave out a cry which was followed by a curse that won't be repeated here. The Scharführer on duty who was standing nearby grinned across his whole face:

"Always getting hoofed in the back you dozy lot, you'll learn soon enough!"

And so we raced to the drill square. What with all the rush I joined the wrong squad, now I didn't recognise a face and had no idea where to go.

"Good Lord!" called the squad leader, "another ass that can't find its stall!"

Luckily, I saw Haas waving at me from out of a squad that was marching off. I raced after it and was able to join them without being seen.

We hurried across fields towards Kolbermoor. The mists were steaming across the morning fields and drifting here and there in clouds of fog. A wonderful freshness came into our lungs. Soon many of us were out of breath, and the formation grew ever longer. Us new arrivals were hanging the furthest back. We went in a wide curve back to camp.
Coming back to the drill square, the Scharführer waited until the last man caught up. He stood in front of us with his hands on his back with a nasty grin that we reached in last place panting.

"Well then, you lame ducks, we'll heat your arses yet."

Me to him:

"You're the biggest arsehole yourself."

Yet I said it so quietly that I could barely hear it myself. A rough atmosphere prevailed here which I'd have to get used to first.

Now we hurried into the washroom. Like pigs in a pig pen, you had to fight a place at the long troughs for yourself in the rush at the beginning. We let the ice cold water trickle over our naked torsos. We shrank together instinctively but soon a tingling warmth ran through our bodies. Once we were in the sleeping quarters again, we got into our drill uniforms and went to the drill square again where the quickest were already waiting for us. We went past the kitchen bunker in single file to get our bread. There was a whole loaf for each man per day. That seemed an awful lot for me and almost too much to cope with, but after a few days I thought quite differently on this.

After getting our bread we gathered in the canteen. All of it was precisely controlled in regards to time because always only a restricted number of people could use the room.

At eight o'clock we gathered for our first drill practice. Us new arrivals were assembled into our own group for the drill duty. We were taken on by one of the most malicious slave-drivers that I got to know in my time in the Legion. Squad leader Ender, a stocky man in his forties from Lustenau in Vorarlberg.

In our washed drill uniforms we surely didn't make much of a military impression on him.

"Well then let's see if we can make men out of you slouching Esaus," Ender began his address to the dithering little group in front of him.
"What a pitiable lot you look standing there, it'll be a tough bit of work."

He went along the front, shaking his head at all of the unmilitaristic posture which insulted his view.
I was the smallest and was at the end of the row as a result, a particularly thankless place, the first man and the last man stood out the most.

"First we'll practice standing to attention! Heels together, toes out, hands to your trouser seams. Those with outturned knees turn them in, those with inturned knees turn them out, understood?"

Ender went along the line, stopped in front of me.

"Name, age?"
"Poschacher, eighteen!" I shouted loudly.
"Poschacher eighteen what?"
"Eighteen years old!" I shouted once again.
"Good God, 'Eighteen, squad leader, Sir,' understood?"
"Understood,"
"Understood what?"
"Understood, squad leader, Sir!"
"Well then," Ender looked me over from head to toe, "somewhat pale lad, well that will soon change."

He scrutinised everyone in the line like this, and had something to moan about with each of them. After the wingman he took five steps back and yelled his first command.

"All of you listen to my command,.. attention.. ."

We clapped our legs together, it thundered like at a gun club burial salvo.

"Jesus wept! At ease!"

It lasted the whole morning until we had been half-evenly turned into puppets, whose movements were operated by Ender's shrill commands as if by a taut string.

When we were dismissed for lunch break we already felt half like Frederick the Great's guardsmen, we still had no idea how much sweat lay between that and where we were now.

The pea soup tasted like a king's dinner, to which our halesome hunger was surely the best condiment. Everyone got a five pack of cigarettes with the midday meal. I had barely taken a hold of them before Malzer turned up, surely in the fear that I would find another recipient.

After the meal there was an hour's bed rest. It was obligatory for everyone to lie on his straw mattress during this time.

The afternoon saw us on the parade ground as well. We practiced: "Come to attention!...eyes front.. and fall out!.."

It all looked and sounded so easy, but Ender always had something to say.
He stood in front of the wingman and looked along the front.

"Marker!" with which he meant me,
"stomach in!" I tried my best.
"Curse it, just your stomach in, not your head out!"

I pulled my head back obediently, how could I help it that my stomach came out again as a result?
Ender stepped up to me, held the chin of my head back with one hand and at the same time with his right fist pushed my stomach back, but with that my whole bottom went backwards.

"Keep your arse still, man, for Christ's sake," Ender screamed. But now I got into a right muddle and eventually no longer knew what was supposed to go forward or backward.
"Totally tense, everyone at ease! Pull yourselves together men, we could do things quite differently if you want you know..."

I wasn't the only one whose stance wasn't right thank God, the squad leader had something to complain about everyone as he went along, nobody came away unscathed.

"This is not on, men," Ender shouted,
"you urgently need some warm up exercises. Well then...Lie down, ...up! .... lie down.. stop moving like old women! ..... up! .... down ...get your ass down for Christ's sake! .... up, five minutes smoking break."

After the first day we were totally exhausted in the evening. We thought that surely it would only be like that for the first days, but we had well and truly miscalculated there as well. The beginning was harmless in comparison to what followed months later.
We wouldn't be getting any leave for the first two weeks, first, we had to learn how to march and salute properly.

We were able to go back to our squads after three days of extra training. We had mastered the basic concepts to the point that we could join in with the other comrades without standing out in particular.
But what was right with one instructor would bring the ire of the others.

I soon figured out the way around it, you just had to not stand out, neither for good nor for bad reasons. Though drill practice was soon hated by everyone, it was still the activity that we would pay homage to most often in future.

The morning runs through Kolbermoor slowly grew longer. Soon our lungs fit the requirements. As some of the instructors were already much older, while the majority of us were around twenty, it wasn't difficult to keep up after a few weeks. On some days even our instructor's enthusiasm for jogging left something to be desired, then we'd take a break in a bit of forest and take a shortcut that shortened the run considerably. But those days were exceptions.

One day we climbed down into the brewery's deep cellar vaults. Here, totally shielded from the outside world we had the Karabiner 98k rifle pressed into our hands for shooting practice with live ammunition for the first time. The long vaulted cellars provided ideal shooting galleries. The gun echoes were corresponding to be sure. I was somewhat uneasy before the first shot, as the older guys had told tall tales of the kind of smacks on the cheek you get when you don't hold the butt against your shoulder tight enough and such like.

But when the first short was fired and you were still on the wooden platform unharmed, you felt a good bit more manly.

After a few days Malzer came to me in the evening.

"Hey Otto, I'm getting transferred tomorrow. I'm going back to Munich first, then I'm pretty certain I'll be let into a civilian job."
"Well aren't you lucky?" I remarked a little jealous.
"Just wait a few days," said Malzer,
"then you can simply apply to be let go."
"I can try that, but it won't be any use."
"They can't force you to stay if you don't want to," I strongly suspected that Malzer didn't believe what he was saying to me himself, surely it was supposed to be more of a parting word of consolation for me.
"And Otto, keep your cigarettes safe for me, I'll write my address down for you, you can send them to me from time to time."
"Sure," I answered, but I knew that I'd find a better barter for my cigarettes, I could do with a few more marks as well after all. And cigarettes were a sought after item.

There was daily shooting practice in the brewery cellars now. It thundered incessantly for the whole day, and we asked ourselves if we were all to be trained up as marksmen. We were under the

strictest instructions to give no notice of our activity to the
civilian population.

On a Saturday morning, it was the thirtieth of June thirty four, we
were already a bit past the camp on our morning run, when a
dispatch rider from camp caught up with us.
We had to turn around immediately, go into our sleeping
quarters and for that weekend and the following Monday we
weren't permitted to leave the camp.
What had happened?
SA Chief Röhm had been deposed from power and shot and they
feared a possible uprising of the entire SA.

A few days later they said Lutze was our new SA leader now,
Röhm had been shot for personal transgressions and for treason
to the Führer.

Up until then we had known neither much of Röhm and we had
even less of a notion of Lutze. This course of events left us quite
unfazed.
Once the matter was closed everything went on as before. With
one exception: there was no more shooting practice in the beer
cellar with live ammunition any more. There wasn't any more for
the following years of my affiliation to the Legion either. In our
existence they surely didn't see any more possibility of liberating
Austria of the government there by force. As it turned out later
the plans went in a completely different direction.

We had been in Bad-Aibling for about three weeks when we went
on an excursion to Chiemsee. They took us as far as Prien by
truck. I can remember that it was a swelteringly hot day. Your
eyes were sore when you looked across the shimmering water. I
had never seen such a big lake in my life. I would have given
something to be able to enjoy this experience as a civilian. But we
were forced into the extremely hot brown uniforms, our feet

squeezed into long jackboots and we were sweating heavily. We were ferried across to the main island, "Herreninsel island" at midday. We visited the Herrenchiemsee castle of course. Built by King Ludwig II of Bavaria, it cast all of the splendour that I had seen up to that point into the shadows. I was particularly impressed with the great hall of mirrors and the opulent bedroom. But this splendour was also overwhelming, and you felt a little liberated when you stepped out into the daylight sun again. With our uniforms and heavy boots we fit into these rooms like a square peg in a round hole. Despite the slippers our appearance en masse was accompanied by disparaging looks from the custodians.

To these gentlemen we must have looked like bulls in a china shop.
You could read the dislike for us on the face of the small white haired man who took over leading us, especially as a number of comrades found very little understanding for the architectural artwork and constantly interrupted the guide's lecture with the most unsuitable remarks. But a few of us listened to his comments with rapt interest, we wanted to make a consolatory little ray of hope as compensation for the poor behaviour of our comrades. But as always, three misfits are taken more notice of than ten with good intentions. At any rate, the contemptuous looks of those in charge spoke volumes, and you could see that these gentlemen were glad when these art philistines left the castle again.

Each weekend after coming off duty, we marched past the paymaster in single file, signed our names off of a list and received our week's pay of two mark's fifty. The rate of pay stayed the same for the year. There were corresponding increases by rank of course, but they weren't particularly serious. Of course with this small wage you couldn't really live it up especially when you also had to pay for necessary toiletries. At the time it was around the earnings of a skilled worker for two and a half hours work.

Malzer was transferred with some older men back to Munich. But he wasn't let out of the Legion as he'd hoped, instead he went into office work in Munich for a higher bureau in the Legion. He stayed in this role for a whole year. Mother received an excursion permit from the Austrian government in the meantime and was able to move with my brother Alfred to Malzer in Munich. Through this Malzer was now also able to obtain a residence outside of the barracks.

After a few weeks I made a written application to be discharged from the Legion.
My application however, only got as far as the desk of my own unit.
I had to go and report in the morning, which was always taken by the Sturmführer. I have forgotten the name of the man and only know that the arrogant way in which he treated us was always loathsome. The Sturmführer now gave me a good and thorough dressing down as they say.
My application was declined.
My desire was seen as treason against the Führer and the Fatherland. In the days that followed I was assigned to cleaning the rooms and peeling potatoes in the kitchen suspiciously often.

Months later, precise guidelines came out for the circumstances under which leaving the Legion was possible. For ninety percent of us none of these circumstances applied.

For as far as it had been there, our initial enthusiasm for service soon disappeared in the Legion.
An early march into Austria wasn't to be expected.

The duty was anything other than inspiring.

We exercised and exercised until we could perform all the movements in our sleep and still for over three years the drills didn't stop. We made up for the moods of our instructors, which grew ever worse over time as well. We were the lightning rods for their sudden outbursts. Sometimes there was a lot of trouble in the air, but things always went on.

One Saturday, a few trucks drove up, and we went on a mountain excursion to Wendelstein. We travelled to Fischbachau in order to climb further up the mountain on foot from there.

Equipped for the field with satchel, blanket, tarpaulin and spade, the climb was quite exhausting. But we took a lot of enjoyment and fun in the affair. For me it was the first big mountain which I'd climbed to the top of and it was a really exciting adventure.

Once we'd thoroughly enjoyed the panoramic view and fortified ourselves with our field rations, we went back down again.

Scattered on an alpine meadow a few hundred meters below the summit, we built up our tents to camp for the night. That of course was the highlight of the whole excursion. For the first time, we built a tent for each group of four men. Each consisted of four triangular tarps that were buttoned together. Each of the four rods were pieced together to the middle tent pole. Then after that there were tent pegs made from a light metal to secure the tent to the ground. The tents were furnished with a small trench that went around them, so that we wouldn't have water under our backsides if there was a sudden rain shower. As we had four blankets altogether, two were used as bed sheets and two as covers.

We made a decent campfire, sang a heap of patriotic songs and in our high spirits we talked a lot of daft stuff. We kidded around and teased each other and we still yarned a lot in the tents once lights out was ordered.

When I woke up very early in the morning I lay alone in the tent with Bittermann, the other two comrades, Haas and Berndt were missing.

I stuck my head out of the hole. A thick morning mist was lying across the whole meadow, you couldn't see the mountain summit at all. The sound of cowbells was ringing out from all kinds of different directions. A bit off, behind a dip in the ground, there lay an alpine shieling.

The shieling was only partly visible from where we were. Only the shingle roof, weighed down with stones, and part of the chimney towered up over the dip in the ground. Greyish blue smoke rose up to the sky out of the flue.

But where had our two comrades gotten to?
All the tents were still lying in tranquil peace. No sound could be heard from out of them.

All of a sudden there was a woman's loud scream from the direction of the hut. It was a shrieking voice, which in a tizz interrupted the morning calm so abruptly.

Now the rest of the tents came to life. Heads were poked out into the open in curiosity, what was going on at such an early hour?

Out of the morning mist, suddenly two figures formed which came running towards our tent. It was Berndt and Haas. Each with his canteen in his hand, the cursing, warbling voice of the indignant dairy maid resounding after them.

The mystery behind all the commotion soon came to light. The dairy maid had caught Berndt and Haas while the two rogues had been milking her cow, as calmly as you like. The fresh milk, squirted straight from the cow's udders into their canteens.

The maid's commotion lasted for a while yet, but we had a luxurious breakfast with healthy, fresh alpine milk. To our surprise, squad leader Ender didn't make a big deal out of it either.

After a rich breakfast we took down our tents and left the meadow, leaving an unpaid bill for two litres of fresh cow's milk behind us.

Singing, we wandered down to the valley again, full of beans after the wonderful experience of this hike in the mountains.

Our trusty Opel-Blitz stood ready in the valley and we travelled back to our camp through wonderful summer countryside.

Suddenly the rumour came up that we would be transferred to another camp. This immediately raised our spirits. Finally again a bit of change from everyday monotony. We would surely go to a nicer camp, the old brewery wasn't appropriate accommodation in the long term after all.

And sure enough. It was only a few days until the rumours were confirmed. Unexpectedly quickly we departed from Bad-Aibling.

About three hundred of us were loaded onto the trucks and left the camp in a northward direction. Across Munich, Regensburg, we went ever northwards.
We travelled through Nuremberg and Bayreuth and ended up lastly in Marktredwitz, not far from the Czech border in the Fichtel mountains.

We were more than brought down to earth when we left our vehicles and moved into our quarters. Our new camp was no more than an abandoned cement factory. Well, it really couldn't get any more primitive than this.

We slept sixty men to each warehouse, where sometimes the mounts for the machines were still present. The huge windows up high, in iron frames, the panes clouded with years of cement dust, iron bed frames, iron lockers and coarse wooden tables and benches made up the only equipment. So we were supposed to be housed here, our hair literally stood on end. Even our superiors I had never seen as despondent as they were here in this hovel. Even the ranks up to squad leader had to sleep with us in the warehouses.

But we just had to deal with the conditions now, we had become second class people apparently, to whom you could give any hole to sleep in.

The camp in Marktredwitz was despised from the beginning. But the hard training went on unabated here as well, how pointless it was grew more obvious to us by the day. Exercises in the country took increasingly tougher forms. Every week two marches from thirty to thirty five kilometers were carried out. We were so exhausted when we got off duty that we were happy for them to just leave us on our straw beds in peace.

Squad leader Ender grew into ever more of a sadist who daily came up with new forms of harassment. He never missed out on an opportunity to hound us and humiliate us and to show us what little arseholes we really were.
We did forced marches up to the border, non-stop night exercises and drills over and over.

At the time Marktredwitz was a little hovel where there was nothing going on at all.

We were already beginning to complain about the whole business of Legion service during this time. We were drilled until we could have fallen over but we couldn't see the smallest point in the affair. The soldiers at least had weapons in their hands and because of that their service would have been a bit more interesting.

We on the other hand hopped around the countryside like crazed rabbits day after day, we were hounded and chased until sweat ran over our faces, but in case of emergency we would have barely been able to handle a gun properly. We spent years throwing wooden hand grenades but barely got to see a real one face to face.

Everything apart from physical fitness remained pure theory.

We only had one wish in those days, to soon be able to leave this despised, uncomfortable camp.

One night, we had slept for maybe two hours, there was another alarm.

We jumped out of our beds, in a quarter of an hour we were all standing in full marching order in the yard. We grabbed field rations for a day and marched into the night. We rushed off towards the North-East.

There was a large woodland area around the camp which was just perfect for these kinds of exercises. If the taller guys at the head of the squad were hurrying on, us short guys at the end of the column had to go at nearly double time so that we wouldn't lose them.

After a two hour march Bittermann was the first to fall victim to this increased pace and lost the man in front of him. Little by little ever more comrades fell behind. It wasn't always the strongest, or the tallest, who were the most enduring.

We had our first break. Some of those left behind caught up again, some were nowhere to be seen and could prepare themselves for extra training the next day.

After the break we went off the road and over rough ground. The whole crew broke off into squads, we fanned out and took up a defensive position. "Everyone dig in!" was the next command. So it seemed the only thing that had any real use for us was the spade.

Luckily we had rather sandy ground in front of us, mostly just interspersed with fist-sized stones. Haas puddled about next to me, Berndt was next to him and after Berndt was Plank.

Plank was a sturdy, strong lad, he was like a red towel for Ender, probably because he hardly ever managed to belittle this tough lad.

Although Plank had a cheeky mouth, apart from that he was good nature itself.
He couldn't be belittled by physical bullying, his endurance was unheard of and he let Ender's dressing downs go over his head with unheard of patience.

While we were puddling around in the sandy ground like moles, Plank was having such bother digging through the roots of a large bush that he was far behind us with the size of his hole. Ender, who always went up and down behind us during our digging and continually had something to moan about, stopped and stood behind Plank.

"Of course it's Plank again, the strongest but also the laziest, well you wait my friend, I have an extra hole ready just for you, while the others have their break, understood?"

Plank didn't answer, just kept working quietly. In order to clear out the many roots, he straightened up his body, so that he could take a bigger swing with the spade.

"Keep your backside down you shit!" Ender screamed furiously, "the enemy will make a sieve out of your arse!" Plank didn't change the way he worked, and acted as if he hadn't heard Ender's angry outburst at all.
"God damn it, your arse down I said," as he raved on, he shoved Plank in the backside with the tip of his boot.

That seemed to be too much even for him.
While he was in full swing, he turned with the spade and hit Ender with force in the hollow of the knee with the flat side.
Ender collapsed like a sack of bricks.

"Forgive me squad leader," said Plank, surely with a wicked grin on his face in the darkness,
"I couldn't see you in the dark, Sir."

Ender picked himself up, his face white as a sheet, rubbing the backs of his pained knees.

"I'm reporting you Plank, physical assault against a superior, that'll cost you solitary confinement!"
"It wasn't intentional squad leader, Sir," answered Plank.
"Not intentional eh? There are numerous witnesses stood about you, it'll cost you dearly."

With that Ender disappeared into the darkness to report to the Sturmführer. All of us around Plank grinned, pleased as punch.

"You showed him who's boss," said Berndt.

"It was high time that arsehole got a slap at last, I would have smacked the sharp side of the spade into his backside rather than the flat side of it."

"Pst, Ender's coming back," whispered Berndt.

We busied ourselves with our foxholes.

"Everyone up, gather around me!" Ender stepped in between us and gave the following speech:

"Well gentlemen, your digging was like that of a girl's boarding school, we'll be practicing this in the future until you're blue in the face men. At this pace none of you would survive a day on active service. Our squad was the last one finished, which will have consequences over the next few days," Ender buckled slightly at the knee, pressed his arms to his hips and tried to look as serious as he could.

"Next time we'll be in first place, understood? Else I'll boot your arses so high you'll hear the angels singing in the heavens," with these words Ender narrowed his eyes, which was supposed to show us his resolve.

"Drill dismissed, the squad will return under the leadership of Scharführer Koller. I'll be with the Sturmführer at the end of the column."

With that Ender disappeared, which was always a pleasant sight for us.

The march back took place at the same swift marching speed. The Sturmführer marching with his squad leaders at the end of the column was also a clever ruse. That way anyone who couldn't keep up the pace anymore and had reached his limit had to let his superiors march past him, of course for understandable reasons everyone wanted to avoid that as much as possible. Sturmführers and squad leaders of course could keep up easily without any rucksacks.

We arrived back at camp totally whacked out. The early duty was postponed by a few hours, so that we could sleep for another few hours.
The following day the kitchen only had limited service. Only warm drinks were served, otherwise we were provided for with the provisions we'd gotten the previous day.

At morning roll call, the Scharführer on duty announced:

"SA soldiers Plank, Haas, Berndt and Poschacher to morning report."

As we lined up in front of the orderly room, the Scharführer reported to the Sturmführer, Ender was also amongst the party. The Sturmführer inspected our line, stopped in front of Plank:

"SA soldier Plank, you are charged with assaulting squad leader Ender, I hope that you know what this allegation means for you, what do you have to say about it?"
"I did not assault him Sturmführer, Sir!"
"So you lie?"
"I am not lying, but it was completely unintentional, Sturmführer, Sir."
"But you swung your spade behind you, your foxhole lay in front of you did it not?"
"I swung far back in order to chop away roots."

Ender butted in.

"You knew that I was right behind you, don't lie."
"In the dark, I couldn't see how close you were standing," answered Plank.
"You're lying!" screamed Ender, "I shoved you with my foot, so I

could only have been right behind you."

"I didn't notice that squad leader, Sir," Plank couldn't be put off his stride.

"SA Soldier Berndt," the Sturmführer weighed in again, "You were a few meters away from Plank, how did the affair take place?"

"I didn't see anything Sturmführer, Sir, it was dark and I was busy with my own foxhole."

"Oh yes," Ender fumed, "You were all so busy, that's also why you were the last to be finished digging, Christ you saw how I collapsed from the blow!"

"No I didn't see that, I mean I didn't directly see it."

"What do you mean, 'not directly?'" The Sturmführer wanted to know.

"Well yes, I mean for sure I saw the squad leader getting up off of the ground, but I didn't see how he got there," a shrewd statement.

"Haas, Poschacher, you saw it as well," Ender turned to us now.

But we kept silent, as neither of us had been spoken to directly and we couldn't both answer at once.

"So then, you saw nothing either," the Sturmführer was annoyed and put an end to the matter, which seemed to be turning into a circus.

"Dismiss them," he addressed the Scharführer on duty and as we walked away we heard him saying to Ender:

"Next time get yourself better witnesses or leave the whole circus be."

The Sturmführer was no doubt happy that it had all come to nothing, otherwise he would have had to pass the report on higher and that would have painted the whole troop in a bad light. No doubt in private he didn't grudge this pratfall for Ender, his unpopularity was no secret to the Sturmführer either.

We on the other hand would come to understand Ender's fury, we knew that we would have to suffer under it for a while, but it was worth it for us. We reckoned that he would bully Plank in particular over the following days. But strangely enough, none of that sort of thing happened.
Instead, over the next field exercises, the entire squad barely kept their faces out of the dirt. But we could be stubborn too. A number of comrades feigned dizzy spells and even Ender was fed up of the constant stress eventually and service took its usual form again.

There were very few leisure activities you could do in the camp besides doing service.
We spent the evenings mostly playing football or voluntary sports activities in the yard. Very few people made use of the opportunities to go on leave. We had a small camp canteen where we could swap our few marks for tobacco products or alcohol. One of the few who preferred to go on leave to the town was Berndt. He had befriended a girl and was away ever free hour. He was the Casanova in our company and was much teased for it.

Every day at twenty two hundred hours the last post was blown by the bugler. Most of the time Berndt only came through the camp door at the very last minute.

One evening we wanted to arrange something moist for Berndt and we prepared his bed accordingly. Berndt was in the upper bunk above Haas. We took a tin bowl, made a fitting hollow in his straw mattress, filled the bowl with water and pulled his bed sheet taut across it. Haas, who lingered in the canteen until last post, had not been informed of the plot against his bunkmate.

At the last minute as usual, Berndt came back from leave. Everyone lay in bed and the lights had been extinguished. But it wasn't totally dark yet, all of us could still observe events very well.

Berndt swung himself into the upper bunk in his undershirt and underwear, climbed up at the bottom end, took his blanket and pulled it up under his chin then finally, with a soft thud, fell back onto his straw mattress.

"Holy shit!" he jumped up again,
"You bastards, you damned bandits!" Berndt yelled out, tearing the bowl out from under the bed sheets and hurling it in a high arc across the room in fury.

Unfortunately the bowl landed, spraying the rest of the water, on Tobler's head, who was sleeping in the distance and had absolutely no idea of the whole affair and was well on his way to a good snooze. Tobler chucked the bowl at his neighbour's head, who he had mistakenly suspected. This neighbour was Hartwig, who we called beanpole because of how tall he was. Hartwig jumped down from his bed and yanked Tobler down from the top bunk to the floor, a good and proper punch up now began at the other end of the room.

While Berndt was still cursing, Haas was swearing because the water was trickling down to his bed from above the place of the goings on had moved far away to the other side of the room. Tobler like Hartwig, each with his own supporters who were now getting thoroughly stuck into the affair themselves. The wildest scrap was now underway. Tables and chairs were crashing about the place, a window pane smashed.

"Stop it!" shouted some of higher rank.

The Scharführer on duty trilled on his whistle at the top of his lungs. But sparks were flying at the other end of the room. Those men involved were too busy to notice commands or rebukes.

Then the Sturmführer came, lured from his room by the tremendous racket in our hall. He had barely set eyes on the situation before he had the bugler, who had just come back from calling last post, blow the alarm. He blew at the top of his lungs and that had its desired effect on the room. Now we all dashed out of our beds, those who were fighting broke off from their opponents and we rushed into our uniforms as fast as we could. We were driven back and forth across the yard for an hour. They had us jumping, crawling, clambering until our temper was cooled.

Those of us who were responsible kept very quiet, we were far too physically inferior to the men at the other end of the room to be boastful.

There were no further consequences over this evening scrap however, it was sensibly classified as cabin fever.

After staying in Marktredwitz for around three months another transfer was in store for us.

But we longed for the day we could leave the old cement factory forever.

As soon as we learned that we were to be transferred to Bremen, our joy knew no bounds.

We had long wanted to go to a bigger city, you could at least do something decent with your free time there.

As we cleared out from camp and got on our truck for the trip to Bremen, the next troop that was taking over after us stood in the yard already. Well then, they'll have fun here, won't they?

It was a long, pleasant trip to Bremen. It was almost dark as we came through the Ruhr area. The fires from the chimneys of the huge factories blazed all over. We were speechless and overwhelmed by Germany's mighty arsenal. In our homeland we had never seen factories this size.

The whole Ruhr area seemed to us like one big city, an unbroken, endless collection of residential buildings and factories.

It was already late when we arrived in Bremen. The long streets seemed empty and deserted. We stopped finally in front of a row of low, elongated buildings. Our new quarters were provided by the Lloyd emigration halls. Here again as well only comfortless large rooms.

"Shit again," Bittermann said to me.
"Yeah well," I answered, "just wait a bit, it's night after all and even tropical birds would look grey in the dark."
"The birds in Bremen are supposed to be really gorgeous," Berndt intervened.
"Hopefully one of them will peck your eyes out soon," Haas angrily threw his knapsack onto the bed that was assigned to him,
"these huge rooms all the time, the stink of dozens of sweaty feet every night, it disgusts me."
"There's not much you can do about it," I pulled my blanket over my head with this last remark, it was the first night in Bremen.

We spent the following days setting up the camp permanently. We were assigned in squads to the kitchen, the medical barracks, the vehicle hangar, bedsteads were carried back and forth, the crates from the orderly room brought along and unpacked. The rooms of our superiors were set up.

A few days passed like this until normal duties could begin. The space provided for exercise was very limited, only the large paved inner courtyard was available for that.

"It's just perfect for your flat feet," said the Scharführer.

After a few days a spot of moorland ideal for our field drills was found north of Bremen. We called our exercise grounds "Rabbit Moor."

A wonderful late autumn began. The way to the moor was so far that we were transported there by truck. The drivers spent the time waiting for the journey back with driving lessons so they said. But we were convinced that most of the time they were just lazing around on the sun warmed heather.

Ender was in his element again here on Rabbit Moor. Here out of public view he could abuse us to his heart's content.

"That damned sadist, one day I'll give him a good hiding, no matter what happens after!" every day someone got such or the same comment off their chest.

The Lloyd halls were surrounded completely by a wall. Wooden guardhouses stood in front of the two entrances. The guard room lay inside a little off to the side. Guard duty here was really entertaining. There were always constant passers-by on the street. You always saw something and the two hours passed quickly.

Soon the girls showed up too, they sauntered past us with all kinds of intentions.

Bremen was thought of as a dangerous place. In the beginning there were almost weekly lessons from the staff surgeon. Time and time again he gave us detailed explanations of the dangers of love in harbour cities. The cooks also did their best to protect us from too much activity with all kinds of secret extra powders in the coffee and the stew.

There were many fights between sailors and legionnaires during the course of our stay in Bremen. The sailors were rightly unhappy to see an invasion into their domain and the lads from the Alps were certainly not averse to occasional fights. For this reason there was sometimes a curfew lasting several days for the whole camp.

One day we had an orientation trip in the rural area north of Bremen. This trip was supposed to be tied up with smaller open country field exercises. The lack of space in the truck also meant that Ender's squad had to be split up. But at our end destination we, who were driving with Koller's crowd in Wallmeir's squad's truck, were supposed to join Ender's squad again.

We travelled in the second last truck, Ender came in last with the rest of his squad.

We went across Lilienthal, Falkenberg and Trogermoor onward towards Zeven.
The column stopped for a toilet break before Tarmstedt. Ender's trucks hadn't caught up yet. The Sturmführer called his squad leaders around him. They determined the theatre of operations on the map and briefly discussed the course of the exercise. The break was prolonged a bit, but the rest of Ender's squad didn't arrive.

The rest of Ender's squad were surely stuck with a puncture or engine problems.

Our journey was supposed to continue to Hepstedt. In the area to the East of the town we were to defend a line of railway track, holding off advancing enemies until the arrival of reinforcements. These were the instructions as they were given to the squad leaders.

In our troop we had a little guy from Bludenz, he was called Paul Wolter and he wasn't the sharpest tool in the shed.

Scharführer Koller was ordered to assign a man to relay the following Sturmführer's order to Ender.

"Squad Ender follow the unit to Hepstedt, take up position on the railway track to the east of the town, hold position until further orders."

God knows why Koller chose, of all people, our genius Paul to convey this message to Ender.

After a while, we boarded our vehicles again. Since Ender still hadn't turned up, Paul had to stay on the road and wait for Ender's arrival.

"What's the name of the place Ender's got to travel to again?" Paul asked Plank who stood next to him.
"Wilstedt, Paul," Plank answered him.
"Hopefully I'll remember," said Paul not altogether convinced.
"Wilstedt, it's not difficult, now don't piss your pants Paul," Plank gave Paul a good natured slap on the shoulder and clambered up to us in the truck.

We headed off, poor Paul was left behind at the edge of the road with his dilemma.
We travelled through Tarmstedt, just behind the town we came to a fork in the road. To the North it went to Hepstedt, to the South it went to Wilstedt.

"Ender will have a lot of fun when he ends up in Wilstedt and can't find a whiff of us," Plank whispered these words to me with his most unashamed grin.

"You're getting poor Paul into a lot of trouble as well though," I said, a little sceptical of his plan. "God no! Precisely because Paul is so gormless, and everyone knows it, you can't touch him. You can't punish him for being thick!" Plank was right there again.

We were unloaded in the little town of Hepstedt, the trucks were supposed to drive under cover where possible. We on the other hand marched a few kilometers to the East and began the scheduled field exercise.

The Sturmführer ranted about Ender, whose absence made a mess of the whole exercise.

So we got into position and slowly drew back in stages to Hepstedt. Here the railway line was to be held until the arrival of the assumed reinforcements.

In the meantime we now expected Ender to have long been in position on the railway line already, and thus to have already built a rear position.

But far and wide nothing was to be seen of the rest of Ender's squad. Now our lot had to occupy the strips of land that were intended for the entire squad. We were spread far apart, and we had a great laze around since we were so little supervised. We lay idly in the sun, guzzled our field rations and thought the war to be good fun.

The exercise was only abandoned in the late afternoon. We went back to Bremen, with no sign of Ender on the way. We had already been in the camp for two hours when Ender finally arrived back to the camp with the rest of his squad. As soon as our comrades came off of the truck we saw on their faces that they had had a miserable day behind them... For half the day Ender had travelled through the countryside with the rest of his squad like a madman, albeit without finding us.

There was no railway line to the east of the town in Wilstedt, on the contrary it ended up on the western side. Eventually he took up position on this railway line and waited for further instructions. But no orders came, nothing happened at all and Ender suspected that he was in the shit. Understandably, he let his fury out on our comrades.

After his return, Ender had to go to the Sturmführer immediately. His face was contorted with rage when he came back, he had surely been given a thorough bollocking.

He went to Koller now first of all, who he gave a real bawling out for the supposedly false report. Of course, Koller then let his anger out on Paul.

"You blockhead!" Koller shouted at him,
"what did you report to the squad leader? What sort of place did you tell him to go to?"
"Hepstedt," said Paul, suddenly remembering the correct town again.
"Wha.....aaaaat?" Ender went up to Paul now.
"What town did you say to me?"
"Hepstedt!"
"You reported Wilstedt to me, you shit, too dopy to hold one town in your head for a few minutes."
"I said Hepstedt for sure, squad leader, Sir."
"Get out of my sight you prat!"

Ender was red with fury.

Bu in the end it was one man's word against another's. Paul couldn't be punished either.

"That ought to be a lesson to me," growled Koller, "only written reports will come from me now."
"Not a chance! Written reports!" replied Ender,
"Reports will be given verbally, just don't give them to morons."

I got my first holiday a few weeks after our arrival in Bremen. I wanted to spend it with Malzer in Munich where mother was also living in the meantime.

I had a holiday slip for fourteen days and a free pass for train journeys thrust into my hand and went on my way.

It was a really long journey for those times, crossing through Germany from the almost extreme North down to the deepest South.

The parents had a little flat in Munich near to the Englischer Garten. At the time Malzer had an easy desk job and was back home punctually every late afternoon.

The days were still wonderfully warm even though it was already well into autumn, the trees were starting to go brown. I wondered at the fantastic grounds of the Englischer Garten I often went for walks there in the morning hours.

In the evening though, we visited some cosy Munich bars. We only travelled on Weiß-Ferdl's tram twice, both wonderful experiences for me. I was jealous of Malzer's cushy job in this city where you could spend your free time so wonderfully. The only thing that bothered me about the whole thing was that I had no civilian clothes anymore and always had to go around in uniform.

Malzer seemed to be very content with the way things were going for him. He had an easy job, a little apartment which the Legion was paying the rent for and he was with his wife. Younger brother Alfred was already in Kiel at the time and had an apprenticeship. Malzer often dreamt of a lucrative position which, as a Legionnaire, he would surely get after an annexation of Austria. Mother was happy with everything, just to be with her Franz. Sadly, the holidays passed by far too quickly and I had to return to Bremen.

I arrived at a time when a furious passion for drilling had broken out at camp again.

In Bremerhaven a ship was to be launched.

The Legion was to be part of this ceremony as well. The Führer would be appearing too and it was said that this was the reason why again all of us had to practice drill to our wits end from morning to night.

We really didn't know what we could have improved on but our superiors were of a very different opinion.

At an ungodly hour, we were already on the way to Bremen when the noteworthy day dawned. Just so that the Legion didn't arrive too late.

We stood for hours, until we were ready to drop, on a huge cobbled square. We barely felt our legs anymore and the satchels weighed us down.

Finally, in really elaborate state cars, our lordly rulers drove by. Countless commands rang out, we halted and stood at ease again, the eyes turned right, turned left, the rank grew higher with every command, the braids on the uniforms wider until finally Germany's most powerful man, the Führer, stepped forward.

Despite the faint trembling in our knees from the long wait, we stood so straight that a fly couldn't have gotten between our legs and stared as if hypnotised at the man who had all of us quite literally in his hands. As he passed in front of me, at a measured pace about three meters away, a peculiar feeling crept over me. I follow him with my eyes as we had learned, he seems to take notice of each and every one of us. He had something magical in his eyes.

Hitler was around five meters past me, when there was an awful crash. The Führer flinched, but controlled himself again quickly. What had happened?

A large wooden spectator stand hadn't been built for the weight of so many people and had partly collapsed. A great commotion took hold of the people on the square. Hitler made a bee line for his car surrounded by numerous SS men and left the scene. Apart from a few minor casualties, the collapse of the podium had no worse consequences. The whole fuss was hurriedly cleared up and we went back to Bremen.

An excursion to Helgoland was a particular experience. None of us had been to the sea up until then and so of course we were excited to be allowed this.

I stood on the bow of the steamship for the whole journey and found it terrific how the waves lifted us up almost as high as houses, then dragged us down into the deep again. It was a sunny, but really windy day and a few comrades soon got really green in the face.

But we already reached the roads of Helgoland before they'd finished their breakfast. We swapped over to a smaller boat now which brought us to land.

We marvelled at the high red cliffs which rose so suddenly up out of the sea, the tiny streets, the many market stands.

We painted Helgoland red for a few hours. We were bad customers for the many stall sellers. We made fun of the girls who quickly disappeared into the nearby streets when the brown swarm of young lads came into view.

We let the sea wind waft through our noses good and proper, looked across the vast sea longingly, behind whose crest so many foreign lands, for us unreachable, lay hidden.

The year came to an end. We celebrated the first Christmas in the Legion. One of the large halls was decorated with a huge Christmas tree. A few hundred men took part in the celebrations. There were extra rations of alcohol and tobacco and a bag of sweets. We grew a little homesick when we sang through the Christmas songs.

The winter months went by, one day the same as the other, we were really only able to bear those times with a great sense of fellowship.

And with the new spring, we filled Rabbit Moor with the noise of our shouting again. We fertilised the heather with our beads of sweat again. Soon we knew every rabbit hole, every sandhole, every group of birch trees within a ten kilometer radius.

Ender was raving like a lunatic again. We ran, moaned, cursed and crawled still compelled by his commands again.

Noon came, the afternoon came, we yelled, we were hungry.

"You're what?" Ender asked,
"come on men, up...get down..up march, march!"
we stumbled onward, but shouted in unison.. "We're hungry!"
"Well then get on with it you fools!...move, move...take cover,..move march, march!"

We wheezed with rage in our guts, full of anger at the man who had the power to let us starve and to discipline us as he saw fit.

We stood in front of him, would have most liked to smack him.

"Well what do you think now? Are you still hungry? Of course you're not hungry, no Legionnaire ever suffers from hunger, a Legionnaire has an appetite at most, no more, understood you sissies?" He grinned at us maliciously, tasting his power over us ad nauseum.

Yes, it was like that back then. Ender was a demon, a monster in uniform. At the same time he was so cunning too, he knew exactly the limits of how far he could go, but he always went to those permitted limits and there was ample room for him to play in there.
And so Rabbit Moor was our stamping ground almost every day for the whole of spring and into May.

On a Sunday at the end of May I travelled with a few comrades to Bremerhaven. In a pub on the street there sat a few SA leaders at a table. A Sturmführer invited me to sit at his table. I had to tell him about Austria, of how I came to Germany. Finally the Sturmführer took me back to Bremen in his car. He invited me for a small meal in his house. I actually didn't feel any great desire to do so, he was too high up for me, indeed an SA soldier didn't feel quite at ease with a Sturmführer. But I wasn't strong enough to simply turn down the invitation either. So I went into his residence with him. He had to be a bachelor for sure, I saw neither a woman nor a child there.
He offered me a hefty snack, invited me to come round next weekend again, but sat so close to me that the whole affair slowly grew sinister. I feigned some duty, took my leave, I was in a hurry all of a sudden.

At the door, he suddenly put his arm around me and tried to kiss me, but I was out the door straight away, racing down the steps and breathing in relief once I was on the street.

Well what a fine gentleman I'd dug up there. I had no experience in the matter, but the Sturmführer's intentions seemed to be very explicit to me. In future I was to give every SA leader a wide berth.

When the summer came they said that we would soon be transferred to a totally new camp which had been built for us. If we had at first believed it was some of the usual toilet gossip, the rumours soon became certain.

In Bocholt, somewhere in Westphalia, the new camp was supposed to be built by one of the Legion's groups of engineers.

The preparations began for our handing over. All of our possessions which weren't part of our field equipment were handed in and packed in boxes. A rear detachment was supposed to remain in Bremen in order to organise the rest of the winding down of the camp. Apparently the camp in Bremen was to be abandoned completely.

To our greatest joy, Ender was to be part of this rear guard. Many comrades were in a hurry to untie themselves, as gently as possible, from the delicate bonds they had established in Bremen. With some damsels no doubt tears were shed, many sailors heaved a sigh of relief having rid themselves of their troublesome competition.

With Bremen we left a city in whose walls we had, apart from the somewhat primitive accommodation, felt totally at home.

It was an extraordinarily hot day in June when, kitted out in full marching order, we left the Lloyd emigration halls and marched towards the train station.

The girls marched alongside us on the pavement, sometimes even accompanied by their relieved mothers.

As we climbed on the long train, a last farewell, a last wave to the girls, the city and the good people of Bremen who had so uncomplainingly endured our presence for months.

We rolled out of the station, towards our new camp. And a last look northward as well, farewell Rabbit Moor!

An entire Legion band stood ready for our reception when we arrived in Bocholt.

Loaded off, we formed into march columns and, under the sounds of a Prussian parade march, headed towards the city centre.

The square in front of the town hall stood packed full of people. A stand had been built and, in tight goose step, we marched past the SA Leaders and dignitaries of the city.

We were able to keep up with any elite division when it came to our marching step. Drill practice hadn't been our year-long daily routine for nothing.

We received loud cheering from all sides for our faultless march past, while the rhythm of the music particularly inspired us of course.

We went eastward in a wide arc out of the city again along a street with young trees planted on either side.

We reached our camp after around ten minutes. Indeed as had been reported it was completely newly built. It lay at the end of a pine forest. A wire fence around three meters high enclosed a large square which formed the outer boundary of the wooden barracks.

A wide wooden door formed the entrance, a national motto on a mighty wooden beam over it, but its wording has slipped my mind.

To the right of the door the guard barracks, to the left the medical barracks and supply room and the library. The two long sides were filled with soldiers' barracks. A large dining hall formed the end to the North, the kitchen, a canteen and a number of smaller barracks for those of higher rank. A wide grass lawn the size of two football fields formed the inner camp.

And so we marched into the new camp and took up position facing the entrance. The sun burned down on us from the sky mercilessly.

Soon the sweat was pouring off our bodies. In thick uniforms, without being allowed to take off our backpacks, we stood in the sweltering heat and waited... and waited. The music was marched past next to us. Everything stood ready but the lordly men on whom we still waited took their time, an awful lot of time. No doubt they were all still busy drinking in the town hall. What did these gentlemen care for the few hundred men who were waiting for them in the blazing heat of the sun? Just be steadfast, the Führer needs strong men.

All of a sudden, a musician in one of the middle rows fell over. He remained lying at first, nobody bothered themselves about him. Our Standartenführer Fuschlberger was in front, uneasy and nervous.

Then the second musician fell over, but in the same moment there was the sound of an approaching car. Commands sounded, we stood as one, with a jerk the eyes went left, a tall SA leader with lots of gongs on him came out of a pulled up car. It was the head of the SA Lutze, who had made the effort to personally welcome us to the camp.

A short address, the National Anthem was played, "Sieg Heil" was given to the Führer three times and the matter for which we'd been roasted in the sun to near unconsciousness was over. We could march off, and we took up our quarters. We shared a bedroom between thirty people here as well, but it was all very bright and spacious. There was space for a hundred men in the dining hall and even the laundry room could fit thirty men at a time. We also had a large, spacious room to piddle in, the main latrine formed a front with six perfectly fitting holes and wooden tops with knobs to seal the smell in, everything very well thought out and generously set out. On the back wall, a huge nail was hammered over every hole from which you could hang yourself, or stick newspaper on it, mostly the latter was done.

We went through two glazed double doors to get to the dining room, a comfort that until now we had never had. The double beds and lockers were likewise made from wood. There were swing doors to the individual dorm rooms. Even the canteen, in which a plain clothes host took our few marks, was better furnished. But our expectations were modest as well.

An important point to note is that squad leader Ender didn't appear in our division anymore. We didn't see that nut-buster any longer. In his place came senior squad leader Scheller. Koller became Oberscharführer and the rest of the SA men were named Stormtroopers. I too was amongst them and along with that came a 30 pfennig increase in my weekly pay.

And so I was out of the bottom level, I barely noticed a difference on the drill field, but at the same time it was the first rung up to chief of staff. But by no means did I want to go as far as that, too high up and things became very dangerous again (see Röhm.)

But our concerns were very different. On our first free evening we headed out to explore the area. We fell on the small town and its neighbourhood like a brown swarm.
After the first night out Berndt said:

"The dolls were cuter in Bremen," he was right, everything was a lot more countrylike here, frequently had a healthy smell of barn dung, everything was healthier here, but also sturdier.

"But no bother," Berndt mused further, "once I've got one in hand, I'll learn her good and proper."

Our Casanova was well-versed and after the second night out he had one "in hand," as he put it. The young lads from Bocholt were little pleased about our turning up. It didn't last long until the first signs of tension began, more of that later.

Early morning exercise was taken very seriously in the new camp in Bocholt.

We had to report in the yard for our morning run in the woods within at least a minute after waking up.

After the alarm you jumped out of bed and ran as you had slept, in undershirt and gym shorts in front of the barracks. A short roll call and we went off in squads into the woods. Our new squad leader Scheller was far removed from the slave driver that Ender was, but he was a downright punctuality fanatic. On that he was strict but never unfair and there were no particularly crass swear words with him.

But for early morning drill a Scharführer mostly led the squad, squad leaders barely took part.

We also had an extreme health fanatic in our division. Kropp was his name but we just called him "Sepp."

Sepp missed no opportunity to harden himself up and keep himself healthy for his Führer. So most of the time at night he also slept naked in bed, he said that that helped to toughen him up as well. We teased him about that a lot, which didn't bother him much.

One evening as he was already lying in deep sleep on his straw bed, his things piled up on a stool in front of him, his gym shorts which we normally kept on amongst them as well, his neighbour Slavik cut through the shorts' elastic and neatly put them back on the stool again.

Punctually at half past five the next morning, we sprang out of bed at the whistle of the Unterführer on duty.
Even as we were coming into the yard, Sepp was beginning to pull at his shorts, which had an inexplicable desire to slide down his bottom.
But we were already heading out of the camp door towards the pine forest.

Sepp desperately tried to pull the band of his shorts tighter as he went, it gave way of course and soon he held it in his hand.
So there was nothing else Sepp could do other than keep holding the rebellious shorts with his hand as he ran. He didn't want to lag behind of course, that would have inevitably meant being assigned to kitchen duty, and we loathed peeling potatoes.

Now after a long trek of running it was usual for us to fall in line and the command came: "Arms up...breathe deeply..arms down breathe out...." and that was always repeated numerous times.

But Sepp was impeded from raising both of his arms up now, he had to hold his shorts up with one hand after all. Squad leader Pacher, who was running alongside the squad, thought Sepp's conduct was laziness, he knew nothing of his dilemma after all.

"Kropp you lazy goose raise your arms if you please!"
"I can't Scharführer, Sir."
"What do you mean you can't?"
"My shorts are slipping Scharführer, Sir."
"What you wouldn't say, you pillock! Your shorts shouldn't be

loose understood?"

"But they are."

"Would you maybe like to raise your mitts up you prat? If your shorts are in order then they won't slide, if they're not in order then that's your problem, hands up Kropp!"

With that Kropp was seized with fury, he raised both his hands up and let his shorts drop. They immediately fell down his legs as well and prevented him from keeping in step.
The men behind Kropp who could see all of this found it difficult not to burst out with laughter. Scharführer Pacher, who was not exactly known for his humour, slowly went red with rage, no doubt he thought that Kropp deliberately wanted to make an arse of him.

"Do you maybe want to cover your naked arse you pig?" Pacher roared.

But now suddenly the otherwise good-natured Sepp went white as a sheet. He stepped out of line, stood in front of the Scharführer, his shorts hanging at his ankles in the most fantastic costume of Adam and with a sinister calm in his voice he asked:

"Who's the pig here Sir?"

Then Pacher backed off from Sepp and said very quietly:

"Kropp, stay behind and put your shorts in order...the rest of the squad on the double .. march .... march ...!"

Kropp thought it over, turned around and disappeared behind the pine trees to cover his salacious nudity, he was close to getting physical with Pacher it wouldn't have gone well for him.

Around once a month you were assigned guard duty. One man stood at the main entrance right next to the guard barracks, this position was not in great demand. Two men had to patrol the camp area beyond the wire fence. Such a trip round needed a good twenty minutes and was a lot more entertaining than duty at the camp entrance. You had two hours guard duty and four hours on call over the twenty four hours altogether.

Countless times I wandered around the camp at night while observing the stars in every phase in the sky and dreamt of the future and of soon being let out of this Legion. We only had small calibre rifles for weapons. Amongst our tasks we also had to make sure that late returnees didn't go around the entrance and climb into the camp over the fence. But the path around the camp was long and since the western side in particular was overgrown with thick bushes, time and again comrades came over the fence unseen as long as they risked a sizeable tear in their trousers, since three rows of barbed wire formed the top of the fence after all.

Combat training was very limited in Bocholt and so instead drilling and sport took precedence, along with long marches with backpacks which were on the schedule at least once every week.

For a long time it had been clear to us that they had long thrown out the idea of deploying the Legion to liberate Austria. They could have easily dissolved the Legion and put us into civilian professions, but no doubt as a potent number of refugees we were surely there to make the hated regime in Austria and her methods of oppression visible to foreign countries. And so a discharge, apart from very few exceptions, continued to be denied. And so we continued to perform a duty which had long gotten on our nerves on account of its senselessness.

One day in the course of the summer a committee from the League of Nations appeared in our camp, and looked closely at our operations and the whole premises. But the gentlemen disappeared again just as quickly as they had arrived without asking any questions of us.

At the beginning of autumn the drill exercises suddenly increased exceptionally. The reason: We were to go to the harvest festival in Bückeburg and so we were to be prepared with extra drills. The exercises were so bitter for us that we looked forward to the change that the journey to Bückeburg would bring. And so it went on for the whole day in the camp yard as if it were recruitment training, we were old hands with it already, but our trainers still found weak points that had to be ironed out.

Our camp yard's beautifully laid out turf soon resembled a pounded down mud floor. If we weren't busy drilling we played football, outdoor handball or dodgeball. Despite all of these activities we were still gripped by cabin fever often enough. You can't just do exercise and sport after all.
We constantly cooked up all kinds of mischief. Got up to all kinds of monkey business with comrades in order to find some kind of diversion. But over time these high jinks took on forms that overstepped the limits of the harmless only too often. The snorers most of all had to suffer all kinds of nastiness. Little folded scraps of paper were stuck between their toes and lit on fire. When the severe pains from the resulting burns woke them up, all of their comrades lay well behaved in their beds and it couldn't be ascertained who the evil-doer was. It started out mostly that once the paper had been lit the person affected by it started to thrash his feet about wildly before he woke up, if the pain woke him, with a shriek of pain he immediately sprang out of his top bunk to the ground cursing loudly, in despair hopping around between the rest of the beds on one leg. Often the victim went around with painful burn wounds between his toes for days. Woe to him when on top of that, a backpack march was scheduled. These

terrible habits got so out of control, that in the end only the most severe threats of punishment could contain them.

One Sunday in the middle of August, around evening time I sat with other comrades in the canteen when comrade Hartwig suddenly shouted through the door:

"Come on! There's a huge fight going on in Bocholt, we have to go and help them!"

We raced out of the canteen, reinforcements came out of every barracks and off we went towards the city.

We already saw the huge crowd of people as we arrived in front of the relevant inn in Bocholt. For the most part we weren't exactly given friendly looks.
Unfortunately, the fight had long finished, but the destroyed furniture showed the ferocity of the clash. The cross of a window was fully ripped out of its frame, smashed beer mugs lay around and there were numerous chairs broken to pieces. In the pub the police were already at the scene of the crime and since camp commander Fuschlberger also turned up we decided to disappear as quickly as possible since the battle was already over. We found Plank on the way in an awful state. He had gotten a hefty smack over the head with a beer mug and in the end had to be seen by a doctor in the medical barracks. The whole reason behind the scrap was as Plank put it "dumb bitches." Little by little more and more comrades arrived with greater or lesser heavy wounds. Fuschlberger made a big show out of the fight. He preached a great sermon to us peppered with reproaches and threats.
Those directly involved had a few days of solitary, for all of the other men and ranks up to Sturmführer fourteen days without leave.
Fuschlberger loved taking rigorous action.

After a week confined to the barracks, cabin fever slowly grew close to its peak. Dozens of Bocholt girls stood outside in front of the camp fence, inside a number of Legionnaires hung like monkeys from the wire mesh. The good camp commandant Fuschlberger didn't put in an appearance.

The duties were increased during the day and long marches were scheduled outside in order to tire us out as much as possible and slowly cool our tempers.
During the evenings, the canteen was packed full and a series of comrades would already be drinking their pay for the next weeks.

Around this time, Italy was involved in conquering Abyssinia. We became ardent supporters of Negus then, and wished all kinds of things to the Italians other than good.
Then comrades came to the idea of organising a parade in the camp out of sympathy for the Emperor of Abyssinia. This proposal was taken up with great enthusiasm, it could at least distract us from the dreary life in the camp for a few hours and it would surely be great fun too.
Around a hundred comrades took an active part in the procession, the rest formed the enthusiastic audience. Rarely did we have to find so much oven soot and brown shoe polish as was needed to transform into dark skinned Abyssinians. For Negus there was even a horse brought into the camp.
It must have been five times that Negus went round the camp area with a great retinue while we in the audience constantly shouted "Heil Negus" at the top of our voices. A number of civilians stood in front of the camp fence and watched our insane carrying on, shaking their heads.

When on a Saturday the fourteen day curfew was over the camp was swept empty by midday. But there were no great fights in the future. At the weekends a patrol of Legion and civilian SA had to check all of the inns constantly. Slowly even the lads in Bocholt came to terms with their rivals, particularly since they were wealthier and performed better in the race in the long run. Some girls went back to their former admirers either under their parent's pressure, or because their new partners slowly lost their appeal after all.

But a few dozen close connections will have surely kept for life.

On a Saturday in the beginning of October we were loaded onto a train, we travelled to Bückeburg for the harvest festival. Outside of the city we built camp and spent a night there.

As soon as the crack of dawn the next day we were shook awake. We tore down the tents and marched to Bückeburg to the big festival ground for the event.

Now we could stand here for hours until we were ready to drop. Formation after formation marched past in the next hours, a sea of flags and standards the vastness of which you couldn't see over the top of. Of course we were the first in place again and so had the pleasure of waiting the longest. We were around thirty meters to the side of the speaking podium that had been built, it was a brilliant spot from which we could observe everything. After our curiosity had been sorely tried, little by little the party bigwigs finally arrived. The weedy Goebbels was the first to step up to the stage, some followed that we didn't know until fat Goering clambered onto the podium and claimed a good part of the stand just for himself. We kept standing still, shouted "Sieg Heil" at the top of our voices and were allowed to stand at ease again. Trumpeting and drumming from all sides, the air was filled with the howling of the Jagdflieger planes which passed over us again and again.

Hitler appeared on the stand as the climax. It was a large scale spectacle. The subsequent speech powerful in word and volume as always.

An almost immeasurable mob of people broke out into almost hysterical cheering again and again.

The conclusion of the event was formed by a combat demonstration from the Wehrmacht which was of the most interest to us.

With an indescribable howl, the dive bombers ended the exercise. It lasted ages again until the way was free for our division to march off as well.

We were loaded back onto the train again on the same late afternoon.

One day squad leader Scheller came to us with a plan which immediately gained universal enthusiasm. He suggested ordering bicycles for the whole squad which we could pay off in monthly rates of three marks, assuming we were agreed. And how agreed we were, we were even utterly thrilled by the idea.

Three marks was more than even an entire weeks pay, but what mobility we were swapping it for! And moreover, the area around Bocholt was frankly ideal for cycling excursions. The bicycles would have cost around thirty marks, whereby a decent bulk discount had already been deducted.

And so the order was placed and we could barely wait for the wheels.

An order came from up high to do something about general education and writing skills as well. For this reason every month a little competition with modest prizes was supposed to serve as encouragement.

For the squads in our Sturm, prizes were made out for the three best pieces of work. For the first task we were to prepare a written exercise about reconnoitring land and map reading. We had three hours time to write down our knowledge under supervision. An Agfa box camera was arranged as first prize, the other prizes were comprised of cigarettes and various board games.

Of course the squad leaders were interested and wanted to come off as well as they could with their men and pushed us respectively.

After the essays had been written they were gathered together and brought to the orderly room. We were excited what would come of it.

A few days later after lunch break, Hartinger, our Sturmführer came into the room in which we had assembled with all of the essays under his arm. Flanked by three squad leaders, he began with his appraisal.

"Well then gentlemen, what some of you have written here at times made my hair stand on end! I don't want to talk about the countless spelling mistakes, we're not here to fill in the gaps that are present in your education after all. No, I'm disturbed by the ignorance of matters which we have gone over and over again in your lessons and in the field. There will be some hard work for the squad leaders in the next weeks."

Hartinger took a few papers in hand which he had sought out in particular.

"Endruat!"
"Here,"
"Instead of writing about compass 'magnetic declination' you've written 'magnetic decoration' – I can assure you it has nothing to do with interior design!"

Universal laughter set in.

"Gentlemen, really very few of you have any reason to laugh."

Hartinger turned to Endruat again.

"Your description of how you can correct this declination is so confusing that nobody could understand it. In seriousness I really don't want to be dependent on your compass reading skills, you'd end up going every direction apart from where you're supposed to."

Hartinger took out another essay:

"Slavik!"
"Here."
"Good Lord, what must your compass look like, when one indicator points north and the other end points east? What can you say to that gentlemen?..."

Hartinger shook his head and looked somewhat pityingly at Slavik who stood there embarrassed.

"And about the tides you simply write, the moon pulls the sea up and hours later it falls down again - well you're really making things too simple there. Also tides have nothing to do with tying things up, so please don't write it with a 'Y.' Please look at your compass properly and don't write me such rubbish again understood?"
"Yes, Sturmführer, Sir."

Hartinger took out more essays:

"I can't go into full detail about all of the nonsense that you have dribbled out here, your squad leaders will have to deal with that after this, but I would like to attend to one more sample in particular."

Hartinger looked around the room searchingly:

"Plank!"

"Here."

"Ah yes, well Plank you're really taking the biscuit. You write here about marching at night: In the night time, there is no sunlight, and so you can't see where you're going. So you always follow the North Star and then you'll get to where you want to go."

A universal snickering filled the canteen.

"Well under no condition do I want to entrust myself under your leadership! That there's no sunlight in the night is of course somewhat obvious, but the idea that the North Star always shows the direction you want to travel is truly a hair raising assertion. Take some time and think over the drivelling crap you've written."

The Sturmführer put the essay back with the other blunders which had been particularly looked out.

"Well thank God, there were also essays which were satisfactory. Josefschnig!"

"Here, Sturmführer, Sir."

"You've turned in a good essay, factually however there are a few falsehoods to note. But for the good essay I can award you third prize. I am very pleased with you."

Hartinger took a new sheet to hand.

"Hartwig!"

"Here,"

"Excellent work Hartwig! What's your education?"

"I've a Matura, Sturmführer, Sir."

"That's why, there's barely anything to find fault with in your polished essay, your squad leader can be pleased, I award you second prize."

Now Hartinger slowly took the last sheet of paper to hand.

"Well men, I have an essay here that has somewhat made up for some of the crap that I've read.
In your factual correctness and skilful phrasing a truly outstanding performance, Poschacher!"
"Here,"
"What education do you have?"
"Three classes of Bürgerschule, Sturmführer, Sir!"
"Good for you, there is nothing to find fault with in your essay, truly outstanding. It's a crying shame that you're such a reserved lad. A little more mouth and with your knowledge you'd be a born Unterführer, why are you so modest man? But for the essay you've earned first prize."

Hartinger handed over the rest of the essays to the individual squad leaders for further review and left the room.
So the matter had gone much better than I could have hoped. The competition brought me a considerable increase in respect in the eyes of my superiors. I was barely assigned to kitchen duty anymore and also had other privileges too.
The box camera I'd won was also the starting gun for a newly awakened passion for photography.

There was a great reception when the bicycles that we'd ordered arrived. They were very robust touring bicycles painted with an olive green finish. We rolled our way round the campyard until in the evening the last post was called and we even had a storeroom assigned in one of the barracks.

As early as the following weekend, we grabbed ourselves two days field rations from the kitchen and set out on our first great excursion towards the South. We cycled in fantastic sunshine through streets which were still quiet back then, across Wesel uphill along the Rhein and camped in the late afternoon on the Rhein meadows somewhere between Düsseldorf and Cologne.

They were fantastic hours, although after a few hours our backsides were in some real pain.

We built up the tents we'd brought with us, arranged enough bottles of beer and sang patriotic songs by the blazing fire late into the night.

When, unexpectedly, a few women appeared between the tents, they were promptly chased off by the squad leader. They of all people shouldn't disturb the sociable evening and thereby the camaraderie.

Unfortunately, due to the many bicycles, setting up a guard for that night as well was unavoidable. But enough volunteers were found to give themselves to watching the fire and bikes for the night hours. We messed around in the tents for a long time and came up with lame jokes.

When we crawled out of our tents the next morning, the grass was totally soaked with the night's dew, but the sun was already high in the sky over the Rhein. A wonderful new day accompanied us on our way back. I busily took shots with the box camera I'd won, but sadly all of the pictures were lost in the unruly years that followed. Sadly back then I hadn't known their great sentimental value.

When we arrived in Bocholt again around evening time, despite having taken numerous breaks we could barely sit down on our backsides any more.

"Good Lord," said Berndt,
"Everything between my knees and my belly is burning like it's on fire."
To that the little Haas said mockingly:
"That shouldn't bother you, your broads are always lighting a fire under your ass!"
"I'd rather have a fire beneath my ass than sawdust between my ears," Berndt replied wittily.
"Your soup for brains would be useful to soothe your burns with," Haas laughed in Berndt's face and had a dozen others laughing with him.
"Oh leave me alone you imp!"
"I'll give you imp you blockhead!"
"You children, stop it already," intervened Scheller.

But none of it was meant seriously anyway.
We brought our bicycles to the storeroom and even before the last post was called we lay in our beds very tired.
But both days had been wonderful and finally some change from dreary camp life.

So autumn came to its end, winter came into the land and we began to shiver with cold during our early morning exercises until we had ran ourselves warm after a little while. But when we sat at breakfast afterward we were as fresh as crispy bread rolls when they come out of the oven.

When the first snows lay across the country, we really missed our native mountains with all of the ideal opportunities for any winter sport.
But the snow didn't last for long here, after a few days the white splendour was mostly gone again, and the streets changed to slush and we even preferred to leave the bicycles in the store.

I had been in the Legion for over a year now and still the service only consisted of drills, sport, a little field exercise and some oral lessons and everything was gone over ten, twenty times until you grew sick of it, and there was still no end to be seen. In the meantime the knowledge that you'd gained for your profession slowly slipped away, more and more often the uneasy question came up of how would you be able to hold your ground in a civil profession. Who wanted to when it would still be a long time yet that we would be kept in the service?

On many evenings we sang songs about our homeland and a lot of sentimentality crept in. We suffered from no poverty but still we felt as though we were crammed into a cage from which there was no escape. The worst part was that we didn't know when we would finally be given back to civilian life again.

There were hours when we couldn't stand the sight of each other anymore and were still condemned to endure each other. Sometimes we longed for certain superiors to harass us directly so that we could react to it with fury. We envied some comrades who were promoted to the barracks of the Wehrmacht at the completion of their compulsory service in the summer, luckily we didn't know that we would see them again in two years, still in the Legion.

In the long evenings there was mostly only one topic of discussion, cursing about the "bunch of slobs" amidst whom we found ourselves.

Often our relationships to each other were so strained, that only one thoughtless word was needed to get into a quarrel. The detention cells were constantly occupied, the squabbles within the company constantly increased.

Why couldn't they assign us to an obviously useful occupation? We were happy if in the summer we were posted to help with the harvest for a few days.

I had two weeks of holiday between Christmas and New Year.
I travelled to Hagen in Westphalia.
In the meantime, Malzer had been transferred to this city where a higher position was situated where he was working in an orderly room again as well.
The parents had been assigned a two bedroom apartment in Hagen-Eckesy in an old house on the corner near the train station. I spent the days over Christmas here and the cross over into the New Year. It was a really restless residence, for the whole night behind the house the trains rumbled straight past and you needed a few days to finally not consciously hear the racket any longer.

I got to know a man here in Hagen who often took me with him on a pub tour across the district around the station. We had some real fun times and what with my meagre cash it was fine by me that for the most part he was paying.

He invited me to his house for a day once. He waited for me in front of the train station. We travelled a bit with the S-Bahn until the last stop Langestrasse.
We climbed up several stairs of an old block of flats and ended up in a small, really old fashionedly furnished apartment.
On the sofa in the kitchen living room lay a dog, whose breed I would have classified as a "mutt." In addition the damn dog was dirty, shaggy and especially unkempt. The wife, a strapping, curvy woman in her thirties seemed to me to be good natured, but on first impression not the cleanest. Despite a year and a half's service to the nation, I was still very sensitive on that point. It was shortly before midday, I squeezed myself into the sofa where the dog only very reluctantly made space for me.

Fritz grabbed a mug of beer from a nearby inn. All kinds of smells rose up from the pots on the stove, in all honesty I didn't feel very comfortable.

The sturdy housewife spread dough out on the table and began to spread it out for afternoon cake. The mongrel of a dog, which was looking at me sullenly through narrowed eyes disapprovingly, had to move even further into the corner after Fritz sat down on the sofa too, which further increased its hostility towards me.

Suddenly it seemed the mutt couldn't stand being near me any longer. Without further ado he jumped onto the table and with his dirty, hairy paws ran across over the rolled out cake dough. Good Fritz laughed, his better half just patted the mutt on the backside lovingly and rolled the paw prints flat again.

I was almost sick, and my hairs stood on end when I thought of the coming midday meal and the afternoon cake.

Once the dough had been taken off the table, the good woman already set the plates for the stew on the table regardless of the rest of the flour that was still lying around.

Beads of sweat formed on my forehead when I saw the plates, not exactly clean, which were set in front of us by the same hand that had patted the dog's backside only a few moments ago.

"Get stuck in Otto," Fritz encouraged me, "for my part I love stew, the more leftovers you can get in the better, that gives the right flavour to it."

"Tastes good," I squeezed out with effort and drank a gulp of beer after almost every bite.

"Yeah get stuck in there," said his tubby darling as well, "and later there's coffee and fresh cake."

"Thank you, but no, I have to be home early."

Of course that was a lie, but there was no way in the world I could have tried to swallow even a piece of cake.

"That's out of the question Otto! The fresh cake hasn't even been cut yet, and a cup of coffee will do you good too."

Fritz was incredibly assertive. But I already had goosebumps on my back just thinking of the cake in connection with the dog. A while after the meal which was lying really queasy in my stomach, before the afternoon coffee edged too close, I reminded them again, forcefully, that I need to leave.

"No really Fritz, I can't stay any longer, I promised my parents that I would be back soon, they want to make another visit with me yet."
"Yes comrade," Fritz was really disappointed,
"Well I can't force you to stay. We're only trying to be good to you, no doubt you only get cake in the camp very rarely and my Erna makes exquisite cakes I can promise you that."
"I'm sure of that Fritz, but a promise is a promise."
"Yeah yeah, I won't take it too personally either, it's just a shame, we were so looking forward to it. But you can come past for coffee again tomorrow, deal?"
"Sure Fritz, but now I really have to go, well then till tomorrow and thanks a lot for the great meal."

Once I was on the street again, I took a deep breath first of all.
I didn't go for coffee of course, and I didn't see Fritz again.
I spent a quiet New Year's Eve with the parents.
Malzer promised to help me get into a civilian position soon. I was tired of constantly running around in a uniform and having to salute some buffoon every few minutes.
I travelled back to Bocholt a few days after the New Year.

In the beginning of April '36 our squad was posted to Bad-Godesberg for four weeks to guard various buildings of the Legion headquarters.
Finally some change in the general routine of camp life.

Two trucks brought us into the Rhineland. In Godesberg, we took up very fine accommodation in an old castle-like building in the middle of a huge park. Our straw beds lay on the floor in a small mirrored hall. Our hobnailed boots surely didn't do the parquet flooring any good.

The spring was much further ahead here in Godesberg than it had been in Bocholt. Some of the buildings we were to guard were directly in Godesberg, but some were in Mehlem a few kilometers south of there.

The headquarters building in Godesberg was in a wonderful park very close to the Rhine. The spring nights were fantastically warm as we went all across the park on our patrols.
The air was filled with the intoxicating aroma of the many bushes, already fully blooming, the names of which weren't remotely familiar to me back then.

We had enough free time to be able to look at Godesberg and the surrounding area in detail. Every week we got a few extra marks as guard bonus and the smoker allowance was doubled as well. So we could also afford a few visits to a few restaurants and the cinema.

The food was good, it was provided to us from the headquarters' kitchen, the men certainly didn't eat too badly. Since I always swapped my cigarettes for money, I was able to set a few marks aside over these weeks.
It's a shame that we couldn't take our bicycles with us to the Rhine, we would have had the most fantastic opportunities for excursions here.
Soon all of the plantation's many fruit trees stood in full bloom as well, and with it the warm, mild climate, for weeks on end we felt as though we were living in a fairytale.

One day, there was a real crowd of people in Godesberg. The huge airship "Graf Zeppelin" flew over the city. For me, it was the second time I saw this giant cigar in the sky. The first time I had still been attending the Bürgerschule in Wels. Back then I'm sure all the school classes in Austria which were near the airship's flight path were on their feet.

On a day off, I went on a hike up Drachenfels with a few comrades. From there you had a wonderful view over a wide stretch of the Rhine and the cities of Bonn and Godesberg. The view around Siebengebirge spanned far across the area. At that time it was still a comfortable ascent up to the castle ruins, the whole route wasn't ruined with stalls yet. We saved ourselves the costs of the rack railroad of course.

When with my family many decades later I made the climb again I was disappointed with the negative changes that the years had brought with them. I was disgusted with all the monstrous racket and the cheap tat which dominated the place now and which ruined all of my so romantic memories.

When we travelled back to Bocholt again after the guard duty was finished, we found the departure really difficult. We had to leave Berndt behind. Despite all the warnings he had still messed around with too many easy women and had promptly suffered a sports injury from this hobby as well. Now he was sure for a long stay in sickbay.

Once I was in Bocholt again, I wondered how I could spend the money I had saved in Godesberg. Weeks ago I had had a catalogue from Photo Porst delivered and I studied it now at every free moment.
In the end I ordered myself a "Voigtländer Bessa," almost half of which I could pay from the money I had saved.

The remaining balance for the "Voigtländer Bessa," had to be financed from cigarette money.

In the proud possession of the new camera, I went into the surrounding woods every free hour with Hoffman, an assistant forester from Styria, to photograph the wilds.

There was a whole load of deer, hare, rabbit and fox in the area around Bocholt. Lapwings had their nests in the fields, there were pheasants and snipes galore and every kind of bird of prey.

But taking good photographs of the wild was far more difficult than I had imagined in my enthusiasm at the beginning. There was no such thing as a single lens reflex camera yet and the normal equipment had a focal length that was too short to get the wild all in focus on film. I frequently came to a good shot, but the images were still really disappointing.

At that time there was a well known animal photographer who took the most beautiful shots with a Rollei. But to do that you needed, alongside enthusiasm, years of practice and outrageous amounts of time. I didn't have enough of either, and enthusiasm alone simply wasn't enough.

And so the unsatisfactory results slowly caused my enthusiasm to peter out as well. I now turned my efforts more toward landscape photography and would have surely soon had very great success with that, had I been given the opportunity to map the shots myself.

All of the pictures from this time were left behind somewhere in the course of the troubled years. Nothing remains preserved up to today.
Of course, my passion for photography was also strongly curbed by the chronic lack of money. But nevertheless it had given me

many hours of pleasure and distraction from the very dismal daily routine.

One day shortly after midday we suddenly got the order, "All divisions without exception to report to the drill square."

Around six hundred of us stood on the field, including the cooks, medical staff and all the office lackeys.
This was very unusual, we were all full of excitement about what was going on.
The camp commander Fuschlberger appeared and made an announcement, next to him was a man with a girl of around eighteen years of age.

Fuschlberger gave us the following speech:

"SA Men, an unbelievable occurrence has taken place which threatens to destroy our honour and our good relationship with the people.
One of you men has made this woman pregnant and was too cowardly to give the girl his real name. He has slyly deceived her in order to evade his responsibility. I hope that this man can overcome his cowardice and report to me within the next fifteen minutes and also take on the consequences of his pleasure. I will wait for his report in the command barracks, fifteen minutes and not a minute longer."

Afterwards we were allowed to leave again and go to our quarters. But soon we had to go back out again, and so it seemed the culprit had not gone to report.

You could read the indignation on Fuschlberger's face.

"It is shameful," he spoke again,
"that apparently cowardice seems to prevail here. Well then fine,

you'll have to have the humiliating show of a line up for all of you. Sturmführer, have the first row take five steps forward."

The girl, her father and Fuschlberger behind her, now walked along the first row slowly. She took a lot of time, gave every face a searching look. Had her amorous escapade only taken place in the dark? To us it seemed so, how else could she look at the great number of men so uncertainly?
But the first row returned nothing.
In the second row, she stopped still in front of big Hartwig and scrutinised him for a particularly long time. Hartwig's face flushed bright red.

"From his big stature it could have been him," the girl turned to her father shyly.
"Good Lord, what use is his figure? You have to know him from his face."
"I'm not sure."
"Look at him closely!" the father found apparent hope...
"I don't think it was him,"

Fuschlberger stepped up to Hartwig:

"What is your name?"
"Hartwig, Standartenführer, Sir."
"Do you know this girl?"
"No, Standartenführer, Sir."
"Now I'm sure it wasn't him," the damsel affirmed.
"Well let's keep moving," answered the camp commander a little annoyed.

But even the second row brought no results.
She quickly went past us in the third row, we surely weren't big enough for the image in her mind, she had surely been with a

long beanpole of a man.
But she stopped again in front of Plank.

"Was it him?" her father came quickly to her aid.
"Yes...," she said no more.
"What? You stupid cow," Plank roared off in spite of
Fuschlberger's presence.
"Man control yourself!" the camp commander roared at him.

But Plank was not a man to be intimidated.

"But I have never seen this cow in my life commander."
"Control your tongue you mannerless dolt!"
"Yes Sir."
"So was this the man?" Fuschlberger turned to the girl, now very
intimidated.
"No, mine doesn't have such a coarse voice."
"Then onward."

But the search remained inconclusive.
The commander stood together with the father and his deceived
daughter for a good while yet. The Sturmführers were consulted,
but the case was surely not so easy to resolve. In the end we were
able to go back to our quarters again.
We never heard any more of the matter, but perhaps she went on
to find the father of her child.
When we were still standing in rank and file, Bittermann
whispered to me:

"Maybe it was Berndt."
"Don't talk your way into trouble," was all I could answer him.

After all Berndt had gone into hiding somewhere at the time and
was licking the wounds which his lovemaking had granted him.

So the days went by, and the second summer still found us in the service of the Legion. Then a new task brought some change to the camp's everyday life.

For the first time, the Legion was to take part with a few formations at the Nuremberg party congress.
When this order came from above, and it further transpired that a large part of the team from the camp in Bocholt was to take part, the camp commander was unstoppable.
There was only one phrase from now on: drilling and drilling again. Everything that could walk had to take part in it. The selection was only to be made shortly before the journey off.

For weeks only drilling and uniform inspection were on the schedule, alongside the already obligatory early morning exercise.
Soon even the trainers were "sick to their back teeth" with this circus, as it was so politely put.
It almost bordered idiocy what was required of us here. From a certain point in time our movements became ever more cramped. Our Unterführers saw this too, but they too were kicked and hounded and of course they took it out on us. Soon we wished the whole party congress to hell and all the superiors with it.
When, two weeks before the journey off, those taking part were drawn up, those staying behind were in no way bitter about it. Besides they could surely have a cushy number while we were away.
However us "lucky" ones in quotations marks, had the prospect of being drilled for another ten days.

In the days that were left you couldn't count how often the words "Layabouts...slowcoaches...etc" thundered across the square.

Finally the drill stopped, if they could have, they would have maybe made us carry on all the way to Nuremberg.

We reached Nuremberg in the evening after a very varied journey. We took up our quarters in the huge camping town Langwasser.

A monstrous bustle reigned in Langwasser. Thousands were accommodated in this camp. A monstrous amount of organising was needed in order to stage everything smoothly.

If you left all of the political considerations aside, it was really a unique experience for us young people.
We had neither the life experience needed for a realistic assessment of the politics, nor a conclusive comparison. We just saw the gigantic illusion a facade of splendour, strength and organising thought through to the smallest detail.

While the celebrations took place on the huge party congress grounds, the subsequent march led us past Hitler through the town centre of Nuremberg.

When the events were over we headed back towards Langwasser. We would have liked to look at the city in our own time, but we weren't given any leave.
So we whiled away the rest of the evening in the beer tent that had been pitched up and sang our soldier songs into the evening which with the progressing hours grew louder and less melodic until they degenerated into a hoarse bawling.

We were shaken awake at an unearthly hour the next morning. Still half asleep, we stood around the water trough set up outside and washed our bleary eyes.

Freshened up so we prepared ourselves for the march back. Column after column moved off, an area littered with paper and all kinds of rubbish remained behind, but the first cleaning divisions moved in as we were marching off.

I spent another three week long holiday with the parents in Hagen in the summer of 1936. They had escaped to the green belt south of Hagen in the meantime, in Ambrock. They had gotten somewhat better accommodation here.
Now every time I wanted to go to Hagen, I had to cover a sizeable march on foot on the way back. The street tram ran as far as Ambrock but every pfennig counted back then. During this holiday I also got to know a nice family that lived in Emst. Herr Wedekind had a small factory in Hagen, his daughter was a Kindergarten teacher and his son an engineer with Messerschmidt. Wedekind had an extensive library, which I could rummage through undisturbed. A year later I spent an entire holiday with this hospitable family.

Shortly before the end of my holiday in Ambrock I visited an Austrian evening in the Hagen town hall with the parents. There was a legion camp in Altenvoerde in the vicinity of Hagen. The evening was organised by the occupants of the camp in association with the staff stationed in Hagen.

They presented a lot of folk music, Austrian folk dancers appeared and patriotic songs were performed. All things which were largely foreign to the people of Hagen back then, there wasn't this annual stream of holidaymakers to the South yet after all.
Two girls from Hagen sat at the table with us. One of them was close friends with a Legionnaire, the other was accompanying her friend.

And so I got into a long conversation with the second girl. After the programme had finished we had to clear our tables, the space was needed for dancing. And so a big shuffle around began and we had to find another space.

As chance would have it both of the girls came to sit at our table again. Now we could continue our conversation.
I was invited by Mimi (so the sweet lass was named) to visit her at her parents' house and to get to know her brother as well who at that time was a member of the Hitler Youth in the Haspe shawm band.

I visited this girl from Haspe once in the holidays that I had left. Her father had a building firm in Haspe. So I drank coffee with Mimi and Frau Marschall and in the evening I went with her brother Willi to a shawm band rehearsal.
Before the end of the holiday in Hagen the parents bought me some knickerbockers, stockings and shoes, I wanted to buy a matching jacket for them in Bocholt myself.

In Bocholt the business in camp went on as it had before. A few weeks later, I had recovered enough financially that I could buy a matching Tyrolean jacket to complete my outfit. Now at last when I went out in the evenings I could leave my uniform in the locker. I immediately felt more free and more casual. I got the approval I needed to wear civilian clothes outside of duty without any trouble.

We spent a second winter in Bocholt. But the intensivity of the training slowly reduced steadily.

Seemingly they had lost all enthusiasm even amongst higher ranking staff.
The pointlessness revealed by our continued existence became ever clearer. It seemed all round that everyone just wanted to survive the rest of the time as unnoticed as possible. We didn't

exert any political pressure any more, we felt that our existence had become a burden on the higher leadership.

A general apathy took hold of all of us. We took each day as it came, lacking any motivation for any particular task.

In the spring of 1937, along with other comrades, I got a request to take an aptitude test for the Wehrmacht.
We were brought to Recklinghausen in the Ruhr area.

The notification of fitness for service was pressed into my hand at the same time as the call up orders for the third of November 1937.

At that point in time I was to enlist in Heiligenbeil in East Prussia. My unit was the 9th MG battalion, an independent battalion and part of the third motorised infantry division.

At least I now knew the chronological boundary until which I had to endure being in the Legion for.
For sure, also bound up with it was another two years behind barrack walls. Two more years in which I would grow ever more distant from my civilian profession.

But we weren't as far as that yet.
For the second time, we drove to the Rhein for a few weeks to fulfil our guard duty at the headquarters. It was a few weeks earlier than the previous year, but nevertheless we again had beautiful warm days where the work was enjoyable. There was still always something to see and the days passed quickly. But there were no particular events to note.

Once we had been back in Bocholt for a few days we were loaded onto the truck again. We went to the little town of Balve in the Sauerland.

A heavy snowfall that had set in in late spring, along with a heavy storm, had brought down large parts of wooded areas around the Sorpesee.

We took up accommodation in an open industrial building at the northern exit of Balve. It had a lot in similar with the miserable quarters in the camp at Marktredwitz. We stayed in Balve for around six weeks.

Every day we were brought by truck to the surrounding woods. Here, over the course of the weeks, we were trained into near-perfect lumberjacks.
We learned the working and handling of saws, wedges, axes and draw knives.
Finally an activity with practical use for once.
You could have long employed us in such practical activities. Working in the gorgeous outdoors was a real joy. We engaged ourselves with corresponding enthusiasm. After we'd finished work, we took a refreshing bath in the Sorpesee on an almost daily basis. Back then the tranquillity of the forest landscape was still rarely disturbed.
Balve itself didn't offer us much to do with our free time. So we spent our evenings solely in the camp. On days off I was often with other comrades in the beautiful area around Hönnetal.

Once we had cleared up a large part of the storm damage, much to our disappointment we headed back to Bocholt.

A feeling of listlessness for every kind of service spread all around here. Even the superiors were ever more laxadaisical when going about their tasks, barely anything was done with joy anymore. Even the camaraderie slowly crumbled away. Signs of disintegration became noticeable everywhere. Everything was geared to somehow scrape through the rest of the time.

The only diversion was made by our squad's occasional cycling trips which we made to the area further afield, to the castles in the lakes on the Dutch border in Münsterland. Otherwise Bocholt was dull as dish water.

When autumn came, as a group of around sixty men, all liable for military service, we were transferred to camp Deggingen in the rugged Alps.
Now I had to part from many comrades who I had been together with since joining the Legion. I was the only one from my squad who had to leave the unit.

I took my leave of Haas, of Bittermann, Hartwig, Plank and all the rest of them. For three years we had shared joy and sorrow together. We were chased through the mud, ran and crawled together, but also had a lot of fun together.

As our truck left the camp they stood at the gate and waved to me one last time.
I never saw any of them again. In the years ahead, the moloch of war would have devoured many of them in the Balkans, in Africa or in the steppes or Russia. Their traces are blown away, time has passed them by, but in my memory they live on.
We left Bocholt, the camp in which I'd spent two years, my time in the Austrian Legion came to its end.

We came into the new, and last camp. It stood on a hill, high over the little town of Deggingen on the Swabian Alps.
Notably smaller than Bocholt it was a transit camp for everyone who would shortly be leaving the Legion. The majority of us were being handed over to the army.

Everyone in camp was just slouching around. The duties were curtailed to an absolute minimum, we were put on standby. The days crept on slowly and without any highlights.

Most of the time we lay around lazily in the sun, were bored of everything, the weeks stretched on like elastic. Even the town of Deggingen didn't offer much diversion other than a visit to the cinema.

For some time I had been exchanging letters with Lina, our apprentice girl with Hapala in Enns.
She told me that in the meantime she had been employed in her parents' bakery. The boss had died of a stroke a half year after I'd left, the son had gotten an infection on a trip to Africa after which he also soon died. Frau Hapala had sold the house along with the shop and rented an apartment in the city. The good cook Anna had bought herself a little old house and retired. So a lot had changed in these few years in Enns as well.

After several letters I arranged a meeting with Lina in Rosenheim. She had to apply for approval to cross the border first though. So I had to wait until I got the corresponding notification from Lina.

In order to quicker bridge over the boring weeks in the camp, I applied for a voluntary position with a farmer. But I got hold of a downright stinge who only wanted to take advantage of me. I was left to sleep in a wooden pen right in the horse's stable. I had to begin the stable work at four o'clock in the morning. That wouldn't have been the worst. But the food was miserable and the farmer constantly confused me for being a fully trained agricultural assistant. But I couldn't fulfil his expectations in this matter. Since he was always in a bad mood as well, I packed my bits and pieces and went back to the camp a week later.

In Deggingen we had a little library which I made active use of. Of course I had taken my bicycle with me from Bocholt so I could take some trips out into the nearer and further surroundings.

Since I couldn't find anyone who wanted to go with me it wasn't any fun in the long run.

Finally the notification came from Lina that she had received the authorisation needed and we settled on a time for the journey. It must have been the end of September or the beginning of October. I got eight days special leave without difficulty. As my holiday budget was very modest I wanted to undertake the journey with my bicycle. I got a day's field rations, for the rest of the days I could cash in on my allowance.

Pleased as punch to at last be on a new adventure, I started pedalling at the crack of dawn.
I had a really hilly stretch in front of me as far as Ulm.
I'd copped a cool, but still sunny autumn day that was only a little too windy. After around three hours travel, the tower of the Ulm Minster appeared in the distance. I travelled around the southern side of the big city and stopped for lunch in Ichenhausen. I ordered myself a glass of beer in a little country inn and spread my rations across the table. But absolutely nobody took exception to it.
I don't know if it was a hard sausage or a hard crust of bread, in any case I had the bad luck of biting something terribly hard, I felt how a hot pain went through my molar. But the pain passed and soon I was charging off on my bicycle again.

The ground was consistently flatter now and I got on well without any great difficulties. I avoided Augsburg to the South, travelling onward across the Lech until just behind Mering.
I took up accommodation for the night here in a little inn. It was a primitive but also cheap dump and that very much suited my finances. When I wasn't paying attention while I was eating, the damned tooth began to throb again. Of course I was constantly

fraying around it with my tongue which didn't help to calm it either.

I was tired from the journey and went to bed early. But I woke up in the night, plagued by toothache. That was all I'd needed.
I stood up, took some cold water out of the wash jug and numbed my tooth with it for a while. Soon afterward it grew even worse. The rest of the night wasn't made for me to rest from the hardships of the previous day.

As I looked at myself in the mirror while taking my morning shave, I thought I saw a little swelling on my left cheek. But the pain wasn't as piercing anymore, it was more dull but steady.

What bad luck that was. For months I hadn't had any tooth pains at all, of all times I could get them it had to be now. But what use was it, I had to keep going, I couldn't postpone the meeting with Lina anymore. So with the most extreme care, I ate my breakfast and made myself on my way again.

Because of exertion, particularly when going uphill, the tooth began to make itself ever more known again. The pain was easy to endure however, it wasn't piercing, more overlaid by numbness. But as I touched my cheek, the bulge became ever larger. A fat cheek, just what I'd been missing.
My route went across Fürstenfeldbruck south past Munich. As I was travelling along the ramrod-straight street of the Hofdinger forest towards Bad-Aibling, my toothache had almost disappeared, but the lump already filled the entire palm of my cupped hand. The skin across the lower cheek was visibly stretched.
I arrived in Rosenheim around evening. I had a whole day's time yet, Lina was coming on the next day on the afternoon train from Salzburg.

But on the next day my cheek swelling had barely disappeared. Darn it again! Wasn't that a nuisance?

I found a hotel not far from the train station which suited my modest financial circumstances and yet still made an impression of cleanliness. I rented a single room for myself and ordered a second for the next day.

Thoroughly tired from the long journey, I soon put myself to bed, also to let my injured tooth calm down as well.
I barely felt any toothache anymore, but as I said I was really tired, so I soon fell asleep.

When I woke up the next day, all the pain had disappeared but unfortunately the cheek had grown even bigger. I didn't dare to eat the fantastic, fresh bread rolls at breakfast out of fear that the tooth would cause me difficulty again. I just scooped out the soft inside of the bread roll, I put the rest in my trouser pockets.

I spent the majority of the day on a sun warmed bench in a nearby park. I skipped lunch, which did good for my holiday budget.
I checked the size of my cheek every few minutes, but for all the will in the world I couldn't find it getting any smaller. I thought back and forth of how I could get the swelling to recede but nothing sensible occurred to me.
It was incredibly embarrassing to have to greet the girl with such a distorted face. If there had only been some possibility of moving the meeting by a couple of days.

My heart was really hammering when, in the late afternoon, I stood at the station to greet her.
I had taken a look at myself in the mirror beforehand and practiced the most favourable facial expression I could.
Most of all I wasn't allowed to laugh, I made the most stupid face

of all when I did that, I had to remain friendly but at least halfway serious, a difficult task.

I thought of feigning a wound with a big plaster, perhaps that would have looked a little more masculine, but I couldn't hide the swelling, which was up to my mouth, with that either.
So I just had to chance it, Lina couldn't run off afraid at the beginning and I hoped that a day later my face would look a little more pleasant again. Good Lina probably wouldn't be for kissing straight away. It made me sick.

I positioned myself on the platform behind an advertising board. From behind this cover from view, I wanted to let things take their course first.

But Lina was already getting out of the train and coming along the platform. Now I was forced to give up my hiding spot and set myself up to welcome her despite my fat cheek.

I recognised Lina immediately. She hadn't actually grown any taller, but unfortunately had become a little more portly. Not fat, I would be doing her a wrong there, but she was well built.

"What's ... wrong with you?" were her first words, whereby she put a disappointing tone on the.. "you.."
"Well what else, when I've a fat cheek. Toothache of course," I answered. I took her luggage from her, forgetting to shake hands in all the fuss.
"It looks really bad," was her further comment, I could have jumped down her throat for that. In the end I knew best myself how dumb I looked.
"It's on its way out though," I tried to play the matter down, "tomorrow there'll surely be barely any of it left to see, I'm not in pain any more either."

"The main thing is it's not sore," she said in conclusion, but I felt it clearly, there was something awkward already, there was nothing to be done about it.

"Have you found a hotel already?"

"I've had that all dealt with," finally I could bring up something positive.

"How was the journey?" I asked it to bridge over the first embarrassing minutes, nothing more sensible came to mind.

"Good and you?"

"Well what do you think? When you look at my cheek?"

"Sorry, I didn't mean it like that."

"It's fine, I'm so angry I could kick myself even."

"You can't do anything about it now," but I noticed a little disappointment in her voice, could I blame her for it?

We went to the hotel. Lina wanted to get dressed up, when I asked for the key to Lina's room, the porter grinned at me stupidly,

"Tough luck eh?" he said teasingly, very rude I thought, well when you had to stay in a cheap place, the louts will come out with all sorts of stuff.

So that I wouldn't have to look at the stupid porter anymore, I paced up and down in front of the hotel and waited for Lina. When after a very long time she came down, we started off on a stroll through town.

We visited a small cafe, Lina told me about Enns and I always had to make sure that the bill didn't grow too expensive.

"How long can you stay?" I asked.

"Three days, that means I'm going back on noon of the fourth day."

"Then we have time," I replied.

I calculated in my head that it would mean spending five stays overnight, and so during the day I had to live very frugally in order to get through it.

Of course Lina took care of her own expenses, we had already agreed on that in the letters.

In the first two days I only ate very little and pretended to be paying attention to my sore tooth. The swelling had receded a lot by the next day and I immediately looked a little more respectable.

The days with Lina were a disappointment. Aside from my injury which wasn't exactly sexy either. No, it was a certain estrangement that didn't allow for any real warmth to develop, we simply didn't click, which was needed for us to be in harmony with each other. We both felt it very soon but couldn't do anything about it.

We had imagined the days so beautifully in our letters but they didn't leave us with any blissful memories. We suddenly lacked that spark of unfettered affinity which, before the journey, we had anticipated.

Lina said it aloud a day before her journey back, at that moment we both knew that we wouldn't be meeting again. We simply didn't find the right contact with each other. We had imagined something which in reality didn't exist between us.

When, on the last day, we parted on the platform, we both knew that there wouldn't be another meeting. It was lost hours that we had spent together. Disappointed, we travelled away from each other in opposite directions, not even the exchange of letters was continued, why would we bother?

As early as the next morning, I left Rosenheim behind me and went on my way back to Deggingen. The return journey passed by without any events of note, my cheek had returned to its original size.

A journey to new shores.

The last days in camp Deggingen dawned. As a group of four, we had a journey to East Prussia ahead of us. The rest of our comrades were distributed to garrisons in the rest of the Reich.

We'd already been exempted from all duty for a week and had had ample time to make the preparations for our journey.
A few days more for which the Legion had me under her wings, soon I would be given a different meal ticket.

In the last days I also found someone to buy my bicycle. The uniform had already been handed in, I proudly went about in just my civilian clothes for the last days. Finally I could leave that dull crowd, I wept no tears for the Legion.

On the first of November 1937, a Monday, I left the camp with the other comrades, a cheap cardboard box in my hands with the few belongings which made up my entire estate.

There were few comrades to whom I had to say my goodbyes, my time in the camp was short, there weren't any close attachments.

As I stepped through the entrance for the last time, a three and a half year episode came to an end.

It was a journey to new shores. With two days field rations and some money in my pocket I went on a new adventure.
I was newly becoming dependent and returning into a civilian profession moved far into the distance again, but once more I was going out into the world.

East Prussia was distant, and I was lured by adventure. When we reached Berlin in the evening and came into the train station, the Legion already lay long behind us.

We reported to the Bahnhofsmission, were given warm soup, brought our luggage into storage and tried to take down Berlin.

But first of all, we only got as far as the first cinema.

We tried to go chasing tail in a bar afterwards. But the girls must have surely seen that we weren't particularly in the money, and without the dosh the girls in Berlin were untouchable goods for little dalliances. You needed a few bottles of champagne just to get these dolls on your lap, which certainly went far beyond our financial means. Cheap merchandise on the other hand was too dangerous.
And so we put a brave face on and contented ourselves with cheap beers in a smoke filled pub.
We wore civilian clothes but nevertheless we promptly attracted the attention of an army patrol that inspected the pub. In the opinion of a fat Feldwebel, the quickest connection to East Prussia certainly didn't go through Berlin's inns.
We cleared out so that we wouldn't risk any trouble, only to disappear again behind the next pub door. Under no circumstances were we in a hurry to reach our new employers.

So we promptly missed the next connecting train too and for a few more hours we bummed around near the station. But we went back into the train station again eventually, especially since pubs in Berlin were closing as well.

The exceedingly nice sisters in the Bahnhofsmission had a lot of understanding for us. We squeezed a hot morning coffee and a few cigarettes out of them.

But since we couldn't stay in Berlin forever, we eventually brought ourselves to get on board the next suitable connecting train.

We went onward towards the East. In Schneidemühl the train doors were closed and the windows were covered, the journey went through the Polish Corridor.

Just behind the border we reached Marienburg, in East Prussia. From out of the train we could see the mighty castle lying on a hill, an absolutely immense construction which left a strong impression on us.

The journey went onward to Elbing, then north towards the Vistula Lagoon across Braunsberg towards Heiligenbeil.

With that we had reached our journey's destination. Heiligenbeil, a little town, founded by the Teutonic order, lay in a lightly hilled landscape only a few kilometers away from the harbour.

The barracks lay outside of the town. It was a totally newly built building complex. An astonishing sight for us as up until now we had scraped by in wooden barracks and abandoned industrial buildings, they were real buildings of splendour.

We actually arrived in the barracks a day too early. If we had known that in Berlin we could have still gotten up to something. And so we were forced to spend another night as civilians.

In the course of the next day, it was the third of November, more recruits continuously arrived in the barracks. In groups and as individuals, with trunks or Persil cartons depending on financial circumstances and social class.

It was tremendously reassuring to us that so many comrades shared the same fate. Shared suffering is half the suffering, that would hold for us in the future too.

Finally around a hundred of us assembled in the barracks square. It was a long and tedious procedure that now followed and lasted until well past midday.

We were examined critically, checked, registered and finally divided up into separate divisions.
I went to the fourth heavy company.
An Unteroffizier from our new division received us and led us to the drill square in front of the company building.
We took up position in three rows. It was a really civilian crowd in the middle of which I, having already been trained in drill exercises for years, felt like an outsider.
A Hauptfeldwebel stepped out of the company building, slim, tall in an immaculate uniform, the Unteroffizier reported:

"Sixty five men reporting to the division as new recruits."
"Thank you."

The Hauptfeldwebel, who was indubitably the Sarge in Chief of the company took a long list to hand, examined us superficially and gave his first speech.

"Recruits, I am Hauptfeldwebel Schenk, your Sarge in Chief and so to say the mother of the company. You can come to me with all, I repeat all matters of concern. I will always have an open ear for you. Now then, to the division of dormitories: You have the fortune of getting a completely newly built barracks for your quarters. Without question, cleanliness is very important here. I hope that you're taking a good upbringing in with you, if not, we'll break it into you, you can count on that."

Now the Sarge called out the dormitory assignment. Everyone pricked up his ears so that he didn't miss his room number. It was a long list but finally I had my turn too.

"Room 54, Kiwitt, Becker, Poschacher, Kahle, Kubuns and Nölle. Unteroffizier for rooms 54 + 56 Unteroffizier Gläser."

So room 54, with that I first knew where I belonged. But the Sarge in Chief continued:

"You will now go to your room and wait until your Unteroffizier takes you to get your equipment from the uniform store. You will also get your straw mattress there. The more carefully you fill this up with straw, the better you will rest on it, and what is still much more important, the easier your bed building will be in the next weeks."

And so we were only six men to a room, a comfort that was utterly alien to me. The rooms had parquet flooring, the halls and washrooms as well as the bathroom facilities were laid out cleanly with tiles.

While my dormitory comrades Kiwitt and Nölle came from the Ruhr area, all the rest apart from me were real East Prussians. I was the only Austrian in the company, the others were assigned to the rest of the divisions. But this allocation was surely just chance.

In the uniform store, the distribution of equipment definitely didn't take place by the book as it is often said, rather things were very carefully selected, all items were widely available.

In a large room a warehouse straw was piled up in heaps. We stuffed our straw mattresses here. This was no longer new to me and I could give my first useful tips to my dorm comrades.

Building a good bed was only possible with an excellently stuffed straw mattress.

A lot of what was done in the first days I already knew back to front. From the bed building to the drill exercises.

As I was the oldest in years in our dormitory, the task of dorm senior fell to me too. The Unteroffiziers were two to a room at a time, despite having a room of the same size only one Feldwebel could be fit into his.

Around evening on the first day I was ordered to report to Unteroffizier Jeremias. This man shared his room with Unteroffizier Gläser. The room lay directly across from us. Freshly clothed in the finest field grey uniform for the first time, I reported to them.

"Schütze Poschacher reporting for duty."
"Do you know where the cigarette machine is located?"
"Yes Sir, on the wall at the end of the corridor, Unteroffizier, Sir."
"Good, grab me a packet of 'Juno,' but on the double, understood?"
"Yes, Sir!"

So I tore off, grabbed a packet of Juno and was back again just as fast.

"Soldier Poschacher reporting with a packet of Juno."
"Good, dismissed!"

I wanted to go straight out the door,

"Halt!"

So I remained standing, turned around again and stood to attention, the Unteroffizier grinned at me, while he opened the packet.

"Poschacher, why are Junos round?"
"I don't know."
"Get down!... Up!"
"Well then, why are Junos round?"
Jeremias threw the packet at me and waited a few seconds.
"Well?"

But I couldn't think so fast, no answer came to mind. I also had no idea what I was supposed to do with the cigarette packet.

"Well then?"
"I don't know, Unteroffizier, Sir."
"Get down... five press ups.......one..two... up.. well you prat.. can't you read? ... 'The reason's sound why Juno's round'...get it into your head..understood?"
"Yes, Sir."
"Now, shove off already."
"Yes, Sir, shove off, Sir.."

With that I scarpered off immediately. I went to the machine, pulled out a packet of Juno and took a look at it in peace. I realised now that the slogan was written on the packet.
What crap.
I'd get him back for that one day, I'd certainly see to that. So there were monkeys like this in the army as well, trying to compensate for their own stupidity by bullying their subordinates.

In the dining room we had female staff of elderly years who served the meals and cleaned the tables. There was also an excellent canteen available. We soon made extensive use of this facility, since for the first weeks we weren't allowed to leave the barracks.

The fourth company was a so-called heavy company. We possessed 3.7cm anti-tank guns, while the rest of the divisions were equipped with SMGs. Hence the entire battalion had tremendous firepower at its disposal and in addition was fully motorised.
Each anti-tank gun also had a light machine gun to defend at close quarters. The first weeks in Heiligenbeil were also completely filled with drill exercises and salutes. Of course this was all old hat to me and my pre-military training didn't escape the notice of my superiors either.

Our trainer Jeremias was one of the few who went to the all too extreme swear words when something didn't work out. But he intentionally avoided coming out with all the swear words past the permitted limit as soon as the head of the company Leutnant Hornig stood nearby. Soon the men who were supposed to learn to drive were also sought out, we needed an awful lot of them in the division after all.

My bed building was soon made out to be the model for the dorm which I didn't really like, but my comrades had understanding, they knew that I had already been practising this activity for many years after all.

The duties were much more interesting compared with the Legion of course, particularly because it was complemented with the training in various weapons.
Early morning exercises were performed in Heiligenbeil as well but not as intensively and extensively as in the Legion.
We had a lot of really robust, strong farming lads in our company, real tough cookies as they say, but even they were out of breath after a few hundred meters. They were as strong as

bears, but in all their movements they were often still really awkward.

For dorm comrade Becker, a farming lad from Zinten, his call up simultaneously constituted his first train journey.
Kubus, who came from a farming croft somewhere amongst the Masurian Lakes, had never known a cinema before, his parents were poor cottagers in the service of a large East Prussian landowner.

One man who was affable in every respect was Unteroffizier Gläser, also an East Prussian. The East Prussians could be really stubborn, but in my observation only rarely acted unfairly. Our platoon leader Feldwebel Jankowski was strict, but no real slave driver, that was at least my impression in the first weeks. Hauptfeldwebel Schenk our Sarge in Chief, made himself look pretty big, from his height as well as from his mannerisms.

During basic training we only rarely saw our company commander Hauptmann Stracke, more often we saw Leutnant Hornig who watched over our drill exercises now and then. Hornig was also a giant of a man.
Just like in the Legion, during normal service we also had an hour's break at midday in the barracks. Before being marched off into the dining room there was the issuing of orders with the post in the barracks hall.

A few days after reporting for service the order came that everyone who was paying instalments to a company had to report to the orderly room.
Unfortunately that applied to me as well. At Photo Porst I had exchanged the "Voigtländer Bessa" for a "Robot" spring motor camera and had entered into further instalments. That was still from the time that I was in camp Deggingen.
I had to go from the Sarge in Chief to the Hauptmann. To him it

seemed the payment obligations were too high to be ignored. The result was that I had to send the camera back in order to swap it for a cheaper camera that was in keeping with the payments that had been made.

I got a simple 35mm camera which totally didn't meet my expectations, but it was paid for. Payments through instalments were not permitted during service.

After three weeks of basic training we were granted our first leave. Only dorm comrade Becker hadn't made the cut and had to continue his salute practice for a week longer.

But we certainly weren't allowed to walk around town ourselves now. The appropriate Unteroffizier took the lead and we recruits followed him like ducklings after their mother. With most of us our salutes were really cramped but it was our first proud trip out.

We didn't stay in Heiligenbeil though, instead we continued on to Rosenberg, a small town directly on the harbour.

We visited an inn with a little dance hall. The premises were filled with the smoke of hundreds of cigarettes but the whole inn tightly in the grip of the German Wehrmacht.

A three man band played the dance music. Only soldiers were to be seen, girls were only sparsely represented. We were proud to be there, even though we weren't taken seriously by those who had already served two years, mostly Gefreiters.

Of course there was barely a girl who wanted to bother herself with us grunt Schützes. The Gefreiters were firmly at the helm, they reigned over the scene with pleasure and ignored us, and they still trumped themselves up as superiors where they could.

So we drank our beer and hoped that that would yet change. In a year at the latest, the old ones would go back to their home towns and the girls would have to be given over to us, and then we would assume the inheritance for a year.

In good time, so that they reached the barracks before the last post, the Unteroffiziers made their way back with their following. Soon we were found worthy enough to go into the city without accompaniment as well. Mind you constant army patrols took care of that too though, that things went on in an orderly fashion.

Once the basic training was finished, service became more interesting. The budding drivers were taken into special schooling and we were trained in anti-tank guns. There were plentiful lessons in weapons proficiency, battle expertise and gas protection. The first smaller field exercises in the smallest group formations were organised in the area around Heiligenbeil. The first shooting exercises with silhouette targets in the open field followed.

There were lots of drills with anti-tank guns and if you wanted to drill us particularly hard there were exercises in formation with the anti-tank guns and with our gas masks on. Then we literally watered where they wanted us to, that was supposed to be the point of the exercise.

One day the whole battalion stood gathered in parade uniform on the barracks court, we recruits were swearing an oath to Hitler. A standard was given over to the battalion, everything was very celebratory, the division's marching band had travelled in from another garrison.

At this time the first smallpox vaccinations took place. For me the vaccination caused a heavy swelling of my arm around the injection. I went to the sickbay for three days until the swelling had passed again.

Around two months after we'd begun service there were the first holiday passes over the weekend. Since we had a lot of East Prussians in the company, the barracks were rather empty over Saturday and Sunday.

On Saturdays and Sundays, along with the butter, sausages and tomatoes at supper we often got cocoa as a drink. In every room we had a big tankard in which we gathered the drink for the whole room. We just filled the can up out of a large tank in the kitchen, nobody asked how many people the drink was meant to be for.

Often I was only with Kiwitt in the dorm over the weekend we then had a full can available and drank until our bellies almost burst. One Saturday that was too much for my stomach. From that point on it went on strike against the taste of this otherwise so wonderfully tasting drink. You really shouldn't overdo yourself. On the other hand I learned to eat tomatoes in East Prussia, which in any case had disgusted me before. And so from then on I didn't like cocoa anymore and a joy on Saturdays had passed.

If an Unteroffizier really didn't like someone, then alongside drilling, weapons and uniform inspection, bullying was best suited. If your superiors wanted to find something here, it was impossible to get away unscathed. During uniform inspection your trousers were turned inside out and the smallest speck of dust between the seams was enough to be written into the notebook for some particular task, or to be chased around the barracks block several times there and then.

I was very rarely affected by such extra tasks. Through my years in the Legion I had slowly learned all of the ruses for how you could avoid these embarrassments.

Some comrades had a particular knack for falling into such traps set up by their superiors. The poor devils who had really stood out once, would repeatedly get caught in the snares which had been laid for them. It was like a chain reaction for them, one mistake already had the seed of the next in it.

Over the winter months we went on smaller exercises in the surrounding area. For these we mostly had our light-coloured drill uniforms on and after returning we looked like pigs that had been wallowing in filth.

On one Friday, uniform inspection was on the rota again. Sometimes the Sarge in Chief also saw to a row and this was to be a black Friday for me too.

As customary we had our timetables spread out in front of us on which lay the designated items of clothing.
Unteroffizier Gläser had taken on our group's inspection, he'd already inspected a few men without having any complaints. To the Sarge, who was going up and down in front of the row, this certainly seemed very odd. He intervened and went up to me, as it was my turn at that moment.

"Well Poschacher, show me your trousers, inside out, turn your pockets out."
"Yes Sir, Hauptfeldwebel, Sir."

I turned my trousers round, pulled my pockets inside out, my stuff was safe.
Schenk led along the longways seam with his thumb, embarrassingly inspected the trouser cuffs with precision, but far and wide no bit of fluff could be discerned. He got to work on the trouser pockets, but no fault could be found there.

"Now your socks!"

Certain of victory I presented my two pairs of socks. But Good heavens! As I unbundled them I found a huge hole in one of them, which almost made up half of the heel.

I didn't doubt it for a moment, a comrade had played a wicked trick on me.

The Sarge in Chief put both hands on his hips:

"If we had words for that, man, a hole that you could fit your whole fist through! What did you think you were doing, do you want to make an arse of your superiors?"

"No Sir, Hauptfeldwebel, Sir, the hole must have completely missed my notice!"

"You don't say! Missed your notice, good Lord, I think you'll need some glasses prescribed by the doctor in the medical barracks....missed your notice....could you have thought of anything more stupid?"

"No Sir, Hauptfeldwebel, Sir."

The Sarge took his book.

"Well Poschacher, that will mean a pleasant activity over the weekend, leave is cancelled and you will report to me on Saturday midday before the end of duty for a special punishment understood?"

"Yes Sir, report on Saturday for punishment, Sir!"

"I will think up something nice for you Poschacher."

I was certain of it and I was livid at the wrongdoer who had played this trick on me. But as I never found out who it had been I could only pay better attention in the future. My first task after finishing my duties was to sew a tag into all of my socks as well, like we had done for our underwear.

At one end of the long barracks hall stood a large wooden box with a hinged lid which was marked, "scrap metal collection." All of the metal refuse went in here from the toothpaste tubes to all sorts of empty cans.

On this Friday there were now sardines for supper, the empty cans also ended up in the box.

On the next day, a Saturday, around midday, while most comrades were picking up their leave passes, I reported to the Sarge in Chief for the promised punishment.

"Schütze Poschacher reporting as ordered."
"Good, wait in front of the door, I'll be there soon."

I waited in the corridor, curious as to which activity was intended for me.
The other comrades went in and out continuously to collect their leave and excursion passes.
Unteroffizier Jeremias came along the corridor, as he passed he tapped me on the chest with his index finger:

"Why are Junos round?"
"The reason's sound why Juno's round!"
"Yeah, man," Jeremias laughed as he went on.

It lasted at least half an hour until the Sarge stepped out of the orderly room. He thrust a toothbrush into my hand:

"So, Poschacher, I have a wonderful task for you. During it you can reflect on what condition the socks which you bring to uniform inspection should be in."

We went along the corridor to the opposite side.
The Sarge stopped in front of the wooden box marked "scrap metal collection." He hinged the lid open, and gave me a sign to step closer.

"Poschacher, do you see the many sardine cans in the box?"

"Yes Sir, Hauptfeldwebel, Sir."

"What do you think happens if they sit in this box for a week?"

"They start to stink Sir, Hauptfeldwebel, Sir."

"Quite right Poschacher, they start to stink.

And so that that doesn't happen, we don't want a stinking barracks after all, you will now go to the kitchen, grab a bucket of hot water and make every can spotlessly clean. I have given you the toothbrush so that you can get into all of the corners. When you are finished, come to my room and report to me, understood?"

"Yes Sir, Hauptfeldwebel, Sir."

At that moment I must have had the most stupid look on my face in my life.

So I got hot water from the kitchen, a stool from our dormitory and put myself to work. This task didn't just violate my nose, the smell of fish had always been disgusting to me, no, it offended me to my core.

All of the comrades that passed me by rang out with laughter at the work, so worthwhile to the public good, that I was doing here.

In silence I thanked all those who, through their abundant appetite, had already licked the cans real clean beforehand.

Once I had this unsavoury task behind me I reported to Schenk.

"Hauptfeldwebel, Sir, Schütze Poschacher, reporting task complete."

"All clean?"

"All clean Sir, Hauptfeldwebel, Sir!"

"We'll see about that!"

The Sarge accompanied me to the box, gingerly checked all of the cans lying within sight and cautiously felt his way a little deeper too.

"Good Poschacher, you are dismissed. Let this work be a lesson to you. Such a thing is not permitted to happen again, always keep your eyes open, hopefully you've given the culprit a good hiding."

So it was clear to the Sarge as well that someone had taken me for a ride with the socks, but what did that help? I was still the idiot in the matter.

Once, while we were receiving our post again, I was finally one of the lucky ones as well. A card from Mimi from Hagen was handed over to me.
I had long forgotten Mimi from the distant Sauerland.
The card had come a long way, as it was directed to my address in the Legion.

A few days later I wrote back, but I didn't content myself with a card, it was a long letter, yeah well, I always liked writing and I had time too and I had experienced enough in the meantime as well. So I wasn't lacking things to tell.

Christmas slowly approached. I don't recall what context it was in any more, but somehow my modest poetic streak became public and I was commissioned to write a comic newspaper for the Christmas celebrations. That was a fine thing and earned me some leave from duty in the next days.
The Christmas celebrations were arranged by the company in the large dining hall. Along with the comic newspaper I had written

up a song for the company which could be sung to a known marching tune.

The head of the company was so enthused by the lyrics that he had them copied and distributed to all the groups. The song was sung for the first time on Christmas Eve. I have long forgotten the wording, it was surely written very patriotically.

In the meantime a series of recruits had taken their driving test and with that followed the first rides out into the surrounding area.

In the meantime I had become Schütze Eins on LMG, which was actually envisioned as the protection for the anti-tank gun against enemy attack.

The first small night exercises were held. A thick blanket of snow had laid itself across East Prussia in the meantime and a very severe cold reigned. Nevertheless for the most part the duties took place in the open. A little diversion was formed by the modest dance evenings in Rosenberg, where we recruits were mostly just spectators though. We preferred Rosenberg over Heiligenbeil because there were two very comfortable pubs there that were firmly in our grip. We made great use of our canteen by the by, only we were always grouching over the prices which to us seemed too high.

On Monday the fourteenth of March 1938 we had a small night exercise on the rota again.
We camped scattered in the forest near the barracks, I myself was behind the LMG to secure the anti-tank gun.
Then our platoon leader Jankowski came over and told us that German troops had marched into Austria. This message brought forth considerable excitement of course. A universal fervour

seized us all.

Now I was suddenly very sad that I wasn't in the Legion any more, our comrades were surely already on the march towards Austria. They could see their homeland again and I was sat here in East Prussia. I followed the breaking news which constantly came through on the radio with suspense.

On the next day, the fifteenth of March I had to go to the orderly room at midday.

"Poschacher," said the Sarge,
"With immediate effect you are given leave of the army and are to return to the Legion. You will travel this evening, your march papers are being issued now."

Was that not a delight for me? Finally I was going home. I had enjoyed Heiligenbeil, but nevertheless I was wildly overjoyed at the prospect of returning to Austria.
I gave back my uniform and all my equipment and received my civilian clothes again.

When I said farewell to the comrades of dorm 54 I thought I would be leaving for good. I checked out with all of the superiors. Hauptmann Stracke pounded me on the shoulder and shook my hand.

"Well Poschacher, you've been lucky eh?"
"Yes Sir, Hauptmann, Sir."
"Yes well, say hello to your homeland for me, no doubt you will have to complete the rest of your service in Austria, don't forget East Prussia, and keep your chin up."
"Yes, Sir, thank you, Hauptmann, Sir."

Adieu, Heiligenbeil. The sun lay deep on the horizon as we four Austrians saw the city disappear behind us on the way to

Braunsberg.

Braunsberg was an express train station. We left the passenger train here and changed over to the connecting train going towards Berlin.

We didn't stop in Berlin long this time, we didn't want to miss the Legion's march to Austria at any cost.

We arrived in Mainz on the next day around midday. Here we had to change over to another train again. We travelled onward to the Legion camp in Wackernheim where we arrived in the early afternoon.

Absolute bedlam dominated Wackernheim camp at the time of our arrival. New comrades were constantly showing up, the camp management seemed totally overtaxed, nobody knew which unit he belonged to.

I met a few comrades again with whom I'd already been together in Bad-Aibling and Bocholt, the majority of those present were strangers to me though.

After us four from East Prussia had already been in the camp for two days, we still didn't know our crowd. It had already cost considerable running about until we even appeared on the rationing list.

Finally we were referred to a barracks store where we were to be kitted out. A few trucks with uniforms had arrived in the days before. But the clothing lay around the barracks in a wild mish-mash. Nobody found himself to be made responsible for a regulated issuing of the uniforms. Every new arrival rummaged around blindly through the supplies, took whatever seemed good to him and trampled all over the rejects. Sadly, all the uniforms were consistently worn out, you couldn't get dressed up with them anymore.

Finally on the third day, they had arranged us into units, pitiful drill exercises began so that they could at least bring a little order into the crowd.

And so more days went by in a real shambles, there were no preparations for marching off to be seen. Day after day went past, the second week appeared, but still there was nothing to be discerned about when our departure would finally take place. The German Wehrmacht had long been in Vienna and the first excitement was over, but the Legion made no move to take up the march home. The leadership from above seemed to have long written off our band of troopers.

After we had been in the camp for almost two weeks, they suddenly said:

"All those belonging to the army report to the drill square."

The camp commandant appeared with a paper in his hand.

"Comrades," he began his speech,
"Unfortunately our return home is delayed every day. But men, the Führer will have his reasons for that. Sadly I now have here an order from the highest leadership of the Wehrmacht in my hand, which with immediate effect removes the permission for leave from all those in service and orders the immediate return to your divisions."

The camp commandant made a short pause.

"I know, comrades, how hard this order affects you, but you are the Führer's soldiers, the Führer's soldiers are hard, and can endure hard knocks too. We will greet our homeland in your name. Comrades, long live the Führer, long live Greater Germany.. Sieg Heil......"

This decision hit us really hard now. We had arrived in this camp with such happy expectations, and how quickly all hopes of a return home had been reduced to nothing.

But none of it helped, we had to go back and home vanished far into the distance again. At least we could hope for a holiday, the borders to Austria were open now after all.

We took off the brown uniform for the last time and put on our civilian clothes again. With new marching orders and provisions we made our way back towards cold East Prussia.

We weren't in such a hurry on our way back from Berlin. We visited numerous cinemas and went into a little vaudeville where beautiful girls' legs somewhat bettered our bad moods. The financial resources came to an end, we travelled onward.

They were very surprised at our return when we arrived in Heiligenbeil. They hadn't received any orders about us being reintegrated again.

Without orders, the wheels of the army didn't turn either. For the time being I had to keep on my civilian clothes, I could sleep in my bed, received provisions as well, they weren't so hard as to let me starve, but I was excluded from all duties. The Sarge in Chief was convinced that there must have been some kind of mistake and I would no doubt go back to the Legion.

So I lazed around Heiligenbeil for a whole week, until finally the Wehrmacht remembered her lambs again. Now the Sarge was in a rush all of a sudden. He chased me to the uniform store and an hour later I was again frantically busy.

With that the chapter of the Legion also came to a definitive end.

Post from Mimi in Hagen had also arrived in the meantime. I was expected to spend my Easter holidays in Hagen, but for that the matter of accommodation had to be settled urgently. Malzer had long left Hagen and found himself in Friesland. Then I remembered the good family Wedekind in Hagen-Emst. Since staying in a hotel wasn't affordable for me I wrote a letter to the Wedekinds asking if I would be allowed to spend my Easter holidays with them.

In the meantime the duties had changed over more and more towards combat training. Shortly before Easter, we went for the first field exercise as a whole company in the south of East Prussia. It kept us busy for days, polishing weapons, instruments and vehicles until they gleamed, we asked ourselves why we were bothering when we would soon be rolling around in the open country with them, but the wisdom of our leadership was unfathomable in that regard as well. And so we polished and we scrubbed, someone else had to puzzle over what use it was.

At the first dawn of the morning we left the barracks heading towards Zinten. I sat with Becker and Nölle in an off-road vehicle handling the LMG.
First we went through rather flat countryside alternating partly between fields and pine forests. As we reached the small town of Hermsdorf the countryside became really hilly. The whole column came to a standstill between Hermsdorf and Zinten. Unteroffizier Jeremias drove past us with Kiwitt, Kubus and Kahle.

"Comrades, I think the enemy is close," said Kaiser our driver.
"All the better," I answered,
"finally we'll get some action for once."
"Ach whatever, fuck the enemy," Becker interjected,
"I'm just hoping we'll stop in Zinten, then I'll get to swing past my house."
"You'd better not do that," said Kaiser,

"or are you going to catch up with us on your bike?"

"Well you'll be waiting just as long with the motor anyway, you can pretend it's broken down."

"Oh sure, I'll go in the clink then, just so you can go see your mummy for a few minutes!" Kaiser answered,

"'Mummy,' don't make me laugh," Nölle butt in,

"it's no doubt a girl whose bosom he'll be laying his head in!"

"Bosoms here, bosoms there," I said, "on we go again, it seems the enemy is withdrawing."

Slowly, and at intervals, we moved forward along the road to Zinten. We travelled through the town. Curious farmers' wives stepped out of their doors, a few children ran alongside us. On the edge of the town another stop.

"Dismount! Anti-tank squad secure the town exit! LMG take position to the right of the road!" Unteroffizier Jeremias shouted these commands to us.

"Park the vehicles concealed in the farmyard!"

"See you lads, I'm off to see mum!" Kaiser shouted to us and turned off the road into the next farmyard entrance.

I raced into the ditch with the machine gun and went southwards into position behind a milestone on the edge of the field.

"I could get away easy now," said Becker,

"Our yard is right there behind the barn."

"Well ask Jeremias," I advised him.

"At best he'll kick my arse."

"Maybe not, maybe he'll let you nip in there for five minutes,"

Then the Unteroffizier was already coming down the road to check our position.

"Poschacher, do you have enough field of fire as well?"
"Clear field of fire," I answered.

He lay down next to me on the edge of the field.

"Good," Jeremias got up again,
"and if the company commander comes you'd better report else I'll bust your ass."

Jeremias went off again to the anti-tank guns up front.

"I'm off," said Becker, and then he had already disappeared through a front garden.

Now our platoon leader Jankowski came back down the road again.

"Ten minutes break, everyone gather around me on the road."

We left our posts and formed a circle around the Feldwebel.

"So that you're not running around the field like headless chickens, I'll explain the combat situation to you in short,
Well then!
The enemy is staving off attacks and retreating on both sides of the road towards Rositten. We're following after them in around ten minutes time, constantly on standby for combat. Our battalion is taking up position to the south of Rositten, standard front facing formation in the area around Stablack. Larger bands of enemies are suspected to be around the castle hill. Here we can expect more resistance."

Jankowski turned to the squad leader.

"Have the men mount up again, everything remains fully combat ready."

"Poschacher," Unteroffizier Jeremias turned to me,
"Get the vehicles from the yards, everyone mount up again."

I informed Kaiser and the driver of the anti-tank gun.
We mounted up, only Becker was missing.

Jeremias, who saw the gap in our crew standing in his front car,
shouted back:

"Where's Becker?"
"Becker's sucking his mum's tit!" shouted Kaiser.
"What's that supposed to mean?"
"Becker's home is here, he's no doubt at his mother's."
"Are you mad?"

Jeremias's face turned red, he sprang from the car and ran back to
us.

"Is the man gone crazy? Go, Nölle bring the damned scoundrel to
his post!"
"Yes Sir, bring damned scoundrel to post, Sir," Nölle sprang from
the car and ran to the yard.

In the meantime at the front of the platoon Jankowski standing in
the car had raised the signal which meant:

"Attention, motors on, column prepared for march."

Then Nölle came with the fat Becker racing along in tow.

"You wait, boy!" shouted Jeremias,
"we'll speak in the barracks later....squad!...march!"

We continued towards Rositten between a thick lane of trees.

"The Unteroffizier will give you a good hiding," said Kaiser,
turned to Becker,

"did you at least take some decent sausage with you?"
"I did."
"Then all is forgiven, brother, we'll cook his goose at the next break."

And that's just what happened as well.

Shortly after Rositten the exercise was abandoned, the platoon could dismount and we spread ourselves out on either side of the road. The four of us from the LMG got tucked into Becker's sausage.
When Jeremias just so happened to be nearby Kaiser said:

"First class farmer's sausage, Unteroffizier, Sir. Do you want to taste?"
"Well a little bit then why not."

Kaiser who had taken over the sharing out of Becker's sausage cut a decent bit off, gave it to the Unteroffizier.

"Not bad," said Jeremias,
"and who's is it?"
"Becker's, Unteroffizier, Sir," answered Kaiser and laughed roguishly.
"Damn it!" shouted Jeremias,
"The man ought to be shot against a wall, but the sausage doesn't taste bad," with that he turned his back to us and marched off.

With that this case of desertion was cleared up too.
What good sausage wasn't capable of.

"See," said Kaiser to Becker,
"you just have to treat the guys right, it'll solve every problem, but you'll never understand that."

In the meantime post from the Wedekind family had also arrived with the invitation to spend the Easter holiday in Hagen with them. So that problem was solved as well.

So I applied for holidays and had them approved for fourteen days as well.

The weather wasn't the best. Easter fell on the first week of April, it was still cold with snowfall at times.

Regardless I was excited for the journey to Westphalia.

In the army you weren't allowed to wear a coat after the first of April, the weather had nothing to do with it, what decided it was the date.

With my holiday pass, a free travel pass and some money in my pocket I journeyed westwards again. I left cold East Prussia and hoped to find more warmth and sunshine further to the West too.

I was received very warmly by the Wedekind family in Hagen. I was hosted in a small guest room and was even given a house key. It was a lot of trust that they gave me and with it my freedom of movement was helped a lot too.

And so one day after my arrival I set out to meet Mimi Marschall. She worked and was employed in the office of a shipping agency in Hagen. We had already come to an understanding on the time and meeting place the day before. Who I did not meet at the agreed location was Mimi. I still don't know today whether she missed me or stood me up. If the latter was the case she's of course never owned up to it. Dumb as I still was back then I waited for almost an hour, after which in anger I first went to a nearby inn and drank a beer. Then I called by Mimi at home, her mother answered, as far as I can recall, nothing was clarified further that day.

So I headed back toward Emst around evening.

When I returned the Wedekind family were sitting gathered in the living room. So I had to tell them everything first of all, had wine served up to me, a drink of which I could only dream otherwise. Even without girls it was still a beautiful evening and I could still read for hours afterwards in my room.

The next day I slept until almost noon.

I went into the kitchen for breakfast. Wedekind employed a cook who was also very nice and obliging.

For lunch we gathered in a large dining room at a table which had space for a good twelve people.

Only in the late afternoon did I make my way to Hagen. Mimi had time in the evening to meet me.

This time the hour and the place were right and so we met. Mimi's father didn't know I existed, he was a little old-fashioned and strict and so we had to meet up outside of the house.

It was really cold, during the day it had repeatedly snowed a little, a really cold April weather and I froze to the bone without a coat.

So we whiled away the hours loafing through the area real aimlessly, it remained a very cold, sobering affair.

Around midnight, I had covered the way back by foot, I reached Wedekind's again, hungry and frozen.

Everyone had long gone to bed here, I crept into my room and slept until the late morning.

The next day was even less pleasant than the one before. I went with Mimi through adjoining streets that went past garden allotments. I felt a great desire to break open a little wooden house or something to at least find some kind of shelter from the unfriendly weather.

With a little more money in my pocket things would have been better, but I had to count every mark and Mimi was surely not well flushed with money either. In those days we no doubt visited a cinema a few times but not much more, we just didn't have enough.

I stayed at Wedekind's on Saturday and Sunday. At that time two older women from Holland were also visiting my hosts. They acted very stiff and priggish.

We sat at lunch and towards the end of the meal Frau Wedekind asked if I wanted anything else.

"No thanks, I'm full," I answered.
"Oh," called one of the Dutch women,
"you're full? You don't do that where we're from, that would be a great social offense, as a guest you don't eat yourself full."

Of course I went red as beetroot after this remark, but I didn't know what to say. The Wedekinds ignored this comment, which also didn't exactly imply a good upbringing.

As regards the weather, towards the end of the holidays a few somewhat more pleasant days followed. But altogether the whole holiday was a very cold affair.

Mimi's mother invited me for coffee a few days before my return. The father was out of the house, I only got to know him much later. So I went back to Heiligenbeil again.

In the area around Stablack, we had our first target practice with live ammunition at the end of April. We drove into a large wooded area beforehand where there were hundreds of munitions bunkers. Here we were equipped with everything we needed as a Panzerjäger company to fire the first live ammunition on wooden dummy tanks.

So for two days we really cracked away at them so that wooden shrapnel flew around all over the place. Eventually we took shots at some sheet iron as well and convinced ourselves of the penetrative power of the little 3.7cm shells.

We had an Unteroffizier in the company, a real pig headed East Prussian Kowalski. He had a red face and fire red hair. When he grew angry, his colour grew to a ripe tomato red. He was responsible for the vehicles and in the wide stretching vehicle hangars he led the cleaning schedule too.

The distance between the company building and the hangars only amounted to a few hundred meters, but Kowalski always had us start up a song on the way there. We didn't take this Unteroffizier totally seriously, his intelligence wasn't very profound and he substituted it with a loud, incredibly powerful voice that always served the most ribald language.
When we set into our march, his first command was:

"A song!" the frontmost wingman repeated,
"A song!" and called the beginning to us.
"Soar high you red eagle,"

To us this song was a clear allusion to his bright red tomato head, his red hair, and how easy it was to get him worked up. Kowalski wasn't so stupid as to not realise the ulterior motive behind the singing of this song, especially since we only seemed to know this one song when we were with him.

And so the same spectacle was almost always repeated, Kowalski shouted:

"A song."
"A song, 'soar high you red eagle!'" Kowalski to that: "Another song you damned sods!"

The wingman to that: "Another song, not 'soar high you red eagle.'"

"I will soon you arseholes," Kowalski's head swole up ominously. The wingman again: "A song, ...'high over the wide pine forests'..."

"Get moving!...up!...march!...march!..."

With that we had mostly all reached the vehicle hangars.

The second set of lyrics was from the same song after all. We had been able to take him for a ride with that for several times already. Sometimes we joined in with our favourite song so quickly that we could catch Kowalski by surprise, then we sang so loudly that his next commands were drowned out. If we managed it then for the whole hour of cleaning he went between the vehicles with a bright red face and had something to complain about everywhere. But we had our fun with him, especially since we soon noticed that even the other Unteroffiziers didn't take him seriously.

Around the middle of May we were transferred to the military training area in Arys in the Masurian lake district for a week.

At that time, the last still existing cavalry regiment held their exercises there too. Every morning their military band came through the vast camp area on horseback and cheered us up with their brisk cavalry marches. Here we held our first exercises grouped up as a battalion. We had to make use of the week for which we had the square and we got properly knackered. But all the same it was a fantastic week. The weather was warm, the sandy ground glowed, the birches in their freshest green and we were young, high-spirited and thoroughly in love with life. We crawled around the countryside a lot, but as we were fully motorised (which we were more than a little proud of) we remained spared from long marches. The 9th motorized MG battalion belonged to the 3rd motorized infantry division.

At the end of July there was the first larger exercise while grouped up as a division. East Prussia offered enough moorland and forests to be able to host a military exercise even before bringing in the harvest. There were a few really adventurous days of military exercises. Even the march from Heiligenbeil across Zinten, Preußische Eylau, Barteinstein and Rastenburg until the Masurian Lake District was an experience.

The East Prussian country folk were exceptionally friendly to soldiers. As real border folk they were always ready to defend the homeland. We were received very amicably every time we camped out on the farmyards. And there were enough soldiers romping around the countryside really. Almost every little town had a garrison.

With its hilly countryside rich in water and forests, the Masurian Lake District provided an excellent area for military manoeuvres for the whole year. The many sandy pine forests were ideal for all field exercises.

Our military manoeuvres stretched across the areas of Lötzen – Angerburg – Arys.

Over the weekend we camped out in a huge tent camp in the forests near Lötzen. There was a military ball held for the division in Lötzen which was also frequently visited by the local populace. I was invited along with Kiwitt by a family who invited us on a boat trip across the Löwentinsee on Sunday.

With the most marvellous weather, we spent a wonderful day with our hosts.

On Monday the march went onward grouped up in divisions across Goldap, Gumbinnen, Insterburg and Wehlau back to

Heiligenbeil. The individual battalions of each division set themselves down close to the positions of their march columns.

Even larger exercises followed over the summer which led us across the whole of East Prussia.
I always thought this land was beautiful and fell in love with it. This summer was a wonderful, adventurous time, packed full of new experiences every day and the best camaraderie. As the only Austrian I actually felt really bloody good in this purely Prussian company.
That a certain yearning for my homeland still always remained awake in me was a different matter.

In the course of August I received another fourteen days holiday.
It was the first holiday that I could spend at home again after many years. I had given the address of my parents in Wels as my holiday destination.
I wasn't all too happy about travelling to Wels, but I had no other relatives who I could have stayed with in Austria.

The parents got a room in a nearby guesthouse for Mimi who also had holidays and wanted to come a few days later.

My relationship with my parents in Wels was by no means warm and they had no time for me either, so I went my own way. More often than with the parents I stayed with Auntie Kathi, at whose I could also sleep.

The time passed more quickly once Mimi arrived as well. We were also lucky with the weather and were able to go on many walks. We often only put in an appearance with the parents at meal times. Since they didn't have their own living room we were always forced to sit in the kitchen and you were always in the way there.

One day we made a trip to Linz. There wasn't enough time in the day for us and so we stayed over for a night. Father made a wry face when we returned, he had surely forgotten his own youth by that time.

Since I was tired of things in Wels and absolutely wanted to see the mountains again, I travelled with Mimi to Grünau in the foothills of the Alps. From here we hiked in the most marvellous sunshine, really magnificent weather, along a little route to the Almsee. Mimi played on the mouth organ, I sang along with her, and so we travelled like two vagabonds carefree in the moment. That was really something different from sitting around in the kitchen with the parents in Wels.

At the end of the Almsee there stood a large old guesthouse, the "Seehaus." We found our accommodation for the night here, it would have been difficult to find a place as quiet again. For now we could strengthen ourselves heartily with milk, butter, bread and meat. Mimi was overjoyed that she could spread the heavy country bread so thickly with butter. We had had a marvellous day of hiking, right through the middle of a wonderful mountainside, and we decided to not travel back to Wels the following day, rather to press on with the hike through the mountains.

Breakfast the next morning tasted marvellous. As we looked out of the window, the mountains in the morning sun were greeting us and inviting us to go wandering again. The overnight stay and the meal were dirt cheap, which came in really handy for our meagre travel budget.

I had grown used to constant money difficulties in the course of the years. I could expect no support from the parents in Wels in this regard.

But our meagre travel budget couldn't spoil our good mood.

We had another hefty snack prepared in the guesthouse for the day's provisions and made ourselves on our way again.

From the Almsee we wanted to go over the so called "high road" across to the Offensee.
The journey began on a lightly ascending track right through the middle of marvellous mountain forests. After around an hour's walk, we came to a wild stream that could only be crossed over by a fallen tree trunk. I went to the other side first and waited there for Mimi.

But Mimi didn't think to follow me. She sat down on the trunk and waited for me to take her by her little handie and guide her, as a gallant, to the other side. I on the other hand thought that a little test of courage would do Mimi a lot of good, sat down on the other end of the trunk and waited as well.

Now I hoped that she would get over her fear, she in turn found it mean that I didn't straight away come to help her.

And so we waited for a long time, like two spoilt children who couldn't get along.

We sat, and sat, but I had far underestimated Mimi's stubbornness. She didn't make the smallest attempt to overcome her fear, she sat on the tree trunk and sulked. Slowly I ran out of patience after all.
In the end, as would happen again many times later in life, I overcame my heavy heart, gave in, went back across the trunk and held out my helping hand towards her, but my help was only accepted with much protesting.
But the day was so sunny, the area so marvellous, so the ill

feeling didn't last long and we soon continued on our way again, reconciled.

Wonderful panoramic views were to be seen on either side of the path.
To the North with a view of the many mountains at the fore like the Weißeneck, the Ball-Kogel and the Roßschopf, to the South the imposing Totes Gebirge mountains.
After we had crossed over the Nesseltal stream which had caused so much difficulty for Mimi the track went on almost flat for a long time. Marvellous new views were still offered, we took in all we could see, we had time, so much time. We could very easily make the way to Offensee until the afternoon.

We came to a hunting lodge and stopped for a long rest. In front of the lodge, which was locked, stood a coarsely carpented wooden table with a bench round it. We made ourselves comfortable here. In front of a wayside shrine, a spring bubbled merrily providing delicious, refreshing water free of charge. I got stuck into the meat mainly, Mimi into the butter, to us it tasted like a meal fit for kings.

The path ascended a little more steeply again behind the lodge. We reached a mountain peak. The Gschirrek towered high to the right, to the left the Himmelsteinkogel. As we crossed over the peak, we saw the Offensee lake lying deep below us. Far to the North-West the water of the Gmundnersee gleamed up to us. From now on it went steep downhill until the Offensee.

We found a nice little guesthouse at the Offensee too, which offered excellent accommodation until the next day. The rucksack, our only travel pack, was quickly stowed in the room, whose colourful curtains and bed covers made a really quaint sight.

We also went on a long tour around the lake which made us really tired and then came back to the guesthouse in the evening. But now we were really hungry and I was looking forward to a hot meal. Despite my objections Mimi ate bread and butter again. But I chose a hefty juicy goulash with bread dumplings. A marvellous meal after such an exhausting day. The dining room became really lively later on. Local lads appeared, a zither was fetched and with that as accompaniment there was a performance of sentimental songs of love and climbing through lover's windows.

But our tiredness made itself apparent to us and we headed back to our grand chambers.

I let myself fall into the flowery bed with a thud but the structure, somewhat old and weak, took this rough treatment badly. The carved fixture at the top of the bed could only be stopped from burying my face under its massive rustic woodcarving with a hurried hand movement.
The merry lads' singing came up through from the guest room and thundering smacks on wood indicated that they had started to play cards.

The next day was warm as well, marvellously blue and full of a delicious summer aroma. It smelled of pollen and hay everywhere.
After the hefty breakfast, we wandered along a long valley ever accompanied by the sound of a stream. It went uphill steeply on both sides of the path. Alpine meadows that soon merged into mountain forests lined the way. Suddenly the valley unexpectedly grew wide, we reached an open scattered village and on a flat road it went on into the Ebensee.

On the ship's moor we realised that we still had an hour's time until the next boat left. We found a little cafe, both drank a fizzy pop and spent the time so until the boat departed.

The ship that brought us to Gmunden was only very sparsely occupied. And so on all sides we had the peace we needed to enjoy the journey. We couldn't stay much longer in Gmunden itself, we hurried to the train station where the train to Attnang-Puchheim was already waiting to leave.
Attnang-Puchheim didn't offer anything worthwhile seeing, so we spent the half hour until the connecting train to Wels in the train station.

We spent perhaps another two uneventful days with the parents and then made ourselves on our way back, every holiday comes to an end eventually.

I made part of the journey back together with Mimi. We made another short stop in Nuremberg and looked at some of the city. I then travelled onward towards Berlin, Mimi took the train across Würzburg, Frankfurt-Cologne back to Hagen.

On one of the first days after I was back in Heiligenbeil again, I was summoned to the Sarge in Chief.

"Poschacher," said Schenk,
"I have an order here, that all former members of the Legion are to be given the opportunity of soliciting a transfer to a division stationed in Austria. Do you want to make use of this opportunity?"

I was totally surprised by this announcement, but I answered without considering for long.

"Yes of course, Hauptfeldwebel, Sir, I would like to make use of this opportunity."

"Well? Didn't you like it here with us?"

"Of course I did, Hauptfeldwebel, Sir..."

"It's good Poschacher, I understand, well then draft up an application and hand it in as soon as possible."

After only a few weeks the authorisation arrived for a transfer to the 1st. Battalion of the 137th Gebirgsjäger regiment.

Now the die was cast. I couldn't have foreseen back then that this transfer had in all probability saved my life, that I would have no doubt never been able to write these lines if I had remained with the 9th MG battalion.

The transfer to Salzburg was to take place at the end of October. So I had almost two month's time to prepare myself for it mentally.

At the end of September there was another large military exercise grouped up as an entire military corps. Only fully motorised units took part in it. Our march column stretched across through the whole of East Prussia. It was the largest movement of troops that the land had ever seen, so they said to us at least.

Finally my last day arrived, in a unit in which I had completed almost a year of army service, and which I had very much enjoyed. I had found a lot of comradeship and as my last day came I was almost sorry to have to leave this in every respect exemplary company. Not once did I feel like a foreigner although I was so to say the only Southerner in a northern crowd.

At that time I couldn't have known of the bitter days and weeks that many comrades of this division would have to overcome in a few years. Nothing of the great annihilation, by which the 9th MG battalion would be literally snuffed out.

I think on comrades Kiwitt, Becker, Nölle, Kaiser and whatever they were all called, on some superiors who in every situation had behaved correctly and commendably.

It was a beautiful year that I'd spent in East Prussia. In this time I'd grown to know and to love this land, a land so unjustly described by some as a cold, rough place. In no region had the population greeted us so warmly and so openly as they had in East Prussia. In this land in which so many Salzburger people had settled who Frederick the Great gave refuge to after the Archbishop of Salzburg had exiled them.

I think on the wide pine forests, on the moorlands and the many crystal clear lakes of the Masurian Lake District. On the harsh frosty winters, which were still more than made up for by the many warm summer days.

To conclude my memories on East Prussia and in view of the many beautiful hours and exemplary comradeship which I had experienced in the 4th company I would like, in a few words, to go over the continued course of this division's destiny, a division on which I will always think with the greatest warmth. Years after the lost war I first heard more of the whole bitter journey which the 9th MG battalion had to endure.

Gone with no coming back.

As part of the 3rd motorised infantry division, the 9th MG
motorised battalion fought first in Poland and afterwards was
deployed to the Netherlands and France.

In the spring of 1941 they were transferred to the East.
When the campaign against Russia began they were marshalled
into the 6th Army. They crossed the river Bug, moved towards
Kiev, Poltava and Kharkiv.

At first they withstood the hard winter of '41 to '42 under
severe casualties. In the summer offensive of '42 the bttl. was
again involved at the forefront of the advance to the Don River.

In the night of the 22nd of August '42 the battalion, as part
of the 14th Panzer corps, crossed the Don advancing towards
Stalingrad. North of Stalingrad, around 18:35 the next day, they
reached the Volga. With this, at the fore of Stalingrad, the
sorrowful ordeal of the 3rd motorised infantry division began.

Those parts of the 14th Panzer corps which had surged
ahead were temporarily encircled. With that the weeks long
struggle for Stalingrad began. With the forces available, the
objective could not be achieved.

When the Russian full-scale offensive began on the 19th of
November, bringing a collapse of the fronts to the north and to
the south of Stalingrad, the encirclement of the 14th Panzer corps,
and with them the 9th MG motorised battalion, began again.
The days of great suffering for the battalion began. On the 10th of
January the Russians succeeded in breaking through deeper to
the north and to the south of the 3rd motorised infantry division.

The division had to retreat as far as south of Gumrak airfield. The encirclement grew ever tighter, every day the casualties greater.

The suffering which was left to those who remained was indescribable. They were no longer able to take care of the wounded, there was no longer any fixed shelter, the support was wiped out by the fronts of the Russian tanks surging forward. The bread rations were fixed at 50 groschen per day, the temperature sank to minus 30 degrees. The 6th army was split up into two encirclements. In the northern encirclement those parts of the 9th MG battalion that still remained fought and braced against the Tartar wall.

The ground was frozen so hard that no more digging in was possible. Death without hope of reinforcements began.

Around the 24th of January the battalion's last radio signal reached the headquarters of the 6th army in the centre of Stalingrad.
I quote from the book: "Stalingrad" by Heinz Schröter, war reporter of the 6th army. The radio signal said:

"9th machine gun battalion wiped out."

A curtain of fire, two hours long and four kilometers wide, fell on the tartar wall. After that there was no 9th machine gun battalion anymore and no fighting troops of the 3rd motorised infantry division either. Those comrades were ground up below the earth, consumed by the most senseless battle of this war.
The mortal remains of those comrades in Stalingrad have long decayed, the memories of them remain preserved in me, and the further the years continue, the clearer their figures return to my consciousness.

– . –

On to the Gebirgsjäger!

At the beginning of October 1938 I left Heiligenbeil and made my way to Salzburg to my new division. I crossed through all of Germany from East to West, and from North to South at the cost of the German Reichsbahn. Such a long journey was always a particular experience considering conditions back then.

I still had a year of service ahead of me and then I would finally return to a civilian profession. The prospects of finding employment had already improved to a large degree, many were in work and earning their keep again, having born the bitter lot of unemployment for years.
But I still had a year as a soldier ahead of me and I was excited for what awaited me in my new division.

As I left the train in Salzburg it was dominated by that well known deluge of rain. Not exactly weather for a happy start. The barracks were supposed to be in Salzburg-Glasenbach and so I made my way there.
I had to cross the bridge over the Salzach to get to the other side of the city. When I arrived in Glasenbach the first disappointment was that the barracks were wooden ones. Newly built admittedly, but all the same nowhere near as comfortable as the newly built barracks in Heiligenbeil to which I was now accustomed.
The whole camp presented itself as a gaping void.
As I soon discovered, the battalion was somewhere in Lower Austria on the Czech border and only a sparse rear guard had remained in Salzburg.

I was assigned to the 4th company, was given a bed where I could rest my weary head for the time being, apart from that I was left completely to my own devices, I had to see how I could kill the time, nobody bothered themselves about me. I found the whole affair to be really rotten and I was close to regretting the whole transfer.

There was actually only black coffee for breakfast, a hangover from the habits of the Austrian army. Two whole weeks I loafed about without anything to do. Spending most of the time outside of the barracks area in the city. I stood in front of a certain clockmaker shop in the Getreidegasse dozens of times and marvelled at a watch on display which particularly pleased me. But I could only stretch my budget so far, I simply couldn't afford to buy it. At that moment my financial circumstances were really miserable as well.

Lots of free time, and no money in your pocket, those are two things which always go badly together. At the same time there were so many beautiful pubs in Salzburg where you could have really had some fun over the evening hours.

Finally at the end of October, the units came back from their deployment in the South. With them life came back into the (until then silent) barracks as well, and the dawdling about was done with.

More and more instructors from the so called "Altreich" arrived, recruits were also drafted and the company took on its definitive form. A few men of older years were let go again, most of them had already taken part in the First World War and had been deployed in the South.
The 4th heavy company was of a considerable strength both as the number of men as well as the number of horses was concerned. Day after day trucks drove up with new equipment and weapons. Finally I too was newly kitted out in uniform. I swapped my infantry cap for a mountain cap adorned with the

Edelweiss, my boots for heavily nailed mountain-climbing boots and was also given some proper ski trousers.

I went to the mortar platoon under platoon leader Armsdorfer, Oberjäger Stefan Wieser had our squad. Wieser had also been a member of the Austrian Legion, but I didn't know him from that time.
We Gefreiters were assigned to the drill training of the newly arrived recruits as well. Due to the total reconstruction of the units, all the training measures were somewhat improvised.
Our company had considerable manpower at its disposal as it had a mortar, SMG, artillery and signals platoon at its disposal. If we went out on an exercise with all the support, we took up a respectable length of the street.

On the 27th November 1938 we gathered together, suited and booted in all our splendour on the Salzburg cathedral square for the takeover of the new regiment flags.

Delegations from other garrisons of the 2nd mountain division had gathered for this as well. A great tension had preceded this first troop inspection. All the recruits that couldn't be shown yet stayed hidden in the barracks.
No less than Generaloberst List appeared at the square, giving over the flags to the new regiments where of course he had to give a pithy speech. Conscious of our yet insufficient training, we refrained from marching past the generals attending. But our regimental music band played the Radetzky, the Kevenhüller and Kaiserjäger march so that our hearts were bursting with courage. Hohensalzburg castle shone above us, the rattling of the flags which had just been handed over mingled with the drum roll, the Generaloberst spoke of loyalty and heroism, we stood to attention and the brisk marches got our blood pumping, while a shiver of emotion for the Fatherland took hold of us.

The breaking winter had peppered Salzburg, the Untersberg and Gaisberg as well as the grounds of our barracks with its first snow. Overnight the city and its surroundings had been given a totally new image.

Then one day a new endowment of gas masks arrived for the company. Feldwebel Armsdorfer met me in the barracks corridor:

"Poschacher."

"Feldwebel, Sir?"

"You have decent handwriting, you will take over the written work concerning gas protection for me, understood?"

"Yes Sir, Feldwebel, Sir."

And so I was first appointed as a minor gas protection officer. I had to draw up lists, give every gas mask a number and I was consequently exempted from other duties for a few days. In order to not conclude the matter too quickly I studied all of the regulations concerning gas mask protection on the side. Armsdorfer was an official gas protection officer, the work that arose from it, he left to me. Of course the new duty brought me some perks.

In my free time I had begun to draw fat Göring with his imposing, medal-filled chest on primed paper with oil pastels. Somehow Walpert, our Sarge in Chief, had set eyes on the artwork. I was ordered to Hauptmann Hofbauer the following day.

"Poschacher.." said the stern Hauptmann,

"I hear you're good at drawing?"

"Not particularly, Hauptmann, Sir."

"Now, now, no false modesty please. Now then, and this is an order understand? You are to draw our Führer and the other high ranking gentlemen in an appealing size as decoration for the barracks. Find yourself a suitable room in which you can work undisturbed, but don't spend too much time on it, it's not to become a permanent job, understood?"

There wasn't much else I could say other than:

"Yes Sir, Hauptmann, Sir."

And thus given instructions from the highest authority I set out to Oberjäger Walzl, who now had to pay me some money out of the company coffers. Having been given this I went into the city, bought paper and oil pastels and a series of post cards with illustrations of Hitler, Göring and some of the top leaders of the army.
Sarge Walpert allocated me an empty barracks room as an artist studio and I began my work.
Drawing Hitler I found the least difficult, once I had a good grasp of the haircut and moustache the rest was just a trifle. More difficult was putting the not so distinct features of Göring to paper, but instead I emphasised his wide chest with the many medals and honours appropriately.
Hofbauer liked the drawings, particularly since he thought I had captured the Führer well, he was a one hundred percent Hitler admirer after all.

And so I had a series of very leisurely days and my artworks eventually decorated a few of the walls in the barracks. With this drawing task I was also relieved of the effort of having to teach baby steps to the new recruits for a while.

Soon we were far enough that we could practice with live ammunition. We marched out past Grödig for this and, in an open sand pit, cheerfully cracked away with the rifles.
Wonnebauer was careful to ensure no live ammunition went missing here, and we, that the recruits didn't backfire a shot.
During first rifle practice there were hardly any bullseyes but

enough holes were punched around the sides. We used the way there and back to teach the recruits the first hearty soldier songs. We had a lot of mumblers for whom the lyrics long remained a closed book, but there were others who sang, Huhn amongst them, like larks on a bright winter's day.

And sure, speaking of winter days: After many years I was finally able to ski again.
When I found a bit of money in my coffers, I went to "Sporthaus Lanz" in the city and bought myself some ski equipment. In Sporthaus Lanz the famous ski jumper Josef Bradl was working as a shop assistant. Through being served by him personally and through his advice I reckoned that I'd be a better skier if I also used the skis that he was selling. Sometimes you chase after fantasies and let your imagination run away with you.

On the first free Sunday after my new purchase I went skiing on the Gaisberg mountain with Max Leibetseder. After the years of abstinence my skiing ability had seriously suffered of course and I couldn't keep up with Max at all. But it was still marvellous fun and made for a particular kind of change.

The headquarters of the XVIIIth Gebirgsarmee corps was also situated in Salzburg. It was accommodated in a hotel and I had to stand guard in front of it numerous times too. This guard duty wasn't particularly asked after as it involved an almost constant presenting of arms. The red piped uniforms came in and out constantly, it swarmed with all of the top brass.

When we got paid we met in the Pitterkeller in the evening and blew the few marks we'd earned straight away. The Pitterkeller soon became the local pub for the whole battalion particularly because of its value for money.

In the meantime Armsdorfer had given all the jobs relating to gas protection over to me. So I drew up more and more lists, reviewed the stocks and, pleasantly, was exempted from other duties while doing these tasks. Armsdorfer didn't ask about what I got up to much, he was happy to be free of the job himself.

So I got through the winter in Salzburg very well without much effort. I hadn't struggled in barracks since 1934 for nothing, I had slowly learned how to avoid unpleasant tasks successfully.

Around this time I made exceptional friends with Toni Huber. He was an Oberjäger, worked in the kitchen, was a really brilliant skier and came from Wagrain. Toni, not exactly the brightest of the bunch was a marvellous comrade, a sly old dog and couldn't be gotten worked up about anything. But although he had been a ski instructor in Wagrain before his time in the military, he had no sense of direction in the field.
I had a few fun nights with Toni in the Pitterkeller, if Wonnebauer was there as well then a real piss up was on the cards.
Wonnebauer was a Waffenunteroffizier and was much loved by us all because of his straight forwardness. Unless a whole mortar disappeared he barely got worked up about any mistakes. He knew very well how to make these little errors disappear altogether, in real life or even just on paper. A virtue that was highly valued not only by those of us with lower ranks, but rather by the respective heads of the company too.

On one weekend, it was reaching spring already, I went with Leibetseder, Huber and Wonnebauer to Berchtesgaden and on to Königssee.
From there we climbed up to Watzmannhaus with our rucksacks and ski equipment. It was actually already a little too late for this undertaking and the snow conditions weren't so good anymore.

After a cosy evening in the hut we went into the attic and made ourselves comfortable on the mattresses. I woke up several times during the night, Toni snored terribly and each time when I held his nose closed it only helped for a little while.

At the crack of dawn the next day we continued our climb towards Watzmann.

The snow conditions were still good having almost reached the summit. On a rather steep slope, we prepared for the descent. I didn't feel too comfortable. I found the descent really steep and difficult for my ability at that moment. I was shit scared. My knees were still trembling from the long climb up as my three comrades were already off and away without worrying themselves about my concerns.
No wonder: they hang around in the mountains every winter, while I hadn't been on skis for years.

But what did it help, there was nothing I could do apart from follow them. Good God was it a slog though. I was absolutely not used to off-piste skiing any more. I followed the tracks of the other three, but they themselves had long disappeared from my view. I needed to keep my visibility clear, my eyes began to water and the joints in my knees were quivering.

The further I went, the thinner the snow became. The first bare spots appeared and more and more tree stumps stuck out from under the snow.

Suddenly one of my skis got caught on a tree root and I flew head over heels into a pile of brushwood sparsely covered with snow.

I was so exhausted that I could barely lift myself up again. Nothing could be seen far and wide of Max, Toni and Hias, what good comrades they were. I didn't half swear and wanted to pay them back someday when I could.

As I went down further, the snow grew ever more meagre and the skiing ever more difficult. My whole body was in pain from overexertion.
Then I finally reached a track with solid snow conditions, but it was so steep that I could barely throttle my speed.

Since I didn't have enough strength to keep turning I slowed my speed by the most frowned upon method in that I bent over and started to snowplough. A good thing Toni Huber didn't see it.

Finally the path levelled out and I was able to ski the way down to the bottom of Wimbachtal valley in an orderly manner.

Here I met my comrades again sitting comfortably on a fallen tree trunk and eating a snack.

"Is that our Otti?" said Max,
"Ah there he is, look," called Toni,
"we've already been sat here for an hour waiting for you, where were you so long? Shitting yourself?" Toni made his most mischievous face as he said it which he always did whenever he wanted to tease someone.
"I'm not a racehorse and I'm not a ski teacher either," I answered a little angrily.
"You're not a racehorse, more of a lame duck!" Toni laughed so hard that deep wrinkles appeared on either side of his eyes.
"Come here," he continued, burying the hatchet immediately.
"Eat some of this, then your knees will stop shaking."

So I did that as well. Thus bolstered we made ourselves on our way again together. The rest of the path always went gently downhill so that even I could keep up with the rest.

We travelled with the bus again from Schönau to Berchtesgaden and back to Salzburg with the train.
Wonnebauer left us at the train station.

"Will we go for one in the Pitterkeller?" said Toni.

But I had no more money and Max didn't want to go for drinks either. And so we went back to the barracks.
It was still afternoon and the barracks were almost empty. Our comrades from Salzburg were mostly off until last post and the Altreichers were buzzing around the city too. I sat myself down and wrote a letter.

As soon as the snow was all melted and the mountains were bare again I wanted to go with Toni and Max and hike some mountains as well, we had all agreed to, but again things turned out quite differently.

By now German troops had already been occupying Czechoslovakia for weeks. The protectorate of Bohemia and Moravia stretched as far as the border to Slovakia, which was allowed to keep a certain amount of independence.

Soon people were saying that our battalion was going to be transferred to the protectorate as well. "Toilet gossip," we said, but we were proved quite wrong.

The company armed itself to head off. All of our private things had to be packed and went into a separate room of the barracks where they were to be stored until our return. The whole battalion made itself at the ready. A few days were filled with these preparations. Finally, after much commotion, endless roll calls and loading exercises we were ready. We marched to the train station and said adieu to our barracks for an indefinite period of time. With our equipment, weapons and horses our company filled a whole train by itself. The journey went across through Upper and Lower Austria towards Vienna, where we arrived in the Nordbahnhof station. There was a longer stop here where time was made for watering the horses too. Then we swivelled off north, crossed over the former Czechian border and were finally unloaded in Uherské Hradiště north of Brünn, our new garrison. Here we took up an enormous barracks complex of the former Czechian army.

The landscape around the new garrison looked a lot like the Mühlviertel. Very bumpy and yet still very fertile. Huge fields of corn lined the roads and everything gave the impression of being very well tended. Uherské Hradiště was very modest but had a few pubs anyhow and that was the main thing for us.

The inhabitants weren't exactly friendly to us of course, but they weren't particularly unfriendly either. There were no difficulties understanding each other, almost everyone could still speak German from back when the country belonged to the Austrian monarchy. We only rarely came into contact with the population anyway. There was a large pub in the city, it was called "Deutsches Haus" and we appointed it our local pub. It was more of a hotel and it had an excellent kitchen by the way. We camped ourselves here, so long as we were "off duty" and had plenty money.

In Hradiště as well the training went on as usual: we didn't need to do anything in particular to enforce our occupation, our presence alone seemingly took care of that.

The Czechs soon cut their little deals with us. Even on the exercise field the women came with their baskets full of goods like: bread, sausage and all kinds of confectionary and drinks. And it must have been worth it for them, because every day they came again.

We had been in Hradiště for about six weeks, when I was drafted off to a gas protection course in Salzburg. I travelled back to the garrison in one of our Styrian trucks, which were constantly swinging back and forth between Hradiště and Salzburg. That was a comfortable change of course. It was a marvellous day and I had a very jolly journey ahead of me with Schirmer the driver. Toni Huber had provided us with plenty of provisions. We had a proper break in Mauthausen. In a little pub we ate the delicious pork straight from the tin and drank "Poschacher beer" along with it. Back then I wasn't yet aware that I had a very distant relative who owned a brewery. The journey went onward across Linz and Wels until the mountains of Salzkammergut appeared again and we reached the city towards evening.

In Salzburg the barracks were still empty, only the small rear guard occupied a room and were really loafing about. I wanted to grab something out from my stuff that I'd left behind and realised with horror that there was no more trace of my ski equipment. I reported it immediately, Graspointner, the leader of the rear guard, just shrugged his shoulders and didn't have any answers either. Months later, once we were already in the West after the campaign in Poland, Wonnebauer was sent to Salzburg to check and see if everything was OK with our things. By that time the majority of our coffers had already been robbed of their best contents. I was missing my camera as well which I grieved the most. The guys who came after had long taken control of the barracks and what was missing by then was never to be found again.

I found the gas course really boring. What they talked about there I had long since learned on my own. The XVIIIth army corps were still in the city, but otherwise there wasn't much going on at the moment. Even the Pitterkeller wasn't any fun without my comrades. The rest of the detachments from the individual companies formed a really dull crowd altogether. I was happy once the days of the course came to an end again.

I travelled in one of the second company's trucks back to Hradiště. Even before we left the driver was absolutely reeking of booze. Between Lambach and Wels we missed a tree on the side of the road by a hair's breadth. I refused to continue until my comrade was prepared to stop and sleep for an hour. I had intended on making a short stop at my parents' in Wels, but what with my half-cut chum I reconsidered, my parents owned an inn in Wels after all and that was too dangerous for me, I wanted to get back to Hradiště alive if I could. We managed it in the end and I was overjoyed when I got out of the vehicle.

I reported back to Armsdorfer about the furthering of my knowledge regarding gas protection which I had had in Salzburg. Armsdorfer had little idea himself about what this field concerned and with an abrupt hand movement he stopped my explaining.
"It's fine Poschacher, you can save your breath, just keep what they drummed into you in Salzburg in your head."
With that I was dismissed.

One day five of us went into the city as a group and visited the hotel "Deutsches Haus," we wanted to eat some proper schnitzel. And where else was there better wienerschnitzel than in "Deutsches Haus?" We set off with the marks as payment from Unteroffizier Walzl still warm in our pockets. We had to spend our money as quickly as possible, we didn't want it to go off in our pockets. All of those involved I still remember well. We were five Gefreiters: Schröter, Schweiger, Itter, Zopf and yours truly. Schröter, a cobbler from Kassel was a so called Kommandierter and all of us teased him a lot. Zopf was a beanpole Gebirgsjäger from the Lofer area, Itter was small and somewhat round, Schweiger with his ideal military figure was from the Regensburg area.

We found a comfortable spot at a round table in the pub, mostly filled with Gebirgsjäger, which was still free. Then we had the waiters serve it all up: beer and a huge wienerschnitzel with garnishes for all of us. The schnitzel in "Deutsches Haus" was famed because of its size and it also tasted superb. All the spots in the pub had filled up in the meantime. All Gebirgsjäger, the civilians had already retreated from the pub soon after we'd turned up in the city. Of course this bar had lured us in from the beginning with a name like "Deutsches Haus."

And so the five of us sat at the table, drinking, messing around and enjoying the huge portions that had been served up to us. There was such a racket in the pub that you could barely hear what you were saying and the smoke soon lay around our heads like a thick fog.

"I'm about ready to burst from all this guzzling," said Schröter, clearing the last remnants from his plate.
"Yeah that's what suits you Kommandierters the best, guzzling food and drink and lazing about all day," it was Zopf who spoke from the heart on behalf of all of us men in the field.
"That's just jealousy, sheer jealousy," Schröter stroked his full belly with relish.
"The Kommandierters," said Itter, "ought to all be put on half pay, those couch potatoes hardly need the calories."
"We work more with our heads, but you twits wouldn't understand that," Schröter took a hefty swig from his beer glass.
"Oh sure, your heads are very big," continued Zopf, "but brains, there's barely any brains in there."

"Oh shut it you gits!" Schröter stood up, "I'm going to pee."
"Then I'll go with you," said Itter, "else you'll get lost."

The pair of them shoved their way out of the bar towards the men's room.

After a while Zopf said: "Drinking these beers is hitting me already, I could do with relieving myself too, come on Schweiger, keep me company, peeing together is more fun."
"I don't really need to," said Schweiger.
"Oh come on, you could a bit, Otto will be watchdog in the meantime."

And so Schweiger went too and I sat at the table alone.
So now I waited for Schröter and Itter to come back again. But five minutes passed, ten minutes, none of the four of them turned up. Something couldn't be right here. A certain suspicion grew in me, oh those idiots!

I waited till the waiter was at the opposite end of the bar, then I left the table too and went off searching. And so I went to where they'd normally need to be in order to do their business. But far and wide there was nothing to be seen of the four of them.
Just as I'd thought. Those crooks had cleared off without paying the bill!

The guesthouse had a grave construction error to wit. You could head through a corridor out into the open without having to go into the bar again.
Those scoundrels: they wanted to walk out and leave me to pay the bill all by myself. Those hoodlums. What else could I do now other than clear off as well? I didn't want to pay for all five schnitzels myself.

A few hundred meters away from the pub, I met the gang again on the way to the barracks. They stood in the middle of the street bowled over with laughter.

"Did you like your bill?" Schröter had a bright red face and was shaking with glee.
"Who would have thought you were such a pig as to demolish five portions."
"Arseholes," was my only comment.
"I hope you didn't leave without paying the bill!"
Zopf interjected, "Well our Otto is far too honest for that, he wouldn't bail on the check, I'm sure he was a good lad and paid the bill am I right?"
"Of course," I said to that.
"I paid for you five crooks and now each of you owes me a beer and a schnitzel, and woe to you if you haven't paid your debts in a month."
"This rascal is having us on," said Schröter sceptically,
"I bet he hasn't paid himself either!"
"Well go back there and ask them then, go on, push off you crook," I answered as sure of myself as I could, "but you're scared shitless of that no doubt, what do you think the chief would say? He'll give you six days straight in the clink."
"Well then, Schröter," said Zopf, "it was your idea, you got us into this, so go back there and ask them if Otto paid."
"Do you think I'm crazy? You go."
"If nobody wants to go then you'll just have to take my word for it," I said, "and pay me back the debt I tell you, else I'll have to grass on you."

With that the matter was closed for the day.
I pitilessly recovered the debt from Schröter. The others I soon let in on the secret.
Nobody bothered themselves with us when we turned up in the

inn again a week later. In the hustle and bustle they probably hadn't noticed it or they didn't want to ruin things with us good customers. We always paid our bill quite honestly usually.

One Saturday early in the morning some buses left the barracks and took us away on an excursion close to Brünn. We visited a great, world-renowned dripstone cave with little underground lakes which we travelled across in boats. The majority of us had never seen these kinds of caves. As a result we found the day to be acutely enjoyable.

In the meantime we had midsummer. We travelled to a secluded moorland near Střelice on the Slovakian border for rifle practice with live ammunition. We had our first live practice with mortars here too. Wieser, our section commander, herded us through the sandy ground with the heavy equipment zealously. It was some real rough going.

Platoon leader Armsdorfer could show off his mighty voice at its full volume in this deserted area. The nonsense he often spouted off was formidable. While he hounded us like startled rabbits through the countryside he stood with his arms behind his back, like a field commander incarnate and enjoyed the power which his voice had on us lousy maggots. He tried to compensate for a lot of missing intellectual substance through the power of his voice. Our boss, Hauptmann Hofbauer, asked a lot of us too, but his orders made sense and he himself was trained in superb condition and he wasn't afraid of hard work.

And so they hauled us across the barren hills of Střelice. Whether it was in Armsdorfer's mortar platoon, or whether it was with Wiedemann's artillery platoon whose bellowing would sting our eardrums. Even the Feldwebels Schön and Mayerhofer didn't hold back with their voices even though they were nowhere near Armsdorfer's level. These efforts as regards volume would have easily led an uninformed bystander to think that the entire company was hard of hearing.

At the end of June, the names of those who were to be dismissed from service in the autumn appeared on the black notice board in front of the orderly room.

I frequently went past this board every day, but each time I again read my name with particular reverence. At long last, after many years my barracks life was to come to an end. I could count down the days until my release and my anticipation grew from week to week.

I was now forced to reflect on how my life would go on afterwards. Would I even be able to find my feet in my trained profession, having been absent from it for so many years? Where would I live? Where would I find somewhere to stay? All of these unanswered questions slowly pressed to the fore of my mind. It was evident to me that the transition to civilian life would not be all that simple.

But before that, first of all I got another fourteen days holiday. I wanted to spend these holidays, which were supposed to be my last in the army, together with Mimi in Vienna.

We met at the Westbahnhof station and found ourselves somewhere to stay. We eventually ended up in the "Einhorn" hotel, a cheap flophouse suited to our modest travel budget.

In these two weeks we saw a lot of Viennese attractions. The weather was warm and sunny throughout, with which all of the running about was very stressful. The tight travel budget had a big influence on all of our undertakings of course. Nevertheless we were in good spirits, we weren't all that hard to please after all.

Towards the end of the holiday we went on a two day excursion to the Vienna woods. It was a marvellous walk through forest and meadows, uphill, downhill towards Pressbaum. We took up our accommodation for the night in a tiny town with a little inn and perhaps only four or five houses. Schwalbendörfl was the name of this little collection of houses, a really secluded place surrounded by marvellous woods.

We were lucky with our room considering. There were only a few available in the guesthouse and apart from ours they were all occupied by Viennese holidaymakers. In the little country inn you could eat very well and first and foremost you could eat cheap, even food of your own. As usual Mimi contented herself with a stout sandwich and a glass of milk. I already allowed myself a glass of beer, but I ate a tin of sardines I'd brought with me to make up for it. When I gave myself a hefty cut in my thumb while I was opening the tin it didn't matter and it couldn't bring an end to our good mood. Since apparently the washroom was outside, in our modestly furnished room we found two colossal chamber pots to make up for it, made from the best porcelain.

But for all the modesty in the facilities a comfort was offered to us that hardly any of even the most expensive hotels today could provide. We could leave our shoes out in front of the door and the next day we would find them lined up neatly again, freshly polished.

But sadly, as we opened our eyes the next day we heard the rain drumming on a tin roof nearby. All of a sudden the beautiful weather was over. A look through the small window showed us all of the lovely woodland as grey and drab. The rain fell down in a great deluge and we delayed getting up by a good hour. But we had to get out of bed sometime, despite the rain our breakfast, the coffee, the rye bread and the good butter all tasted delicious.

And so our way back to Vienna took place in the pouring rain. But on the way we had two fantastic comrades. Two amusing companions, a tall fellow and a short fellow accompanied us on our way back and cracked a perpetual salvo of jokes and we had some hiking songs too. And so the route was very entertaining and in no way did the rain disturb our merriment.

But the holidays came to an end, and when I left Mimi again our travel budget wouldn't have withstood another day.

Disturbing rumours buzzed through the barracks after I was in Hradiště with my comrades again. The tensions with Poland had heightened, hints of an imminent war appeared more and more often. But we Gefreiters in our second year's service didn't want to give in to all of this gossip. We dismissed all of these uncomfortable rumours as full-blown toilet gossip, only too understandable, we were close to being released and didn't want to give room to thoughts that could endanger these events. But sadly they didn't just stay as rumours. Other unmistakeable signs that something was going on appeared too.

Truck after truck arrived in the camp with medical supplies. Stretchers, arm and leg splints, huge tent tarps with the Red Cross symbol. We slowly started to feel an uncomfortable pressure in our guts when we thought on the coming weeks. Would it all go well? Would we be dismissed? All questions which slowly began to cause us concern. The signs became ever more unsettling, but we were nowhere near willing to think of the worst.

Around the twentieth of August the lists with our names on them suddenly disappeared from the notice board. The company's basic load of live ammunition arrived. Our prospects of a prompt release grew ever smaller. Would my hopes be cheated again as they had been so often? It seemed that I could no longer escape from this barracks life which meant so little to me.

But still we clutched at the tiny straws, still we hoped that the great war could be avoided.

Our division was mobilised on the 26th of August. All preparations for military deployment ran full steam ahead, our hopes for a peaceful resolution sank to almost nil. We still had the tiny hope that the conflict could be contained to Poland and it wouldn't be long before we'd be able to leave the army after all. Hitler's plans had gone too easily so far, so why of all times shouldn't they work now?

The last days before the outbreak of war were full of frantic preparations for our deployment. We found no more time for long palavers and reflections and that was good that way. The whole barracks was like a stirred up swarm of bees. Truck after truck arrived and everything that was missing was brought in. Everything was ready to go.

Weapons cleaning was on the rota once again. It was a hot day. In a large room, on long tables, we made our weapons ready for our last roll call. We had partly filled some empty lemonade bottles with the light yellow, viscous weapons oil which we used for this job. Bottles from the canteen with all kinds of lemonade stood on the tables too. We weren't allowed to drink beer while we were doing this. As I said, the weather was hot and everyone was thirsty. I came out of a meeting with Armsdorfer a little late and had to hurry I wanted to make up for the lost time. Since like the majority of my comrades I was stricken by thirst as well, I grabbed the closest half full bottle of lemonade and took a hefty swig.

But I should have given that a miss.

As I took the first hurried swallow I hadn't yet become aware of my impending doom - but all of a sudden a sinister disgust rose in my throat and like a bolt of lightning I thought:

"Jeez! You've drunk weapons oil!"

A hefty urge to vomit immediately set in which could only be suppressed with difficulty.

"Are you trying to poison yourself!?" shouted little Itter who was standing next to me.

"Jeez!" I hissed at him, "you shut your mouth d'you hear? I'll give you my cigarettes for a week but keep tight."

"What of it?" said Itter, "you drank weapons oil and now you're about to puke, so what?"

"Do you think I want to be the joke of the entire company is that it?"

"Sure thing then, your cigarettes for a week and I'll keep quiet."

Luckily the rest of my comrades were all busy and hadn't noticed anything.

I went to the toilet first of all and vomited. I was sick to my stomach and the rotten smell constantly rose up in my mouth.

"Did it at least taste nice?" asked Itter as I came back from the toilet, very cheeky it seemed to me.

"Shut your mouth," I could answer only with the greatest self-control.

"Well Poschacher, you look pasty," said Schön who was supervising as he went past my table.

"Filled your pants already? The war hasn't even started yet!" this talk angered me.

"No way filled my pants," I answered, "I've just ruined my guts is all."

"That's because you always drink that crap lemonade stuff," said Schön, "you'd be better off drinking a proper schnapps then you wouldn't be sick."

"First of all schnapps is forbidden on duty, also schnapps is too expensive for Gefreiters, only Feldwebels can afford it."

"Don't be cheeky Poschacher!"

"Yes Sir, don't be cheeky, Sir," with that our dialogue was finished.

The weapons inspection which had been ordered didn't end up taking place, our company made its final preparations for marching off.

At the crack of dawn on the first of September we were called into the assembly room. Hitler speaks..the words come out of the radio..... since four o'clock this morning we have returned fire. Now the die is cast.

The entire battalion assembled in the inner courtyard of the barracks complex. The leader of the battalion gave a speech, raised three cheers of hurrah for the Führer, the music played the Deutschlandlied. I stood in the middle row behind Schweiger and feared that at any moment I was going to puke on the back of the man in front of me. I felt so sick. The battalion went to war.

–   .   –

"Let's go men!" the Hauptmann called to us and the company got underway, to march to war. Our first stop was the freight depot in Hradiště, we assembled our weapons here and waited to be loaded onto the train.

Then we lay there on the railway embankment in the warm September sun and dwelled on our thoughts. Sure, we were going to war, but were we cheering about it? No, nobody was cheering.

Slowly carriage after carriage was slid across to the tracks adjacent and assembled into a train for our journey off.

What would the next weeks bring? We were marching into territory where, exactly twenty five years ago, our fathers had marched, had fought and had had to die. All of us were moved by the thought of whether we would survive this adventure, whether we would see our homeland again in good health.

There were optimists: "Ach, in a few days the whole thing will be over and we'll go back home to be celebrated as heroes of the nation."
But the pessimists said: "No doubt we'll soon sort out Poland of course, but France and England, they won't stand idly by boys, prepare yourselves for a long war."

Then there were some really big pessimists no doubt, but they kept their opinions to themselves.

But whoever was right, the machinery that called itself "war" was underway, who could stop this behemoth again, once it was in motion? At that moment none of us could answer this question, we marched into an uncertain future.

But we were still lying in the sun on the railway embankment. Still we were neither hungry, nor thirsty, only there was a heavy feeling lying in our guts. But that weight was drowned out by cheerful, ludicrous sayings, by loud, puffed-up behaviour. Who wanted to let anyone else see how he was feeling on the inside? And the quiet ones who weren't speaking much now, they didn't speak much later either, when fear for their very lives, when hunger and cold lay heavily on their hearts. They kept quiet even in death and endured every sorrow in silent serenity.

Finally the long train stood ready, the carriage's heavy doors were rolled open, we could be loaded on.

All our thoughts of the next days were swept away in a heartbeat. A loud bustle gripped everyone from the simple Gebirgsjäger to the head of the company. Well over a hundred horses had to be loaded on alone, and what with the obstinacy of some of these colleagues of ours this was no small matter.

"Bejesus, get yer arse in ye sow!" swears little Michl Kreuzer from Grossarl and, holding her tight by the halter and the tail, shoves the backside of "Paula," who damn well doesn't want to go through the dark hole into the carriage with his weedy shoulders. But Paula manages to brace herself against his efforts. Only after another two animal handlers joined in and helped were they able to get Paula moving.
The field kitchen's heavy draught horses were a different breed altogether. They were much more docile, calm and more reasonable. They were no way as excitable and stubborn as most pack animals. Paul Fuchs, from Nussdorf near Salzburg, handled his heavy Pinzgauer horses effortlessly. But whether they were stubborn or peaceful, all of them ended up where they had to be

once they were finished. Things went calmly with some of them, with others there was a lot of cursing and shouting. Indeed the platoon leaders shouted most of all, necessarily and unnecessarily, but we little Gefreiters were not in a position to question that.

Once the horses had been loaded on the rest was a pure dawdle. We had rehearsed it a million times after all. Finally we Jäger went on board and the journey could begin. Parts of the division had already taken the trip through Slovakia the day before.

It was around noon when the train slowly got underway. We pressed ourselves against the carriage apertures and let our view pass across the landscape, which had already grown familiar, one last time. The grain fields were still waving golden brown. Only a few had been harvested already. The lighter brown betrayed the harvested fields on which swarms of sparrows were cavorting.

"Shame," said Schweiger who stood next to me,
"I could have gotten through the rest of my service here quite well."
"Me too," I answered, "it would have only been a few weeks for me, God damn it."

"Fucking war!" I wanted to say, but I stopped myself.

"Quit your daft patter, come on we're playing cards!" little Itter suggested, but he didn't find much enthusiasm at that moment.
"Fine then don't, party poopers..." he said, and then threw himself on the spread out straw and turned his back to us.
"The rutting season is starting in our woods now, I should be at home now!" Zopf was clearly feeling wistful.
"Rutting here, rutting there," said Grabner,
"what's with all this wistful prattle? We're marching into Poland, that's all that matters now."

"Get off my back, I'm just thinking of the rutting season, what of it?"

"Just you wait, you'll soon forget all about the rutting season." Grabner laughed quite unashamedly.

"You shut your mouth!" with that Zopf disappeared into the back of the freight car too.

The train took us through the white Carpathian Mountains in many winding turns. Both of the connected locomotives gave off heavy plumes of smoke, working hard to take the long carriages over the hills. We went forwards slowly, but constantly eastward. We had long left the fertile plains behind us, plunging into huge forested areas. Most comrades had lain down on the straw in the meantime, Itter had finally found a buddy to play cards with.

But I still stood with Grabner and Schweiger by the open carriage door. I was still sick, a stink rising from my guts like I'd just cleared out an oil tank, but I just couldn't see enough of the marvellous landscape that we were travelling through.

In the meantime we had travelled across the mountain range of the white Carpathians and the train took us downwards into the Váh valley. And mountains the whole time, and forests, endless forests.

Then we travelled along the Váh valley still north-eastward. We reached Žilina in the afternoon. We took a long break here. The horses were watered, food was handed out and we could stretch our legs.

"It's only afternoon and we're getting our evening meal already?" we asked, astonished.

"Budget it out to yourselves or eat it all now if you want," shouted Wieser, our squad leader,

"but in the evening there'll be nothing."

"The war has hardly begun and already the whole dinner schedule is messed up!" Grabner shouted to him, "thing's can only get better!"

"You'll endure much worse than that yet!" Wieser answered and went back to the head of the train where a carriage had been squeezed in for ranks above Oberjäger.

"You won't get a better answer from that prat," there was no love lost between Itter and Wieser and Itter had no good words to say about his squad leader.

The journey went onward, now along the southern ridge of the high Tatra. The fantastic mountain massif lay in front of us, enormous in all its glory. The famous winter sports town Zakopane must lie behind there somewhere.

It was already night by the time we reached our provisional destination "Kežmarok."

The wheels had barely stopped moving before the unloading began. There was a lot of fuss and shouting as it went on. There was hardly any light in the train station and there was a bit of confusion in the darkness, until everything was out of the train and the company had taken up position.

We left the train station and marched on a narrow, unpaved road northward.

We had mentally prepared ourselves to set up camp for the night soon, but evidently things were to turn out differently. We went ever further into the night. On either side we were accompanied by dark, eerily quiet forests which ascended steeply right at the side of the road.

After around two hours of marching we reached a town. The houses lay there still and dark, no dog barked at us, no window was lit. We kept marching northward through the rows of houses which were staring at us in hostility.

"Where's the hotel we reserved?" said Grabner next to me.
"No hotel for sure, must have burned down," I said.
"Shame, I'd been so looking forward to it, I wanted to have breakfast brought to me in bed."
"Something of a bed bunny are you?"
"Of course!"
"You'll have to get your coffee from the field kitchen too."
"I fear I will."
"You should have been a General."
"You've hit the nail on the head."
"Sepp, I'm afraid we're only lousy Gefreiters, just little arseholes."
"You've spoken a true word there Otto, well let's get the hotel idea out of our heads then."

We kept going for a good hour. To the right and left side of the road you could make out some rock faces, the moon cast a pale light across the rugged escarpments, some of which were almost vertical.
Finally there was the order:

"Company halt!"
"We march again in three hours," he continued, and so we lay down wherever we stood at that moment, every minute had to be used for a wink of sleep. The horses on the other hand had to be relieved of their burdens first.

We tried to sleep, on the edge of the road we were barely able to find the right position to sleep. And so small groups soon sat themselves together, they smoked and chattered. Itter actually tried to get a game of cards going in the dark. As warm as we had been while we were marching, the night was still very cold and we began to shiver. And so you stood up again, walked along the length of the company, ambled back again, so that your limbs wouldn't get completely stiff and you could pass the time.

Before the march continued there was a cup of hot tea at the field kitchen.

"A special treat!" said Toni Huber cockily,
"Damn it," I said, "you pulled out all the stops here, where's the sausage to go with it?"
"You're never happy are you? You'll just have to imagine the sausage."

But the tea really put the life in us again.

There was dew on the grass, we couldn't find a proper place to sit down without getting our backsides wet. But we were moving on again soon anyway, so we were as well staying standing up.

The horses were loaded up again and we continued on a gravel road, ever ascending gently upward, ever stubbornly northward.

Slowly the morning dawn set in. Across the column, a cloud of dust which promptly evaporated upward. Now we went ever steeper uphill. Our burdens weighed us down heavily, the flanks of the horses grew moist, began to steam. Our surroundings didn't change, still just the dark, steeply ascending forest on either side.

We got a very short break. We owed it to the carthorses pulling the carriages, which were exhausted and needed a breather.

Every so often a dispatch rider roars along the column. The curiosity, the lure of the unknown slowly faded, we began to grow more conscious of how tired we were.

With the sun rising over the forests a new day breaks. The gloomy mantle of the seemingly unceasing, unwilling to cease forests by the Polish border is taken up by the sun too.

The 2nd of September, a Sunday, had begun. And it looked to be a beautiful day. The stony, laborious path went up, in many turns, onto a hilltop. A little border-check hut stood in the woods, lonely and deserted.
Soon it lay behind us, we marched into Poland now, with no trace of the enemy far and wide.

After the border check-point it soon went steeply downhill. We heard the powerful rushing of a river far below us. Soon we reached the deep incision of a valley and the river whose rushing we had been hearing before.

We had a longer break now, while column after column of the division passed us by. Apparently we had been set aside as division reserves and so we were arranged onto the end of the endless worm of soldiers.

Well then, divisions reserves: It was fine by us, the generals had to rack their brains over that.
The III./137 passed us by:

"What's this then you slackers? Too feart?" they shouted to us, from out of the rows hurrying past.
"Yeah well," we shouted back, "we'll leave the dirty work to you guys."
"We're just better than you guys, so we have to be held in reserve," shouted others from our rows to those marching past.
We joked back and forth like this until the last of our neighbouring battalion had disappeared into the woods.
For us too, they soon said:

"Prepare to march!"

The path grew narrow, the mighty Dunajec on one side, opposite that rock faces towering up, punctuated by thick leafy forests.

Suddenly, at a great height, a set of planes passed over us, "Polish flight squadrons" they were, but they didn't take the slightest notice of us.

For us there was marching....marching..... . A short break at midday. We could take care of our first blisters.

We had our first pea soup on Polish ground and I have to say it tasted absolutely fantastic after this long march, really, it had never been so good. Hunger was always the best cook. Sadly, after barely an hour's rest we were already off again. And especially now, in the warm sun it would have been so good to nap a little longer.

We heard nothing from the battalion ahead of us, whether they were tangled up in fighting or whether the Poles were retreating without a fight.

At particular bottlenecks in the road we came across the odd hurriedly cleared roadblock, but nowhere could you find any signs of fighting having taken place.

Towards evening, after a long day's march that had brought us close to the edge of exhaustion, we reached Krościenko. An inhospitable dump in an even more inhospitable area. The roads grew worse and ever more narrow. Our heavy convoy including the field kitchen stayed behind, only the horses with the heavy arms and our basic load of ammo accompanied us still.

"Gadzooks! When will the damned march finally end?" cursed Mehrl, a beanpole of a man and a gunner in my mortar squad.

"No doubt as soon as the war is over," I replied, but I wasn't in a laughing mood myself. A sizeable blister on my right foot, my hips chafed sore from the leather belt which, with the weight of the ammo pockets and haversack and spade and bayonet was constantly chafing against my hip bones. I hauled myself about the place no less ill-tempered than all my other comrades.

"We're not cross-country runners," said Grabner.

"Well they seem to think we are," I reply.

"Yeah well," Itter's little figure has almost disappeared, packaged under all of the field equipment, "'marching saves blood' so said the Hauptmann when we stopped last and he should know after all."

"They could have easy given themselves more time the Poles," I say.

"Walking is fun and all, but those muppets could give us a break now and again too," says Schweiger.

"Who knows what's going on up ahead, maybe we'll walk into a trap and all of a sudden the Poles will set about us from our flanks, leaving an empty hole," thought Grabner aloud.

"You bloody armchair tactician," says Schweiger, "just leave the thinking to our Generals, it's the only work they're use for anyway."

"They'll get a fat medal if all goes well, if it goes bad, well yeah, we'll just have to bite the dust then," Itter always saw the glass half empty.

"Better that they get a medal then," says Mehrl, "I'm quite happy to go on living."

But we kept marching, it had long grown dark. At least the pleasant weather made all our struggles a little more bearable.

Finally we were there. We stopped on a wide meadow to the right of the road, between the rushing Dunajec and treeless hills.

The horses were unsaddled, guard posts were set up, we set up our camp for the night.

I went together with Schweiger. We spread out two strips of canvas on the floor, they were supposed to keep out the heavy damp from the ground for the late night hours. Now we had two blankets and we had to get warm underneath them.
We were spared from guard duty that night, the signals platoon had to do it.

"And where is our princely supper?" Zopf wants to know.
"No idea, who knows how far back Toni is with his field kitchen," my stomach was grumbling dreadfully too.
"Well this is a good start," Itter grumbles, "no enemy, no supper, just nothing and they call it a war."
"War," growled Zopf, "don't make me laugh, if things continue like this there'll be no medals for us to earn."
"I don't give a crap about medals, as long as my name's Grabner I'd rather have a good schnitzel."
"Schnitzel? Just stop it you pig, there's not a loaf of bread about and the man's talking about schnitzel, are you mad?" Itter pointed clearly to his temple, showing Grabner what he thinks of his idea.
"Well I can at least talk about it," insisted Grabner.
"You're a God damned lunatic, you don't speak about schnitzel when we don't have a heel of loaf to eat, besides it is very uncomradely, well with that then you can all go and fuck yourselves," Itter rolled himself up, pulled the blanket over his head, showing us that for him the matter was closed.
"Has that lad got the jitters?" says Grabner, "I'm starving too, but at least I can still dream of a big schnitzel with a warm potato salad."
"You must have better nerves than Itter," I say, "and you can go fuck yourself too, OK?"

"Will youse just go to sleep instead of always talking? God damn it," Schweiger turns his back to me, pulls three quarters of the blanket to himself, but I give a hefty tug back and in the end we settle on half and half.

Our stomachs were grumbling, but we were all exhausted and even without dinner we fell asleep eventually.

But we were woken up again in the middle of the night: Oberjäger Wieser came down the rows of those sleeping, pulling the warming blankets off of us,

"Move, get up, fall in line for your food."
"Have they got shit for brains?" Mehrl pulled his blanket up again and slept on. "Eating in the middle of the night, who does that?" Grabner tapped his forehead with his hand to emphasise his comment.

Drowsy and shivering we get ourselves up, walk to the road, the cooking utensils rattling, all around people cursing, but who wants to miss their dinner?

One of our trucks from Steyr stood in the middle of the road. Faschingbauer the driver and Toni Huber had already begun to share out the meal.
The coffee was more of a cold sludge really, but so what, alongside it there was bread, butter and sardines.

"You're here in good time!" I say to Toni. He laughs at me and with his most innocent face says to me.
"Otto you old whinge, be happy you're getting anything at all."

Of course we were happy, and how we rushed to stuff our mouths full, to give our stomachs some semblance of calm again. We had barely finished eating when we went to bed again, the few hours of peace had to be used.

"How late is it actually?" Schweiger asked.

"Nearly twelve."

"Well then we've another six hours of sleep yet."

"Hopefully!" my eyes are closed again already.

A pleasant warmth came up from under the doubled covers. Our stomachs finally had work to do again, that was real good for us and immediately spread a contentedness in us which soon let us slumber again.

Suddenly there was some kind of noise and I was wide awake. Was that not gunfire?

"Alert....!" ..a short silence.... "everyone prepare for battle..!"

High over our heads a short salvo of machine gun fire, a few gun shots from an easternly direction.

"God damn those arseholes," cursed Zopf, "couldn't you start your damned rat-tat-tating a few hours later?"

We swarmed out, lay scattered in the moist grass for fifteen minutes, kept the open hills close in view, but nothing was moving anymore.

Deathly silence all around us. A reconnaissance group went out. We lay in the damp night grass and cursed.

"Alert over," they said after a while, we crawled under our covers again.

"I'll say it. Arseholes," is Itter's final remark.

We dozed off again, but our good, deep sleep was over. We stayed restless and prepared for more disturbances. Half asleep I could still hear a dispatch rider rattling along the street, heard a few shouts from those on guard duty, otherwise things remained calm.

Soon a loud command shook us awake again.

"Get up everyone! Prepare to march!"

It was still pitch dark.

"That can't be right, what time is it?"

Schweiger throws his blanket back.

"Four o'clock," I can barely read the time.
"Gadzooks! You don't wake a tired soldier at this time," Zopf turned over, pulled the covers over his head again.
"Move, move it you slowpokes, up, or will I have to help you with a boot to your backside?" Armsdorfer went along the lines, tearing the blankets from those sleeping. The comrades drag themselves out of their beds like moles, exhausted, with wild hair.

Well, what a night that was.

"Wieser squad! Gather round me!" we gather around our squad leader.
"Well then men, I don't want our squad to be last again understood? And saddle up the horses properly, if they get chafed just the once then I'll saddle the stuff on you even if you collapse, or my name isn't Wieser! And don't leave any rubbish lying about, you know what the Hauptmann thinks of that, dismissed!"

We didn't need Wieser's tip about how to saddle the horses properly and load them evenly. We had practiced this a hundred times and we knew how valuable these animals were to us.

"Move, move assemble on the road, quicker men!" Armsdorfer goes across our army camp, brandishing a torch about.

"And breakfast?" Mehrl asked the question that all of us were thinking about.

"Breakfast? I can't be hearing myself properly, you just stuffed your faces in the night."

"That was our overdue evening meal," soon there are a few comrades making this justifiable objection.

"Oh we're having a little mutiny is it?" Armsdorfer puts his hands on his hips, a position he always adopts when he wants to show his superiority to us.

"Not a mutiny, we're just asking a valid question," Mehrl replied.

"Yeah, a bloody stupid question. Move, up to the road, fall in in march formation, Oberjäger Wieser report to me when the platoon is ready."

"Blah..blah.." Grabner mimicked behind the platoon leader as he left, Wieser heard it, but didn't react to it. Still tired, unslept, with sore feet and real sullen, we took up position on the road.

We eventually stood for a full half hour lined up in formation before we could finally set off in march.

"The same crap over and over," Mehrl cursed, "first hounded like mad and then standing around for hours like idiots, real army life."

Finally we got underway. The sun ascended blood red on the horizon, no clouds in the sky, a beautiful day.

The march still went along the Dunajec directly north. Soon the sun was burning hellishly on our backs and the dust, that damned dust, came back again.

After a few hours we had our first break. The saddles had to be checked, the horses' belts slackened for an hour.

We sat on the edge of the road, dozing while the cart horses and the few cavalry horses were left on a long leash standing on the road like silent statues. They too were too tired to stretch their necks for the few meagre blades of grass at the side of the road.

There was neither breakfast nor cigarettes, the kitchen seemed to have gone up in smoke. The hour's break from marching was over too quickly.

We reached a hill, the road here descended down gently and we could see across a long stretch. In front of us a cloud of dust as far as the eye could see. Our regiment was a great, seemingly endless worm of soldiers that wound its way through the Dunajec valley lying in the morning sun. No trace of the Poles.

And marching...marching.. through the afternoon..legs like lead... tongue dry.. stomach grumbling...but onward.. onward.. into the night..."marching saves blood."

We were on a meadow south of Jazowska in the night of the 5th/6th September. We were finally fed again that night, the first provisions in twenty four hours. We were in a defensive position in the tightest of spaces, the horses in the middle.
We arrived around midnight. With sore feet, cracked lips, eyes burning from a whole day's dust swirling up. We lay underneath our blankets, nobody dared to take his shoes off out of sheer terror that he wouldn't be able to get them on his feet again when we next set off.

While we let ourselves collapse on the ground half-dead as soon as the unsaddling was done, the poor animal handlers had to take care of their horses first. They did it diligently despite all tiredness. If some of them were unlucky, if a horse was crippled, or if despite all the attention to detail they had chafed themselves on the long march, then they still had the way to the vet ahead of them and could only think of themselves afterward.

"Damned army.." Schweiger sits on the floor, his face ash-grey with dust, he waits for me to come so that we can crawl under the blanket together.

"Yeah well.." I answer.. "we have swollen feet, we're filthy...we're exhausted..but buddy it's war and we're still alive.. that's the main thing."

"I only know," Schweiger answers, "that in my whole life there has never been a day where I have been so exhausted, so completely finished I tell you."

"After today who isn't? Even Wieser and Armsdorfer have given up their constant griping and if anyone could be annoyed," I answer, "then it's me. I was in a fully motorised division in East Prussia and I, sucker that I am, have to go and get myself transferred to the Gebirgsjäger."

"What a bloody idiot you were for that Otto,"

"Sepp, where would we be if there weren't idiots every now and then?"

"But that damn stupid, that's punishable like."

"Yeah well you see now that I'm punished for it."

"What did you actually expect from the Gebirgsjäger? Just clambering around mountains and chasing after dairy maids?"

"I didn't actually think of anything at all, I was far away in East Prussia, I just wanted to go back home."

"At least that's a sensible reason...means you'll just have to put up with the long marches."

"I'm just wondering.." Mehrl lying next to us butted into the discussion.. "I'm just wondering how the Poles manage this at all, this crazy speed."

"In truth I don't understand it either..." I answered.

In reality we only had few Poles ahead of us. The majority were on the move further to the north of us. Our job was to outflank the Poles to the South and to reach Lemberg before them.

But back then we didn't know that, since it wasn't custom to explain anything about the sense and purpose of an operation to the simple soldiers anyway. But some hardships would have been easier to cope with if we had been a little more informed. But the soldier should only obey, he should leave thinking to other people.

They barely gave us four hours sleep after a twenty hour long march with a few breaks the day before.

"Nowy Sącz" they said, had to be reached as quickly as possible, the Poles were to be given no time to take up position in front of the city again.

No cursing helped us, we were chased up... on...and forward.

There was still no dawn to be seen as we began marching onward again. The first kilometers were agony.

Our swollen feet bulging in the mountain boots were so painful we could barely endure it. We didn't march, we hobbled..and cursed... and still hobbled forward.

Only after a few kilometers it got better, the piercing pain waned, grew more bearable. We put one leg in front of the other mechanically, barely having an eye for the landscape, staring stubbornly at the rucksack of the man in front of you or the big backside of a horse, depending on your position in the march column.

And the hunger set in again. We simply couldn't understand it. I mean we had trucks that could bring food to the front. We could appreciate that the field kitchen couldn't keep up with this insane marching speed.

But here as well we only learned the reasons much later. All trucks were needed for the battalions at the front, which were being thrown towards Nowy Sącz in a motorised forced march in order to break the Polish resistance in good time.

But we didn't know this context. We could only curse about all the incomprehensibilities in the course of things which we didn't understand.
We marched onward in the glowing Galician sun, for hour after hour we continued to swallow the dust from the men in front of us, over and over we grasped for our field canteens which had long been empty, we moistened our chapped lips with our scant spittle... they had long grown cracked... our faces a pale yellow from the loamy dust... our hair dirty, smeared with sweat, no comb could bring order into these wild knots, we didn't even try...we didn't speak any more we were so tired... we were a silent bunch...only onward.......... onward into Poland.

We had a break at midday.
We were granted two hours. We really had to pull ourselves together in order to muster the strength to unsaddle the horses. We let ourselves collapse into the withered grass on either side of the road exhausted. We lay there listlessly, nobody spoke. To just be able to stretch our legs, to just not march for once, to lie and think of nothing, to just be able to doze. If only we could moisten our dry, chapped lips.
The water of a tiny pond shimmered a few meters away from the road. But we were strictly forbidden to drink from it. No doubt this ban had good reason.

A messenger came along the road from the hinterland. The sidecar of his motorcycle was full of bread, bread for the whole company. But no tea, no coffee, no hot food... not a sausage or a sardine.
Each group had to assign a man to receive the bread ration. This

time Hofbauer, our Hauptmann, oversaw a sharing out which was as fair as possible.

Now even Armsdorfer had finally grown tired, his gestures grew calmer, his instructions were freed from his usual stentorian tone, he became more reasonable.

Our break came to its end.. and we were afraid... afraid of the first kilometers... until our sore feet had been broken in again somewhat and the pain became more bearable.

Half awake.. half asleep.. we dragged ourselves onward till late in the afternoon.. in an uninterrupted cloud of dust... beneath a sun that burned down on us mercilessly.

Slowly the woods receded, a wide open space appeared... Nowy Sącz lay in front of us.

The odd plume of smoke..but no great destruction.
We crossed over the Dunajec on one of the temporary bridges built by our engineers. Rubble from the old bridge blown up by the Polish lay all around. The odd shot up Polish vehicle..but no dead.

We reached an airbase. A dozen shot up fighter planes scattered across the airfield. Destroyed air hangars. We marched onto a barracks complex which was undamaged. From all of this we could see that we were on land formerly held by a school of the Polish air forces.

We found shelter here for a night. I rummaged through a part of the barracks with Schweiger. We came across a classroom, learning materials were scattered around wildly... A very hurried escape had taken place here. In a cupboard we found a number of brand new drawing instruments of the highest quality, "Made in Germany," we could have no doubt found a good use for them, but who wanted to haul them around too? We had enough to carry.

We found some stuff which we didn't need...but what we hoped to find, something edible, wasn't to be found.

We continued on again early next morning.
We left the Dunajec valley now and started marching in a new direction eastward.

The sun burned from the sky staying just as hot. For days we had September weather like in a holiday brochure. Now we went through miserable villages, the "roads" didn't deserve to be called such, what must it look like here after days of long rain? We swallowed dust more than was really reasonable, but certainly it was still better than dragging ourselves through ankle deep mud in this forsaken place. The looks from the locals were furtive and filled with hatred, of course you couldn't wonder much about that.

A greater number of Polish military horses romped around on a great pasture between Korzenna and Bobowa. Some of them were captured and assimilated into the crew, among them a fiery brown stallion.

This stallion was a wonderful animal, full of fire and a lively temperament.
As things went on it was only with difficulty that this glorious steed could get used to being hitched up next to a slow, slightly heavy Pinzgauer horse from the field kitchen. He had perhaps once carried a proud rider from a Polish cavalry squadron and now found it beneath his dignity to serve as a common carthorse. Some horses quickly came to terms with the fate of their capture and served us as additional riding horses on our continued march forward. They offered a welcome opportunity to grant our

sore feet some peace for once and to wear out our backs some more for a few hours instead. Unfortunately, only a few had this opportunity and always only for a short time.

But without pause, ever driven by the need to reach Lemberg by the quickest means we went onward through dust and shimmering sun.

"Marching saves blood," was still the maxim,... and Lemberg was still far.

I think it was between Zargórzany and Jasło. A stretch of the road that we'll never forget. It was still night, after only three hours break, we had set off again, we marched almost without a break for the whole day. We were tortured by hunger, but still worse was the thirst. We went through neglected, miserable dumps, the streams were off-limits, after all the water could be poisoned.

At the crack of dawn they had set us into march with a slice of bread and a portion of sausage that you could barely see. We went over barely discernable roads, through dust and heat, without any long breaks eastward.

That day we managed a stretch of just over sixty kilometers. We couldn't feel our legs any more, our feet burned like fire in the heavy, hobnailed mountain boots. At the end of that day we were completely at the end of our strength.

As we camped on a meadow a few meters in front of Jasło for a longer break we were worn out and deaf to any superfluous words.

An entire Polish army had been annihilated south of Kraków and pushed to retreat towards Przemyśl. We found ourselves deep in the flank of this retreating army. Everything rested on reaching the area around Lemberg before them.

That's why there was this mad rush, these forced marches that exhausted us to the last man. Our faces were covered with sweat and a crust of dust from the road, eyes red, inflamed from the constant irritation from the stirred up grains of finest sand, we fell down like dead men in the few breaks we had. Nobody thought to wash himself, every minute of the break was needed for sleep.

We arrived in front of Jasło very late, but around two o'clock in the morning we continued on again. We cursed, we swore.. we complained non-stop .....but still we marched.
Finally they surely saw the inhumanity of these endless forced marches. We got ourselves a relief, from now on our rucksacks were carried along with us on support convoys. Freed from the burden of our rucksacks we could now make somewhat better progress in future.

In Jasło, we marched across the Wisłoka on a temporary bridge. The rumour went round that mustard gas mines had exploded here in Jasło. It was the first use of poison gas in this war and the last one too.

The march eastward went on. Lemberg became a nightmare for us.

"I'm sure," said little Itter: "My legs are getting shorter every day."
"I've noticed that too," answered Zopf,
"Soon you'll disappear altogether."
"You're cracking daft jokes about it, but it's very sad actually."
You could certainly have sympathy for Itter.

But things weren't going much better for the overly tall Mehrl either,

"I can't even tell if I still have legs anymore, everything's burning, all over, I can't tell where."

You can tell in Mehrl's voice that he's being completely serious with this remark. He suffers from thirst in particular, he takes his field canteen to hand over and over, but no matter how much he shakes it, there's not a drop left to coax out of it. Only with difficulty can he be discouraged from scooping water out of the filthy stream, it's strictly forbidden and if we grew sick from it it would be considered a self-inflicted wound, or at least we were threatened that it would be so.

Sepp Grabner is our company photographer. He was one of the few fortunate enough to possess a camera and what's more rolls of film.
You couldn't prevent him from gambolling out of line at least a few times a day and pointing his lens at us to immortalise our suffering.

"You'd be better off in a propaganda company," Itter said to him once.
"That would be right, then I wouldn't need to march my legs off."
"You could use your footage of us to really fill everyone in in the Wochenschau, imagine their faces in Salzburg."

Mehrl got very excited about the idea.

"I don't know," I thought aloud, "when they see us shuffling along like this? I'm sure we don't look much like national heroes."
"Don't say that Otto..." said Schweiger,.. "even if we don't look like heroes, we'll stir up lots of pity for sure, and more parcels will trundle in in the field post..... if they could see us like this, with our thin faces... crusted in dust...."

"Maybe with the old wifies," said Zopf to that..... "but the young girls? They have very different ideas of what heroes look like... they want to see medals.. flashy uniforms..no, no, they won't be impressed by our swollen feet and dirty faces.... like we are trudging along at the moment.... I wouldn't bet a pfennig that we'd impress them..."

"Well then Sepp, keep taking your pictures, when we're old we can look at ourselves in an album and feel truly sorry for ourselves," said Schweiger.

"Well then comrades, give me a smile so you don't break the camera!"

We went through a totally squalid little hovel, I've long forgotten the name. The village street was an absolute garbage dump. Dogs were prowling alongside us with their tails between their legs. Tall, slim Jews wrapped in long black kaftans, with eerily pale faces framed with black beards passed us by. Their eyes glowed like fiery embers, but to me their lives seemed to be totally wretched.

"No amount of money could convince me to be buried here, never mind live here.." said Grabner and attempted to take a picture of one of the figures.

"By God," I reply... "I'd rather die than have to live here."

We were happy once we had this hovel behind us, the houses from whose half closed windows hostile faces stared after us.

And we were still marching as a reserve division. While for a large part of the journey our sister battalion could lie back, loaded on trucks, we had to march... march... because marching saves blood.

At the same time the Poles were retreating far too quickly for our terribly dishevelled feet.

We reached the San.

We went ever eastward across a temporary bridge. Destroyed bridges... so the forward battalion had made contact with the enemy after all, only we had remained spared from any clashes up until now.

The roads had completely ceased now, from now on we lacked any kind of substructure to walk on. We simply marched away and left a track behind us at least twenty meters wide. The plumes of dust that we trailed behind us must have been visible for kilometers.

Again we went from open countryside into bewildering forests.

Suddenly we were ordered: "Halt!"

"Heavy fighting has flared up ahead," we heard from a messenger. A truck came back, at the double, one of our artillery pieces was loaded on and brought forward with the gun crew.

We on the other hand lay on the edge of the road and waited. Tremendous what a force the September sun still had here. Before we came into this woodland area we crossed over a long stretch of land that had almost been shrivelled up by the sun.

We marched a few kilometers ahead again, already again they said: "Everyone, halt!"

We camped on a wider open area between two parts of woodland.
The day's destination seemed to be reached, or it would be determined through hostilities. But we were happy for every hour for which our terribly tormented feet would be spared, for every minute of sleep.

We learned from yet another messenger: Remnants of two Polish divisions were attempting to delay our journey on to Lemberg.

After a few hours we continued on again swiftly, the way seemed to be free again.

We marched across Krosno, Jasionów and Temeszów.
We spent the night of the 13th and 14th of September halfway between Temeszów and the large woodland area of Borotycze.

The night grew restless. Our guard posts were constantly shot at by individual snipers from out of the woods. Still, every attack in this woodland was pointless in the dark.

We set off again very early.
An exceptionally hot day seemed to lie ahead of us, we noticed that soon after sunrise. It really seemed to grow hotter every day this year, the more that September progressed.

With each kilometer we covered the landscape grew hillier, the forest murkier and more bewildering.

The muffled rumbling of heavy artillery firing could be heard in the distance. All kinds of things had to be going on up front, we couldn't understand why our battalion could keep going on so undisturbed. Why we weren't once loaded onto the trucks and made vanguard. Of course we couldn't see into our generals' heads. Throughout the whole military advance we only learned very little about the combat situation, of course a heap of so called "toilet gossip" resulted from that.

Later it became clear to us why it was always just us that had to march. Since the losses of the forward battalions were insignificant on the whole, they saved themselves the tediousness of reorganising and left things as they'd originally assigned.

The narrow roads led us ever deeper into woods which seemed endless to us. Gunfire could be heard from an eastern direction which lasted all morning.

Around midday a short stop again. Occasional rifle shots from the thickly wooded hills high above us. We didn't bother ourselves about it, it didn't cause us any harm after all.

We went onward, the first signs of fighting that had taken place became visible. Next to the road a dead Pole, he lay stretched out with his face on the withered grass, no discernable wounds could be ascertained on him. The first dead of this war that I saw face to face.

There were holdups again, we stood on the spot for over an hour.

We were ordered to be ready for combat, our steel helmets had to be put on. "And in this heat as well," we grumbled, there wasn't a Pole to be seen far and wide, only these scattered shots far away from the mountain slope.

"They're shitting themselves," Zopf only exchanged his comfortable cap for the steel helmet with great reluctance. "Well get a move on," snapped Armsdorfer who was visibly nervous going along our platoon.
Wieser came up to us, "Take the mortars down from the transports move!... move!.. Speed it up you dozy bastards!" we relieved the animals of their burdens. Base plate, barrel, rangefinder, munitions crates were distributed amongst the individual gunners.

The company set into motion again slowly.

Things couldn't really be all that serious, otherwise we would be getting divided up into our individual Jäger company groups. Surely we were just under orders to be on full alert.

Halt again.

A Jäger company overtook us, was sent to the front.

The woods grew ever closer to the road, the path went downhill gently, the trees on either side came right up next to the road.

We marched around a bend, suddenly the war lay in front of us.

A half dozen jeeps from our forward battalion lay next to the narrow ravine shot to pieces... partly shoved from the road...partly jammed between tree trunks... full of bullet holes... the windshields shattered... the first vehicle was crashed between the trunks of two mighty beech trees...the driver's hand... now sallow white... still clasps the steering wheel.. his passenger hangs out of the rear backwards... his eyes glassy... wide open.... staring into the high forest canopy... a tiny hole in his chest.. a little circle of blood on the uniform...... a vehicle had collided against a tree trunk with full force... the grill...the hood pushed up... the driver hanging over the front... smeared in blood...his chin shattered...his three comrades thrown over each other, shattered by a machine gun salvo....engine coolant dripped rhythmically out of one jeep... a huge pool of blood in front of the vehicle,.. mixed with sand.. congealed to a crust...two dead comrades alongside it...wide eyes open frozen to the sky..next to the road, in dense branches with head hanging down, a dead Pole... at the next bend the same picture, destroyed jeeps... dead Gebirgsjäger...gloomy silence all around... no birds singing only the restrained steps of marching columns. No sounds of battle any more.... no gunshots... only the quiet buzzing of thousands of insects over the trees of these eerie woods... .

Our comrades had been caught in a trap. The disaster had unfolded here a few hours ago... we had been marching only kilometers away.. and were powerless to help.

An eerie silence accompanied our march onward. After a sharp turn we hit the small column's front car which now lay obliterated in these forsaken woods.

The wheels facing upward... the jeep lay with lots of bullet holes on the sloping edge of the road... out from under the vehicle stretched a hand as though searching, into the sunlight..... the body of the column leader half buried.. a Feldwebel.... his face hideously injured... without discernable eyes... .

We marched past these grisly images, no words were spoken, for the first time we felt how close together life and death are in war.

It was the murky woods of Borodycze in Galicia that made us aware of death in all its cruelty, these images were still unfamiliar to us, and so they shook us twice as hard.
And these woods could be so tremendously quiet and peaceful, nobody would expect this cruelty of them, but even the woods were misused for this cruelty.

We marched onward, the road sank into a basin. We barely spoke, the shock sat in us too deeply, everyone was busy with his thoughts, deeply moved by the images that the road had shown us minutes ago. We were unprepared for the reality of war, it struck us with a blow that couldn't be avoided.

We reached the little basin, it lay peacefully in dazzling, brilliant sun, embedded in the eeriness of the rising dark forests behind us, out of which doom had come for some comrades a few hours ago.

From the East to the West, the forest opened up in a semi circle northward. You could make out the edge of the forest well, with the sunlight streaming through, around a hundred meters away.

The company made preparations for a perennial camp. Reinforced guard posts were posted on the hills. Those of us in Wieser squad built our mortar right at the end of the basin next to the road and positioned it targeting the area of the northern forest edge. My task was to measure the range.

Wieser came back from a squad leader's meeting:

"Huhn, Zopf, Grabner and Mehrl as well take over the mortar, Schweiger, Itter, Poschacher come with me."

We followed Wieser up the slope, thickly overgrown with bushes, went past two fallen Poles, who lay with their faces in the floor in the almost impenetrable undergrowth.

This barely ten minute long ascent to the edge of the forest was quite an effort. We were exhausted from the long march, our feet were burning as if they were on fire and we finally reached the edge of the forest totally out of breath.

A wide open field opened up in front of us. Just some bushes around two hundred meters away and to the right of that, but still a bit further away, a little wood.

Wieser assigned us our guard positions. Schweiger was a hundred meters to the right, I was in the middle and Itter went off around a hundred meters to the left.

"Well then you clowns, don't go falling asleep on me," said Wieser..
"And pay proper attention, everyone here has a flare pistol, the password is Salzburg, you will be relieved in two hours," with that Wieser went down the slope again.

I lay down in the withered grass at the edge of the forest, the sun burned on my back at an angle. Up here an eerie silence reigned all around, just muffled noises could be heard from the bottom of the valley. All sorts of insects buzzed around my nose, I yawned, I was tired beyond description. I had marched all day, gone all day without enough sleep, now I could barely keep my eyes open.

I pinched myself in my cheek, my thigh, rubbed my eyes over and over, just don't fall asleep now. Sleeping on guard duty meant a court martial, assuming you got caught.

More tense than was needed I stared across the fallow fields lying in front of me, it took all of my senses to stay awake.

If only it wasn't for this damned sleepiness, again and again my eyes fell shut for a few seconds, with all my strength I fought against this all powerful need for sleep, which threatened to overwhelm me again and again.

A large, blue and green shimmering beetle crawled across in front of me. Strove its way over stones and over withered blades of grass. I tried to block off his way with my hands, to take him away from the preconceived direction of his travels. But he knew exactly where he wanted to go. When I forced him one way with my fingers, again and again he found the direction which he first pursued. Where did he want to go? Was there a good feeding spot for him nearby? A dead mouse for instance? Or was he on the way to his regular hiding place? He wasn't bothered by any war and still he too was constantly in danger. Perhaps even before he reached his destination he would fall victim to the thrust of a bird's beak, even a passing fox would eat him as a tasty little tidbit with pleasure, and so he too lived in constant danger.

And so I took up all kinds of thoughts to prevent myself from succumbing to exhaustion. An exhaustion which weighed on my eyes like lead.

But in the end sleep must have overcome me after all. A burst of fire from a machine gun woke me up with a shock.
The sun was a little lower and more to the side than before, Good Lord, I must have fallen asleep after all.

Again the steady tat-tating of the machine gun, it was far away, coming from out of the wood... a few short bursts... a few little clumps of earth jump up..but far, far too far away to endanger me... then peace again...it was late in the afternoon now, the sun was already low.. slowly I felt a profound hunger.

I hear sounds from behind me, I turn around, but see nobody, I must have imagined it...is something moving there?.. I call out..

"Password!"
"'Salzburg' you prat," it was Zopf who appeared behind me so suddenly.
"I'm relieving you, any news?"
"There's nothing much going on, a few little machine gun salvos but they're far away," I answered.
Zopf lay down next to me, "so it's all hunky dory, well clear off then, our food has come in the meantime, Grabner saved some for you."
"Anything new with the company?" I want to know.
"Nothing, other than that we're to stay the night here, we can get a good kip at last... hopefully."
"Well then so long and don't fall asleep, it's damned warm here and when you're lying on your stomach so peacefully, you're away with it fast."
"So what if you are, there's not a Pole far and wide anyway."

I make my way down to the company. There was a heap of discarded pieces of equipment of Polish origin scattered across the ground.... they must have really taken to their heels in a hurry here.

Zopf was right: we actually set up camp and had the pleasure of getting a whole night's sleep. A new day's sun was already shining in the sky, and we still lay in the same spot.

Even breakfast arrived on time, it was brought out in a military ambulance.

The 15th of September seemed to be just as beautiful and hot as the days before.

Shortly after breakfast Wieser came to our squad along with some medical orderlies, he ran into me first.

"Poschacher!"
"Oberjäger, Sir!"
"Two of our fallen officers are buried at the eastern forest edge, you will find four prisoners at the company command post. Have the Poles dig our fallen out again, bring the dead to the ambulance at the company command post. The medical officer will accompany you, and be quick about it, we're marching off soon."
"Where are the dead exactly?" I wanted to know..
"At the eastern edge of the woods... isn't that enough?"
"Yes, Sir."

So I went off with the medical officer, who had two strips of canvas under his arm, the four captured Poles and two spades.

The prisoners surely didn't know what was going to happen with them, as we moved towards the forest they were looking around really uncertainly. Maybe they thought we were going to have a little court hearing in the forest with them. We had our weapons in arm ready to fire...we didn't want to lose them as soon as we reached the bushes now.

We didn't need to look for long when we reached the edge of the woods. We saw the two freshly raised shallow earth mounds and the birch crosses immediately.

As we handed the spades over to the Poles and made them understand what they had to do with some hand signals, their expressions brightened, they realised they weren't going to die.

They began to dig cheerfully. We gave each of them a cigarette beforehand, which visibly helped their enthusiasm to work.

Barely two shovels deep, the first parts of uniform appeared. Although it had only been dug a day ago a sweet smell of rotting corpses already rose from the grave. I wasn't too happy with the matter, no wonder, the war had only just begun and I wasn't a grave digger by profession either.

We signalled to the Poles to go around with the spades carefully, they didn't need to damage our comrades as well. We pulled a young Leutnant out of his grave first. His face gaunt, yellow like wax, his eyes wide open, the lights in them gone, but it seemed to me that they looked at us with great reproach. Why didn't they close his eyelids? The half open mouth stuffed full of earth, I should have closed it for him, I couldn't do it. We laid him on a spread out canvas, folded the ends over him and pulled the ties together.

The second grave, an Oberleutnant, was soon uncovered too. Again this unpleasant sweet smell. The sun, the warmth had accelerated the decay.

We had just been putting the Oberleutnant on the canvas we'd set up as well, when a burst of machine gun fire threw clumps of earth into the air in little jets about fifty meters away from us. Our captives disappeared into the woods like lightning, before we found the opportunity to stop them from doing so by threat of arms.

Since the next salvo hit much closer, we also drew back behind the closest trees to find safe cover.
That was just what we needed, what a mess.

We looked around for our Poles, but they weren't even thinking of doing a runner at all, they were at the edge of the woods hiding behind the nearest trees and making themselves noticeable to us in a lively way. They could have easily escaped, we didn't know their reasons, but they wanted to stay.

The machine gun that was shooting at us must have been far away in front of the woods, surely there were small groups of enemies scattered there that were still making themselves known.

The shooting had stopped again, we waited another few minutes and then cautiously stepped out from the cover of the trees again.

Once everything was calm the prisoners appeared again too. We finished our work here, gathered up our fallen and, remaining under the cover of the edge of the forest, headed towards the valley again.

I delivered our fallen officers and the Poles to the company command post and went back to my squad again.

I reported back to Wieser, my comrades were busy dismantling the mortar that they'd brought into position and loading it onto the horses, the whole company was packing up already.

"Where were you then?" Grabner asked as I returned to the squad.

"I thought I'd be a gravedigger for a change," my comrades stared at me in disbelief, they surely had no idea about what I'd been up to in the meantime. I told them in short about what I'd done.

"Wieser had to take you of all people," said Zopf, "doesn't he know you're a gentle soul?"

I made a dismissive hand gesture, "he doesn't think about things like that," I answered.

"He certainly doesn't," says Itter fully convinced, "But gentle soul or not, I wasn't best pleased with the affair, who likes digging up dead bodies?"

"Surely nobody," now I start dismantling the mortar too, "but it wasn't that bad either and in wartime we'll have to get used to a lot."

"That may be," Schweiger interjected, "but if the Poles keep running like this, I fear we won't have much more opportunity for that."

Zopf shakes his head sceptically, "Lads, lads, I'm not so sure of that though now, Sepp, you're forgetting the French and the English, they could really give us a hard time yet, that won't be a walk in the park like it is here in Poland."

"Oh come off it you pessimist, where are the French then? They're sitting in their line of fortifications and playing cards, they don't want to get mixed up with us."

Schweiger is convinced that once we're done with this stroll through Poland the war is over for us, and because the majority of us want that to be the case, almost all of us are on Schweiger's side.

"Ach you knuckleheads," Zopf gives up trying to argue with us, "You won't know what's hit you yet, you just wait and see."

"Move! Move you dozy bastards! Load up the horses, and pick up the pace if you'd be so kind, don't go falling asleep on me." Armsdorfer puffed himself up like a peacock again, totally playing the august superior.

The long rest had done everyone good, the men and the horses both, and so we made our way onward light hearted and in good spirits, ever deeper into the heart of Poland.

"The Poles," they said, "are retreating towards Lemberg across the whole line. It is imperative that we reach this city before the enemy."
So forward comrades, forward and stop pretending you're tired, up and on to race to Lemberg.

And we marched onward, swirling up plumes of dust kilometers wide. Soon the dust mixed with our sweat from hour long marches again, soon we were just as dirty as we had been before our long break. Soon we looked like industrious millers who had just come out of the milling room.

And thirst became our constant companion again, and the rations were shared out so frugally, as if the provisions we had were meant to last for weeks. And the sun burned down on us from Poland's sky, good Lord what a September.

The mountains, the woods slowly receded. The region became flat as a pancake. But the roads, well they really didn't deserve to be called roads.
But what did we care? We marched on the clay ground burned hard by the sun and left an incredibly wide track behind us.

And we dragged onward, almost without a break we went from the morning dawn until the deepest night. And again only a few hours of sleep, again only the smallest possible rations, again walking on blisters and sores as our constant companions.

Large Polish units had been squeezed together into a very tight space between Przemyśl and Lemberg, and we ran for all we were worth in order to stop the enemy from breaking out to the South.

One day, we stopped around midday in a lousy, God forsaken hole. I sought shade in a tiny farmer's croft with a few comrades. The little windows let barely any light through the half blind panes, but it swarmed with flies in terrific numbers on the tables, benches and windowsills.

The inhabitants of this croft weren't unfriendly, but the filth, the flies and a stench that insulted our nostrils drove us out into the glistening sun again, to a village green where barely a single tree offered any meagre shade.

The inhabitants here, deeper in South Poland, were no longer so hostilely disposed to us. We were going through an area that was almost exclusively occupied by Ruthenians. Apparently they had no bad memories of the times they had spent under the Austrian Empire.

On the 16th of September, we reached Komarno. We were now to march towards the North-East. We reached the pure German villages of Falkenstein and Dornfeld.

Even from a distance we saw the village of Falkenstein lying on a stretched out plain. It was surrounded all around by an approximately three meter high fence of wooden stakes sharpened at the top. All of the houses were spick and span, with little flowerbeds in front of the entrances. The inhabitants came out onto the street, waving at us in a friendly way. Everything made a tremendously well tended impression, a relief after the squalorous villages of the past days. Around the village were well tended, well looked after fields, which even after the harvest still showed the inhabitant's hard work.

On the evening of the 17th of September we reached Dobryany. We thought we'd get a rest. But we went continuously onward into the night, now directly northward, towards Lemberg. We hurried the bulk of the division ahead. We belonged to Schlemmer group and were temporarily put under the control of the 1st Gebirgsdivision. We, the I/137 now marched with the II./137 in a forced march across Krotoshyn to Vynnyky, to the east of Lemberg.

On the 19th of September in the evening we stood on a chain of hills in front of Vynnyky, our goal was finally lying to the West on a plateau, the towers of Lemberg shone up to us in the evening sun.

She lay there in front of us in the last light of the evening sun, the city for whose sake we'd had week long forced marches until we'd been taken by almost complete exhaustion. The name "Lemberg" had followed us like a nightmare, following by day on dusty roads, following by the short night hours in which we were granted a restless, half deathlike sleep.

And now we were supposed to bring this city into our possession, it was to be decided in the next hours.

We had brought our mortar into position on a backslope overgrown with low bushes and were now waiting for further instructions.

The sun slowly disappeared behind the western horizon, a few meters up, on the crest of the hill, you could see its reddish rays reflected across the many church towers.

Occasional artillery fire... here and there a rifle shot... an unnatural calm lay across the landscape, the calm before the storm?

Night fell, across the city only a gentle veil of mist was rising still, consumed in the darkness.

The calm continued.

We had built our mortar, ammunition lay ready, we also had everything prepared to quickly change our position and move forward.

"No doubt sparks will fly early in the morning, you can be sure of that," said Wieser. He was still restlessly busy with correcting something here and there, inspecting something...he acted as though we'd never seen a mortar, never mind fired one.

It seemed to us as if the whole battle depended completely and solely on our squad, our mortar.

"So make sure everything works when the party starts," he continued, "else I'll boot your arses, and I won't give you a minute's peace."

We were barely listening to Wieser's words. We were battling against exhaustion which lay on our eyes like lead. Hauptmann Hofbauer came past, inspected our position, spoke to Wieser:

"Everything in order Wieser?"
"Yes Sir, Hauptmann, Sir, Wieser squad prepared for battle."
"Good, men who don't have guard duty can sleep a little, further

instructions will follow. In the early morning I expect our attack on the city from the South and the East. And as a final piece of news: a Russian cavalry division will be taking part in the attack following on our right wing."

Of course that was really news to us and for a few minutes it made us chipper again. We'd already heard that Russia had declared war on Poland too and was advancing on Lemberg and the entire eastern part of Poland.

"So the party will soon be over," Hofbauer continued, "especially since there's just the beaten remnants of various forces still holding Lemberg as well, well then good luck."
"Thank you, Hauptmann, Sir."
"So you heard him men, try to get some sleep and then we're on it in the morning!"
"It sounds really simple, hopefully afterwards this insane running about will stop too," said Zopf while he spread out his covers for the sleep he'd been promised.
"Time will tell," Wieser lay down to sleep next to the mortar as well, "and if not, then we'll just run about again, and what do you mean 'insane?' The German Wehrmacht doesn't do anything insane, understood Gefreiter Zopf?" Wieser laughs.. "and after all, if you with your bird brain can't grasp it all then that's not the fault of the Wehrmacht."
Zopf was in the process of crawling under his covers, "all right, all right, we're not Generals after all and we often get told precious little about what's going on around us."
"The Wehrmacht would have a lot of work with that," Wieser answered, "if they had to explain the aims and reasons behind their orders to every dumb grunt."
"Dumb grunts are only allowed to die," said Itter to that.
"Reign in your cheek Itter, and now will you shut your trap at last, we still want to get a wink of sleep after all," with that our

squad leader rolls under his covers and this time we do the same as him post-haste.

In the middle of the night I was shaken awake, drunk with sleep I woke up with a start...."Come on Otto, move, you're on guard duty, you have to relieve Mehrl.." it was Grabner who pulled me from deepest sleep.

So I got myself ready, climbed the circa fifty meters up the slope and met Mehrl there who was already waiting impatiently for me to relieve him.

"Man, at last you're here, you're five minutes late already, where have you been?"
"I was only just woken up, don't piss your pants over five minutes!"
"Five minutes is a long time when your eyes are this heavy."
"You won't be able to sleep for much longer, the party might start soon."
"That's exactly it, every minute is precious."
"Calm down will you, any news?"
"Everything's quiet, even eerily quiet, a few rifle shots, nothing worth talking about."
"Well then clear off, maybe you'll be lucky and can sleep for a few hours yet."
"That'd be nice, well then take care Otto."

The night was full of stars, the outlines of what was right in front of me stood out well, but visibility didn't reach further than around thirty meters. I found myself on the narrow ridge of a hill, after only a few meters the ground, richly overgrown with bushes, dropped off gently to the outskirts of Lemberg. No light betrayed that a city was lying in wait of a military clash a few kilometers to the west of my position. In a few hours this calm would be broken and all hell would break loose.

A gentle wind crossed over the ridge and brought the bushes lying around it into constant movement.

Was it really just the wind?..... Or were dark figures not scurrying across the countryside over there?..... My senses were tensed... I listened to every suspicious sound that became noticeable in this nightly silence...... a nocturnal bird flew close past me... the dark bush a bit ahead in front of me there... was that really only the wind that was playing in its branches? ... Was a man not standing behind it?... Was a head not moving back and forth constantly? .... A rustling in the grass,.. surely a small nocturnal predator on the search for food...a rifle shot far to the east of me... were Poles in front of us? ... Or had a nervous guard fired into the night senselessly? .... And always the bush in front of me... surely there had to be something there?.... I went ten steps to the left... back and then ten steps to the right.. looked on the suspicious bushes from the side... no it was nothing... it was just the wind that was making me believe in bogeymen.

How could time go by so slowly? Two hours could last an eternity... I thought of my childhood... my time at school.. whether the sky back home was so full of stars too? .... When would I sleep in a proper white bed again? .. Sleep for as long as I wanted... put on nice civilian clothing... stroll past bright shops on the street... .. go to the cinema... then a flare went up, for a few moments its pale white glow immersed even the area in front of me in surreal light.

I tried to find the various constellations in the sky, we had learned it all at one time, I was hardly once absent from school... and still my knowledge on the subject was sketchy now. Venus, the Northern star and Ursa Major... any more than that...had been lost into uncertainty... a flare again... our listening posts were far away in front of me after all... something sinister was lingering that night, explicitly because of the somewhat surreal silence.

I heard the sound of approaching steps, they came from behind me. It wasn't yet time for me to be relieved.
A figure appeared from out of the darkness.

"Password?"
"Dachstein," it was platoon leader Armsdorfer who unexpectedly appeared from out of the bushes.
"Gefreiter Poschacher on guard duty, no incidents of note."
"Good, keep your eyes open!"
"Yes, Feldwebel, Sir."

The platoon leader went onward, the night soon extinguished his outline, the thick autumn grass quickly muffled his departing steps.

It remained quiet for the rest of my time on guard duty too. Itter relieved me, it was now two o'clock in the morning, I headed back to my comrades.
Schweiger stood on guard at the mortar position, all the rest were snoring all around in the dewy grass.

I rolled myself into my covers, hopefully anticipating to be able to sleep for a few hours undisturbed now.

This hope didn't turn out to be false. The night went on peacefully until the early morning hours.

We were woken up around six o'clock. We sleepily peeled ourselves out from under our warm covers, we shivered distinctly in the morning cool. But soon movement would make us warm.

A messenger came: Oberjäger Wieser had to go with the platoon leader to the company command post which stood about a hundred meters away in a little hollow. No doubt the briefing for the upcoming attack was taking place there now.

We were very surprised that they let us sleep for so long in the morning undisturbed.
It lasted an eternity until Wieser came back. For sure almost an hour had passed. When he finally turned up at our position again we saw from his face that he wasn't in the best mood.

"Dismantle the mortar, have it loaded onto the horses along with the munitions, the squad will be ready to march in an hour."
"What's going on?" we all wanted to know at once, we looked at Wieser quizzically and incredulously at the same time. His answer came out very brusque and he seemed thoroughly displeased with the events:

"The attack has been called off, the attack on Lemberg is to be left over to the Russians, we're marching back the way we've come again up until close to Przemyśl."

By no means did we make such sad faces on hearing this news as our squad leader had perhaps expected.

"And so more running about again, what did I tell you?" said Zopf.
"Shut it," shouted Wieser, "move, move! Faster you dozy buggers!"
"He's annoyed he's missing a medal," Grabner whispered to me.
"You've hit the nail on the head," I replied.

Fundamentally though, it seemed to be a joke of world history. Here we were marched, often almost beyond our limits, having swallowed dust by the bucketload from the dreadful roads and now at the end of all these efforts, the Russian comes along and walks off with the fruits of all our hardships.

"Well now let's hope we get a really comfortable march back," Mehrl tightened a horse's belly strap, once the mortar and munitions had been loaded on as prescribed, ever under the suspicious view of Wieser. But Itter immediately made a dismissive hand movement,
"I've never experienced comfort in this crowd yet, they'll find something to bully us with again still, to make sure that we don't grow too cocky."

Wieser stood right next to us.

"Oh, and it's Itter again of course, constantly bitching."
"Bitching is the spice of life!" Itter's statement made even Wieser smile sardonically.
"Well come on then...if you washwomen are finally ready, don't think that the war's won already you dozy lot."

We marched the hundred meters down to where the company had gathered.
Once the whole company was gathered, Hauptmann Hofbauer gave us a short speech:

"Men! It has sadly not been granted to us to lead the battle for Lemberg ourselves, a battle for which we were well prepared and for which we had waited with eager hearts. It was not possible this time to bring ourselves honour for our Volk and our Führer, but as heavily as it may weigh on each of you, obedience is the highest precept of each soldier," Hofbauer let a small pause slip in and continued: "For political reasons a demarcation line has been established with the Russians which lies far to the west of our current position, along the San running through Przemyśl. For us this means we will be making the march back with our formation back to front. We will take this bitter medicine with a soldier's discipline, I expect you to continue to give your best, be that for the moment only just your physical strength, the great quantity of marching that will still be asked of you yet. It is our task to reach the new demarcation line as soon as possible. And so men fall in line, and keep your head up."

And so the Hauptmann spoke and we knew what was going on.

"Did you hear that?" said Zopf, "'as soon as possible,' well comfort's out the window then, how could it be any different either."
"Yeah you're right," I agreed with him, "how could it be any different either."

And so there was nothing more for us to gain here in Poland, but we little Schützes and Gefreiters took it with great composure. It seemed that after that the war would be over for many of us and we hoped to return home soon and leave the army.
We believed that France and England would give way again, we believed this, because this belief coincided with our desires of soon taking off the soldier's jacket and being able to return home.

But still we stood on this 21st of September early in the morning in front of Lemberg and prepared ourselves for our march back to the San.

Before we began the long march, we took our mess tins in hand and gathered at the two field kitchens out of whose kettles the hot coffee was already steaming.

At last for once there was breakfast at a normal time again. The support had caught up with us the night before and a normal course of rations seemed to be secured again.

They didn't give us much time, we seemed to be in a hurry to march back to the San. We didn't understand this hectic rush. In our eyes the war in Poland was as good as over. We marched the dusty roads back and we hurried, as if the devil was chasing us. Again we barely stopped for long during the day, and if we did, it was by the need to not overtax the horses. We whirled up the dust again, the roads hadn't gotten any better in the meantime. We had just one stroke of luck, that the weather was still bathed in dazzling autumn days. The weather gods were exceptionally kind to us.

First the march went southwards again, we had the sun in our faces and for a few hours we were accompanied by the rumbling of shell fire from the direction of Lemberg.

Around midday we learned that dispatch rider Schuster was missing. He hadn't returned from delivering a message to the rear guard.

"I bet Schuster's making himself comfortable with a young Polish girl in some secret croft somewhere," Schweiger's suspicion found our unanimous agreement.
"He'll turn up again," said Mehrl, "hopefully the Pole hasn't cut off any of his manhood."
"That would be the worst wound," Itter realised, "and you wouldn't get a medal of bravery for that either."
"Instead you'd get court-martialled for self-mutilation," laughs Zopf, who seems greatly amused by imagining this kind of injury, "picture it in your mind," he continues, "you feel yourself to be in the heavenly realms of passionate ecstasy, when all of a sudden that which no doctor in the world could substitute, is gone."
"Surely that must have happened before already," says Schweiger.

"My God, it happened in the First World War often enough," interjects Grabner.

"I don't believe in these horror stories," I say.

"Yeah well," Mehrl is sceptical too, "it surely happened a couple of times, but people must have lied about it a lot too."

And so we had something new to talk about again, something which could be dragged out for hours, our imagination was stirred and we could forget about our sore feet for a while.

We reached Krotoshyn. Women were standing at the edge of the road, they had been crying, you could already read the fear of what was coming after us on their faces. And so they too had already discovered that the Russians would be coming here to take our place. Back then they would have surely much rather been occupied by us, they didn't yet know what was in store for the Polish under the German Wehrmacht as well, and neither did we.

We made camp between Krotoshyn and Dobryany. An hour after us the support arrived with all the luggage as well. Toni Huber fired up his field kitchen, welcomed enthusiastically by us all, in the twinkling of an eye the tanks were empty and we let the pea soup trickle into our stomachs contentedly.

Schuster was still unaccounted for, perhaps he actually had ran into the approaching Russians, but perhaps he really was sleeping the sleep of the just somewhere, he didn't have anyone to wake him after all.

We were granted around five hours of peace that night and I had to stand for two hours of that on guard duty with Itter. We both cursed Wieser, who had assigned it to us...... good that we could still curse, it let us let off some steam.

We had barely fallen asleep properly after having been relieved from guard duty before we had to get up again, the company was again preparing itself to march onward.

"Are we actually running away from them?" I say to my sleeping buddy Schweiger, "we're running so fast we're nearly losing our legs," I was surly, unslept and exhausted to the point of falling over.
"This urgency seems sinister to me too," Schweiger answered, "I think that really we are running from the Russians.... why else this mad rush?"

We weren't wrong in our assumptions. As we later learned the Russian was really pressing behind us impatiently, he couldn't see us get out of his territory fast enough.

And so between Lemberg and Przemyśl there was one forced march after the other.

The weather remained marvellous though, the sun continued to accompany us day after day.

We went through the German settlements again. There was fear in the eyes of the people here too, who this time were watching our withdrawal in silence with a little bit of resentment in their faces. They were countrymen of ours after all, but how could we have given any words of comfort to them at the side of the road? We were happy once the villages were behind us, but we still felt the reproachful looks behind us for a long time after. Grabner, who was marching next to me and who always considered and tried to analyse everything very thoughtfully said: "I just don't understand it, how can we just leave these people over to the Russians? I couldn't stand them looking at us."

"You're right," I answered, "we're creeping off like burglars, why did we push so far into Poland anyway, if we were just going to give it all up again?"

"Children," Schweiger interjected, "obviously you don't understand, it's all high level politics, far too high up for little reprobates like us."

"I suppose it is," Schweiger says, "those up high must have put a lot of thought into it for sure, but do you think they're always right?"

"The Führer is always right, or haven't you heard?" Itter looks at Grabner interrogatively.

"Oh, I've heard that already," says Grabner. "But?" Itter presses further,

"You can just think about the 'but,' go rack your brains, assuming you've got any."

"Shut it," is Itter's closing comment, with that he blocks off any discussion if he doesn't know the right answer.

"The Russians just give me the creeps I can't help it," Zopf continued the conversation still.

"Who isn't creeped out by them, you twit?" said Mehrl, "our fathers were already really creeped out by the Russians in the First World War and up to today nothing has changed. You never know where you are with them."

"Very true," Schweiger tilts his head, "there's no more to be said on it, you never know where you are with them."

And so we while away our thoughts during the ongoing march, sometimes it was reasonable, sometimes it was unusual, but often it was just meaningless jokes, just real grunt talk, crude, straight to the point and full of irony.

And our heavy nailed mountain boots bore us ever further, ever further westward, back to the San. We had no more rucksacks to carry and still we were exhausted. Thirst gave us the gyp again, not hunger any more, we were getting our meals, even though they were often very late.

We went through the villages that we'd already seen before during our march east, they hadn't grown any prettier, in our exhaustion we barely paid any attention to them.

Behind Rudky, that forsaken hole, close to a fork in the road whose signpost pointed to Sambor, we went past a really dirty farmer's croft. In the yard, teeming with refuse, a flock of ducks waddled around a huge manure heap straight past us.

"Stop for a minute, I'm gonna grab one," said Itter, shoving his rifle into Mehrl's hand. He shot out of line like lighting and chased after the excited swarm of ducks. As he went he showed us a swiftness which we wouldn't have thought him capable of after the hardships we'd been through-

"He's really building up steam," said Schweiger.
"Like Paavo Nurmi!" laughed Zopf.

And Itter actually managed to grab such a bird by the tail, seizing it by the collar and even though the feathers were flying he held the duck tight and wrung its neck with his hands.

"Well, buster," Itter stepped back in line, panting,
"You'll provide us with a first class roast this evening!"
"Otto!" Itter turned to me, "you and Toni Huber are such good friends, we need salt and some butter OK?"
"I'll see what can be done, but slit the duck's throat first of all, the blood has to come out."
"We've time for that until the village is behind us," said Itter.
"Whatever you say."

Then a great yelling soared up from behind us, which was quickly growing closer.

Unfortunately, Itter's attack on Polish poultry hadn't remained unobserved, the farming woman came running along beside us like a furious storm and soon discovered her duck in Itter's fists too. As she ran alongside us she fomented a constant, ear-splitting shriek.

"Will you shut your mouth you old witch?" Itter shouted at her, without the Polish woman being inhibited by it. Another stroke of misfortune was that Hauptmann Hofbauer was riding not far ahead of us, alongside the company. There was no hiding the farming woman's screeching from him.
Hofbauer fell behind until we caught up with him, the screaming woman still running alongside us, we couldn't hide the slain duck anymore either.
Hofbauer immediately realised what was going on.
His face turned red, the veins in his temples swole up. On horseback, he pointed down at the dithering little Itter with his riding crop, so that he touched his chest with its tip.

"Itter, you will report to me early in the morning, and you will give the bird back to its owner immediately, who do you think we are? Are we German Gebirgsjäger or a plundering band of thieves?"
"Hauptmann, Sir," Itter tried to explain, "the duck ran right between my legs and yeah I thought..."
"If you even begin to think, you gnome, you always just come out with nonsense!.. And you have violated an express company order, is that understood?"
"Yes Sir, Hauptmann, Sir!"

With that Itter tossed the unfortunate bird at the feet of the raving farm woman. Then she seized her dead goods, forcing herself through our lines whereby Itter fruitlessly tried to trip her up and, wailing loudly, lifted the dead duck up to the Hauptmann.

She surely expected greater compensation. But this seemed to be good enough for Hofbauer, he stuck his spurs into his horse and galloped away.

"Dirty cow," Itter shouted after her as she withdrew.. "damn woman, you've robbed us of a roast."
"Well then," I turned to Itter, "surely I don't need to get either salt or butter now?"
"Ach go fuck yourself," Itter was mad.
"Your roast duck," Grabner said to Itter, "has gone up in smoke, but don't worry about it, you'll survive."

During our march east the artillery platoon had already refrained from shooting a decent-sized piglet, but even this scheme couldn't get past Hofbauer, even though the squad leader Leutnant Neuschler wouldn't have minded it. But Hofbauer was strictly against any illegal means of improving our provisions.

We got as far as Krukenychi that day. We camped a few kilometers behind the town. It had grown a little chilly that evening and so we built up our four man tents.
I just wanted to head off for a good sleep inside the tent with Schweiger, Zopf and Itter, we had already had our supper in the form of tube cheese, butter, crispbread and tea beforehand when Wieser turned up in front of our tent.

"In five minutes Itter and Zopf are to report for guard duty first."
"Why me?" Itter flared up, "I stood guard with Poschacher last night!"
"Do you have to ask you prat?" Wieser answered him, "surely it's clear that you'll be given preference for things like this for several days?"
"Bullshit!" Itter said nothing more and turned his back to Wieser, crawling into his tent to prepare himself for guard duty. Wieser didn't answer any of this strong language, disappearing as if he

hadn't heard it at all.

It was an order that had come down from above after all, who knew how he thought of the whole matter himself.

"You're going to find that roast duck to be very expensive," Zopf said to Itter laughing, "ach, what do I mean 'roast duck?' It never got that far. On Sunday the duck'll probably be sizzling away in the woman's oven."

"That fucking cow," cursed Itter.

"Yeah well, who likes being stolen from?" said Zopf.

Itter was in the process of crawling out of the tent, equipped for guard duty, he turned to us one last time:

"That woman will have it coming when the Russians turn up, no matter how, but that witch deserves it, for all I care they ought to wring the necks of all of her poultry."

"He's got something against that woman," said Zopf and followed little Itter who was so grouchy.

"How things have changed," said Schweiger, once we were alone and had rolled ourselves under our covers, "in the old days they used to take the women to themselves too, now they get all upset about a lousy bird like that ...... like .. we always sing ....life at arms.... living happy.... it's stupid to sing things like that, ...life at arms.... living rough... that's what we should be singing today."

"Yeah.. yeah.. Sepp, the world is changing ...... and everything's becoming fundamentally different.. but I feel sorry for Itter, he meant well, the roast duck would have benefitted the whole group after all ...... now he has to face the music alone... ."

"He was just unlucky, you can't do anything about that," with that Schweiger turned his back to me.

What a surprise, they let us sleep through the night until it was almost light. As we crawled out of the tent having been called to wake up, the first pale red rays of the rising sun appeared. The sun which announced another marvellous autumn day.

All around in a wide circle, tent after tent stood on the dew wet grass. The horses stood to the side and dozed with their heads hanging in front of them.

Alluring steam rose out of both of the field kitchens. The three cooks were already in full action.

Tent after tent opened, unwashed sleepy faces appeared, heads with their hair completely ruffled. Cooking utensils rattled, tents were folded up, the animal handlers went with their drinking buckets to the nearest stream. The horses had their nosebags put to their mouths.... all over life came into the camp.

I went to the kitchen with Schweiger, I preferred to wait a few minutes than to stand in the long queue later. Oberjäger Huber was still cutting the butter that was left into the fairest portions he could, it was difficult for him he had little sense of consistency and it was a matter of luck whether you got a small portion or a large one. Of course, the officer's and Unteroffizier's batmen stood gathered in front of the kitchen already as well, to our constant annoyance they were always given preference.

The hot coffee really put a swing into our spirits again. After breakfast we immediately began speaking more and clowning about more and even our good supervisors became more lively.... more up for little acts of bullying. But what did it matter, Przemyśl wasn't too far away and there we were finally supposed to get some days rest... assuming it wasn't just toilet gossip.

And so we gathered ourselves on the road for a new, no doubt long and difficult day's march.

We went back along the dusty roads, the sun which hadn't

stopped for weeks now was still gleaming down from a deep blue September sky untiringly.

Despite the strict ban against drinking unregulated water, the ban was often violated. And the consequences soon showed themselves. During the march back the first cases of dysentery arose. And along with this the first visits to the sickbay. Diarrhoea was the order of the day.
Our squad had so far been spared losses of this kind.
But we saw some of our comrades from other squads suddenly breaking rank from the column like a hounded rabbit and, pulling their trousers down as they ran, running as quick as they could across the field. And, despite the quick reaction, some of them didn't get as far away from the company as they'd hoped, had to relieve themselves prematurely and had to endure the teasing of the columns marching alongside them along with the concurrent circumstances. Our battalion had numerous deaths from dysentery, among them one death in our company.

When we reached the town of Mizhenets in the afternoon we swung from here towards the North-West, now we went towards Przemyśl, our destination.

After five days march we finally reached the edges of the city. We crossed the San on one of the temporary bridges built by the engineers and reached the western part of the city. The eastern part of the city was to be occupied by the Russians.

Just one day after our arrival, the first Russians had already appeared on the other side of the San.

But we had reached our provisional destination and were hoping for the days of calm we'd been assured of. We were allocated some private residences as accommodation.

The hosts were acting reticently for the moment but nowhere near as unfriendly as we had feared.

Now first came the days of great cleaning. Weapons and attire were submitted to a thorough overhaul. We cleaned and scrubbed and stood in a long line along the San splashing in the cold water.. in particular our underclothes had bitterly needed to be cleaned. We would have needed more thorough measures in order to remove the weeks long dirt though.

On the opposite side of the San around fifty meters away there were a few trees lined up like a string of beads. The Russian sentries sat well camouflaged in the forks of the branches, all of them were watching our activity with interest.

After a few days of relative calm we began combat training again if only on a small scale. The grassy shores of the San were our practice grounds.

It was on a late afternoon. On the rota stood "Laundry."
In close formation, our squad went with Wieser to the river to subject our uniforms and footcloths to a thorough wash.
Each of us sorted out this business with greater or lesser success, according to the enthusiasm and skill of the individual. Before it grew dark we marched back to the drill square where the results of our cleaning had to hold up to Wieser's critical eyes.
And so we stood in line, our still wet uniforms in our arms, we were in a hurry we wanted to go back to our quarters as quickly as possible since other squads were already heading off with their mess tins. What a soldier wants the least is to miss his dinner.
But Wieser took his time. Precisely since he could see how uncomfortable we were he was irritatingly thorough that day.
Now, it wasn't all that simple to clean a dirty uniform in a cold

river properly, our hand soap was by no means the best quality nor were we trained laundresses and back then we had neither Ariel, Prill nor Henkel to hand.

But Wieser somewhat adapted his standards of cleanliness to the present situation. The roll call went along smoothly up until the squad leader arrived at the penultimate man, Kübler, a horse handler in our squad.

Kübler, who wasn't exactly the cleanest in the company, presented a uniform which had lost absolutely none of its previous greasiness through the washing process.

"Have you gone mad Kübler? Sticking a dirty rag like that in front of my nose?"

"I scrubbed it very thoroughly Sir, Oberjäger, Sir," Kübler protested, acting very astonished that his fine specimen found no mercy before Wieser's eye.

"Oh so you call that clean do you, you pillock?" Wieser held the specimen under Kübler's nose.

"It couldn't be any cleaner Sir, Oberjäger, Sir!"

"You think so? We'll see about that, move Kübler, back down to the San again. In half an hour you'll show me your washing once more, but clean if you please."

"It's almost dark already Sir, I won't be able to see anymore."

"That's your problem you smelly pig, move, march and don't bring such a filthy rag to my eyes again!"

What could he do Kübler took his wet clothes under his arm and raced back down to the San again.

Kübler had been right enough with his objection, by the time he got to the river he already couldn't make out the other side.

In an attempt to not attract attention a second time, good Kübler splashed in the water quite thoroughly, scrubbed and soaked and furiously slapped his uniform into the water again and again. By no means was the Russian on the other side of the river hard of hearing, he certainly heard the splashing in the water, but couldn't recognise the cause of it. He suspected someone crossing the border illegally and fired a few shots in the direction from which the suspicious noise was heard.

As the first bullets struck the water beside Kübler his zeal came to an abrupt end. He scarpered away as quickly as his legs could carry him and came back to our company again completely out of breath.

In the meantime we had queued up in front of the field kitchen as Kübler reported to Wieser again.

"Sir, Oberjäger, Sir," he wheezed.. "I... I came under fire.... "
"You what?"
"I came under fire.... under fire from the Russians.... ."
"You've surely shat yourself have you?"
"No Sir, Oberjäger, Sir, but I won't go down to the San anymore, I'm not going to get shot down over a few spots of dirt.."
"Ach man..." Wieser made a dismissive hand movement, .. "just get out of my face you prat... but tomorrow evening you will report to me with an absolutely spotless uniform, no matter how you do it... understood?"
"Yes Sir, understood, Oberjäger Sir, report tomorrow evening with a spotless uniform."

Kübler left with his dripping wet uniform while we laughed at him.... he gave us something to talk about for the whole evening.

There was often constant border crossing over the San during the night. While we had instructions to not intervene the Russian was not as tolerant. Then shots would whip through the night every so often and the border crossers in the river would turn back around if they weren't brave folks. But still many people sneaked through the thin cordon.

We spent some relatively peaceful weeks in Przemyśl. The combat training, without anything particularly stressful being demanded of us, went on on a small scale, even drill practice wasn't to be forgotten altogether... but the main emphasis was on duty indoors.

We slowly settled in. In the meantime each of us had looked around for a washwoman amongst the civilian population and we had already gotten used to the idea that we would be spending the winter in Poland. Everything remained peaceful in the West, they didn't seem to need us.

The period of good weather had unfortunately come to an end however and it began to rain, for days. Now all of a sudden we didn't find things to be so nice in Przemyśl. In the meantime we had concerned ourselves to some extent with becoming treated as part of the family, we particularly desired houses in which girls of a suitable age also belonged to the family.
After all we had cigarettes, chocolate and even schnapps, and these delicacies opened doors for us, but other than that there was very little to do. And now the rain had come, the roads got all muddy, it grew uncomfortable by the San.
In these circumstances we were happy when signs of a new change in location grew from day to day.

On the 20th of October, a day on which it poured incessantly from every floodgate in the sky, we marched north from Przemyśl in order to be loaded up in a train station in Radymo. We marched the many kilometers to the train station in constant rain. The roads were in an appalling condition. Pothole after pothole filled up to the rim with water, the march wasn't exactly enjoyable.

The train station In Radymo was just as bleak as the whole day. Bombed facilities, destroyed trains, all of it everything other than confidence inspiring. The loading on, often practiced, nevertheless proceeded quickly and smoothly. The train had German staff, which calmed us and gave us hope of getting to our destination without any great incidents.
We had no idea where the journey was going to, we could only rely on toilet gossip and that was of course promising a journey homeward.

Grabner approached the train driver, he wanted to know where we were headed, but the train driver professed to have no idea himself where we were going and we had to believe him.

"Finally we're going home," said Zopf as we made ourselves comfortable in the straw floored freight car in preparation for our departure.
"I wish I had your optimism," retorted Itter.
"Well if you want my opinion," I said, "in two days time we'll know for sure and won't need to wreck our heads about it anymore."
"Very funny," Mehrl tapped his forehead to show what he thinks of my objection, "we'd have never figured that out without you Otto you smart aleck."
But I retorted to him, "Am I right or am I not? You go on with each other all day back and forth with this gossip, and all of it always turns out totally different in the end."
"What would the military be without toilet gossip?" Schweiger pointed out, "these rumours are what make it what it is."
"Yeah well," I say, "you can go believe in a hundred different rumours and be disappointed a hundred times."

"Even if we are Otto," Schweiger has found his place to sleep for the journey and is making himself as comfortable as he can in the straw, "without any rumours at all it would be extremely boring, you would have nothing in your head to think on, no, no I continue to be in favour of our toilet gossip."

"Well fine," I conceded, "then we can keep going with these rumours you love so much even if they are so silly."

"You can't stop them anyway, they grow like wheat in the fields," said Zopf, "at certain times they're just in the air, a soldier needs rumours to live like he does air."

"What a beautiful, auspicious slogan," said Mehrl

"I also find them to be, along with my dinner, the nicest part of this dreary army business."

Since all the air was full of moistness and the rain was drumming on the roof incessantly, we didn't waste any more looks on the dismal landscape when, in the late afternoon, we left Radymo's destroyed train station.

We had gotten our evening meal before leaving, it was left over to us to either polish it off all at once or wait until the evening.

We closed the sliding doors, thus locking out the cold draught and thought to have a peaceful night.

What with the advanced time of year it would be a long night after all and we would be best to spend it sleeping.

We didn't have a lounge car, we rumbled along good and proper and the joints in the track carried up through to the floor of the carriage with full force.

And so we rumbled on through the night, tumbling back and forth on our straw beds, the rays of light from the street lamps shining through the gaps in the carriage doors, lighting us up and dipping us into darkness again. We stopped several times, heard the voices and running of the train staff, the carriage was shoved and shaken.

"We are in Kraków," Zopf called all of a sudden, we lifted our heads sleepily, moist cold air piercing through the open carriage door.
"We've been pushed aside," Zopf continued.
"Close the door God damn it," someone cursed from some corner, "what do we care about Kraków? We're trying to sleep you twit," came the voice from the darkness.
"And I need to piss, is that OK with you?" Zopf answered and forcefully slammed the door shut.

Later we reached Ostrava.

"The quickest route down from here is towards Vienna," said Schweiger, he stood with a few comrades at the open door of the freight car.
"For fuck's sake just close the door you idiots it's cold!" someone swore again.
"Don't be such a pussy," shouted Schweiger, "you waste half your life sleeping."

After some time the train clattered into movement across numerous joints in the track again, the strips of light from the railway lighting grew rarer.. soon they stopped altogether.
And still it rained, we heard it when the train was standing still.
We went through Olomouc, and so the journey went ever further westward.

"From Olomouc we could still go down through Bohemia straight into Upper Austria," Zopf held doggedly tight to the idea that we were going back home.
"It's called the 'Upper Danube' now you moron," came a voice from the background.

"Whatever then 'Upper Danube,' the main thing is we'll end up in Salzburg."

"I don't believe that anymore.." I say, "I reckon we're travelling across through Germany to the West."

"Ach nonsense, you'll see, we'll soon turn southward."

"It would be great if you were right, but I lack faith."

"Otto, we'll be in Salzburg tomorrow!"

"Don't start spouting rubbish now."

"Would you just shut your traps, do you have to blather for the whole night?" Itter lifted his head out of the straw sullenly, we couldn't see it in the dark, but no doubt he was giving us a venomous look.

Since they were constantly whining, we pulled our covers over our heads again and tried to sleep as well.

We really didn't have a luxurious carriage, no comfortable mattress but still we dozed through the heavy rumbles.. bumps.. and shakes time and again, if only for a few minutes.

We were woken again and again, a few of our comrades seemed to have a bloody weak bladder, in ever shorter intervals the doors were pulled open a bit and closed again with a hideous screeching, and each time an uncomfortable, cold, damp draught crossed over our heads.

We stopped again in the pitch dark night.. no light far and wide.... no train station to be seen... only the regular sound that was made by the steam constantly escaping from the tanks of the locomotive.

"I can't make out where we are," said someone who was doing his business, it was already well past midnight.

Then the train jerked forward again... only to stop again after a few hundred meters, blowing steam. Suddenly there was a mighty jolt.. it seemed we were swapping trains.

We took it all while somewhere between waking and sleeping. We got underway again.. travelling through Bohemia half awake half asleep, towards new unknown destinations.

It dawned, the night that had lasted an eternity was over and we stopped at a train station in the dawning light of a new day. I stood dozily with the others at the carriage door, looked into the day, no longer so bleak, and couldn't believe my eyes when I read the name on the sign at the train station:
"Furth im Walde" stood there in large letters.
I remembered back to the summer of 1934, a good five years ago, when I had first crossed the border into Germany here, back then in the company of Malzer.

Five years, a long time when you had had to spend it involuntarily in a uniform and squeezed into a system of command which wasn't exactly much loved. Five years of relinquishing civilian freedom, five years without a prospect of continuing the profession you'd learned.

And now there was the war and I couldn't foresee when it would release me from its bondage.

Now our train stood on German soil and soon it had to decide if it still wanted to take the road southward.

Germany greeted us with an unexpected change of weather. As the last morning mists gave way, the sun rose blood red in the East. After the journey through the night we had also left the inhospitable day long rain behind us. And with the sun in league with it the world seemed a lot more friendly all of a sudden and the general mood was raised.

We had a longer stop. The horse attendants were allowed to leave the train, they stood lined up in front of the large water pump and filled the drinking buckets for the horses.

Both of our field kitchens stood lashed up to an open freight carriage. The smoke curled up promisingly from out of their chimney pipes.

Then we were allowed to leave the train too, soon we stood in a long line to get our breakfast. The cooks stood on the carriage, their thick coats on, their collars turned up, for sure they had already spent some uncomfortable hours on the draughty platform in order to provide us with a punctual warm breakfast.

"Well Zopf," Schweiger said as we went to get breakfast together, "we're not going to Salzburg, no doubt that's clear now at last?" "Crap, God damn it," replied Zopf, "but a small possibility is still there, if we turn southwards now, Otto says we would then go straight to Munich and from Munich to Salzburg is a stone's throw."
"Zopf," Schweiger tapped his head, "you're a bloody lunatic, just give it up. I get it for sure, you just want to go chasing skirt again, but you'll be waiting for that for a long time yet."
"Maybe there'll be a holiday soon, who knows," Zopf replied.
"By the time you're allowed to go on holiday," Itter interjected, "you won't be able to chase any more skirt, they'll all have been poached already and there'll be none left for you."
"What rubbish you speak," Zopf could only shake his head hearing so much ignorance about what things were like in his area.

Grabner stood with his camera in front of our carriage, we all sat together in the doorway, letting our feet dangle down, slurping our coffee with great pleasure and setting about our butter, bread and jam.

"Attention!" Itter shouted, "eyes open, close your mouths, the company photographer is taking a close-up!"

"You arseholes, you've broken the camera!" Grabner called laughing and snapped his Voigtländer-Bessa shut.

As the train carried us further into German territory we soon realised that our hopes of Salzburg, of a holiday back home, were over once and for all. We travelled steadily west. We travelled through Franconia towards Nuremberg.

All of the toilet gossip we had concocted in Poland, beautiful as it was, had gone up in smoke once and for all.

The campaign in Poland was behind us, the heavy, hissing locomotive carried us toward new adventures.

–   .   –

As we were leaving the train station in Furth im Walde, it became clear that we definitely weren't going south, but there was little time to have any gloomy thoughts about it.

The sun was shining and for all our comrades who hadn't seen Germany yet, the rest of the journey became an exciting experience.
The many neat little towns and archaic cities were greeted with the greatest wonder. Some of the Gebirgsjäger from the hidden mountain valleys of Tyrol, Salzburg and Kärnten couldn't see enough of the majestic castles, time-honoured romantic half-timbered houses, and large industrial plants with their mighty smoking chimneys.

We travelled through Franconia, along the Main, arrived at the Rhine with its constant shipping traffic. From the wine-covered hills on either side of the river the many legendary old castles hailed down to us. And the men from the mountains were singing: "Why is it so beautiful by the Rhine...," had grown cheerful and were already over the train not travelling back home.

We went sharply westward from Coblenz, up the Moselle valley. Finally in Cochem the journey came to an end. We were uncarted here.

We would have easily found some pleasant lodging for ourselves in Cochem, but of course considering all of the oat-munchers we had clip-clopping along behind us, such a neat little city was taboo. Who would have suited there better other than the divisional staff, the generals, staff-officer veterinarians, paymasters and whatever other puffed up bureaucrats made up the division?

So then our unloading had barely finished before the order to march onward was given to the division as well.

And so we marched out of the little town again, onwards up the Moselle valley as far as Mesenich. And there where the manure heaps lay in front of the houses, where it stank of cow shit and sewage, we were allowed to stop. That's the way it was and nothing about that changed for the course of the whole war.

But the place wasn't so bad in the daylight either. It was still the time of the grape harvest. A bustling activity filled the whole town. It smelled of wine mash everywhere, in all of the houses they pressed and squeezed. And so for the next weeks we were to settle in here. Everyone got a billeting slip. I took up a tiny room in a really old, crooked half-timbered house along with Mehrl and Odental. The room was on the top floor, a really wobbly, steep wooden stairway led up to it.

Odental turned up in our accommodation last, late and drunk as a ferret. He must have gotten caught up in a wine bar on the way back. He made a dreadful racket, fell down the stairs several times over, until in the end Mehrl dragged him to the forecourt and dunked his head in the cold well water. Odental was an unpleasant friend when he had drank one too many, he was still throwing himself around, but against Mehrl the hulk he was powerless. We were embarrassed in front of our hosts having just moved in but what could we do?

We had our drill square directly on the Mosel, between the shore and a street with walnut trees on either side. As we stood lined up the next day for our orders to be issued, Hauptmann Hofbauer gave an address.

"Men!" he said, "we are here on the Mosel in one of Germany's largest wine producing regions. The Romans once marched here through this valley, ruling the area for almost four hundred years, you will still come across their traces all over the place. The grape harvest is in full swing here. Many of the village's men have been drafted into the army and we are lacking workforce to gather in this precious harvest. At the order of the division we have stopped here to help with the harvest as best we can. I hope that those who are to be chosen for this will also carry out their duty and knuckle down to it properly. The vintners will be able to make their choice personally after every morning drill. To work then people, tallyho!"

"Tallyho!" the company roared back, moved to the best spirits by this speech.

The Hauptmann disappeared and left the rest of the affair to the Sarge in Chief.

The vintners were already standing on the road and were waiting for a signal before seeking out the workers who they thought would be most suitable. Since they didn't know our work ethics their choice leaned towards the muscle men who were present in the false assumption that the strongest people must also be the most hard working.

It was a real feat, putting up a whole company in such a little hovel. The locals really had to huddle up together and surely weren't always best pleased about this, but if they were feeling unfriendly towards us they didn't let it show. After all their sons, who would be happy to get a roof over their heads, were in the field as well. All of the living rooms in the houses were occupied by us. We lived here on the floor in numbers which depended on the size of the room and were happy just to have a warm, dry place to sleep. Along with the crew they also had to accommodate well over a hundred horses. The field kitchen mostly found shelter in a threshing floor, but the cooks often had to content themselves with an enclosed courtyard.

Where possible the orderly room was hosted in the school, Germany's offspring stayed at home then, or had to huddle up together. The Hauptmann lived with the vicar, mayor or teacher and the Sarge and the Leutnant were granted better quarters when available.

"Poschacher," Armsdorfer said to me on the second day, "in the coming days you will take care of the condition of the gas masks. Take an inventory and inspect every mask to make sure it's ready for use, you are exempted from field service for a limited period of time."

"Yes Sir, Herr Feldwebel, Sir," I answered, "will I collect all the gas masks to do this?"

"And how else would you get the job done you smart aleck? But speed it up a little, else you'll soon lose the job, understood?"

"Hurry up a little Sir, Yes Herr Feldwebel, Sir."

"And do it all properly, or you're in trouble."

I went to Wieser, informed the squad leader of my task and made myself at work. But by no means was I intending to carry out the matter in a hurry now. I was counting on even Armsdorfer not being able to precisely judge the amount of time needed.

"You've gotten a cushy job again there Otto," said Zopf, "if you're smart, you can cling onto it for weeks."

It was also a time when the company was swamped with regulations and new instructions. The office lackey's pencils were smoking, the typewriters clattering incessantly for the whole day under Hartmann's somewhat brutal keystrokes, the head of the company himself was up to his eyes in organisational matters.

I was in close contact with the orderly room during this time. My activity supplied me with unhindered entry and I was fresh on the traces of all incoming reports and rumours.

For the majority of my comrades the vineyard operation continued. The farmers came every morning and picked out their flock. Some picked the same as before, others tried out someone new, and so had drawn a blank the day before.

"This is like a slave market here," said Grabner, "all that's missing is us having to open our mouths and show our teeth."
"Slave market that's right," I answered, "hopefully the vintners are happy with their purchases!"
"So long as they don't let our comrades into the wine bar, and keep them away from under the barmaid's aprons, things will work out," said Tiefenthaler, who we also called "Goldtooth" because of his conspicuous gold filling.

On one of the first Sundays, having been paid by Oberjäger Walzl the day before, we went in small groups to Cochem to once more finally find a sensible use for the money we'd gotten.

"We'll piss the lot up against a wall, down to the last mark."

Philips said it in a tone of utter conviction.

The pubs in Cochem were already overfilled with all of the departmental staff and the Gebirgsjäger from the surrounding towns. That day Cochem belonged to the G.D.
The innkeepers had plenty of wine. Sometimes we sure had the suspicion that they kept the sourest kind especially for us.
Rhineland songs were chanted incessantly as we grew merrier with wine, were there Mosel songs too? We didn't know, ... but...
"Why is it so beautiful by the Rhine".... we all knew that one.
This Sunday, many of us were having our first hefty drinking

session after a long time. Who knew when we would get the opportunity again? And so we needed to use every hour we had and even if we only had a little money, it sat loose in our pockets and we were sure to get paid again. What did we need to save for anyway? We were living for the moment, who knew what the next day would bring anyway?

An hour before last post some good Gebirgsjäger were staggering in a wavy line along the road back to Mesenich, the village had long lay in deepest slumber, no lanterns lit the narrow alleys, no doubt the orders for black-out had already come through even though there was never an enemy plane in the sky.

At the village entrance on the bank of the Mosel Herzog, one of our cooks, was lying on a bench totally pissed. He was snoring for all his worth, no amount of shaking could wake him up.

"Well is he hammered or what?" said Philips, "we can't leave him lying here all night."
"Such a drunken pig," Gerl grabbed the cook under the arms and dragged him backwards across the bumpy cobblestones.
"Well? Do none of you pissheads want to give a hand?"
"We're not bloody Samaritans," said Mehrl, "he can sleep off his hangover wherever he wants."
"Think of our breakfast!" shouted Grabner, "You know what? We'll chuck him on the next dung heap we come across, then he'll be warmed up nicely from underneath and won't catch a cold."
"Are you mad?" called Gerl, "tomorrow he'll stink more than any of us can handle!"
"Yeah, so?" Grabner liked his idea, "by God's name let him stink."
"Well on you go, there's a dungheap there, off with him!" Mehrl, a man of action, grabbed Herzog's legs too and between the two

of them they heaved him onto his fragrant bedstead.

"He needs something to cover him," said Mehrl, "we don't want the top of him getting cold either."

"There's a pitch fork by the barn wall there, throw a layer on his belly too, then he'll have a warm, aromatic blanket," Grabner's suggestion was greeted with glee all round. Mehrl immediately set to work while we looked on excitedly. We nearly wet ourselves with laughter as we watched. But I still thought of next morning and pointed out: "Let's hope breakfast won't stink of cow shit."

"Good heavens," said Grabner, "we'll have our breakfast long behind us by the time this pisshead is over his hangover."

"Hopefully," Mehrl considered, "the farmer won't go tipping a whole manure heap on his front when he's working early in the morning, covering up his face and he kills us!"

"Ach nonsense," Philips answered, "he has eyes in his head, just let our comrade have his nice little nap."

"But you keep your mouths shut," Mehrl ordered us, "if Herzog finds out who played this trick on him, then for as long as he's in the kitchen we'll be guaranteed the smallest portions, our seconds will stop altogether."

That was certainly a consideration which couldn't be denied. It was clear, we couldn't say a word.

At breakfast the next morning Herzog was nowhere to be seen. When we asked after him very innocently, the head of the kitchen Toni Huber put on his well-known canny face, laughed very wickedly, but didn't say anything further. In the next days Herzog scrutinized everyone's face over and over, but our expressions were totally innocent.

Unfortunately our stay in Mesenich wasn't for long either. We had barely gotten comfy in our quarters before we had to leave again.

We stood along the Mosel one evening ready to march off.

"Gebirgsjäger let's move!" they called once again. Men and the good horses set off towards Cochem.

We crossed over the river there and took the way a little north of the city up to the hills in front of the Eifel. With that we left the delightful Mosel valley and the friendly wine growing crowd too.

In the pitch dark night we marched towards our new destination, accompanied constantly by our soldier songs, which we untiringly blared out into the night hour after hour. From the "Edelweiß" song... "Erika".. we went through our whole repertoire up to the old Landsknecht songs.

We had a few Rhinelanders in our company who always distinguished themselves in particular when they were singing. I'm thinking here particularly of Karl Huhn from Remscheid, he was part of our mortar squad and he'd let his voice ring out in particular.

We climbed the steep hills coming out of the Mosel valley and went through a series of really miserable looking farm villages on a broad plateau. The wind was blowing around our ears, the climate up here was certainly much less friendly than it was in the wind-protected, friendly Moselle valley.

We temporarily took up camp for a few days in Hambuch and Gamlen, two farming hovels that you can quickly forget. We only finally got accommodation in Mertloch, south of Mayen.

In the end we were to stay in Mertloch for a long time. We spent the winter months there until the beginning of March the next year.

They'd sought out a cold and really windy place for us over winter. The town didn't offer us any leisure activities at all, if you wanted them you had to deal with a long march on foot.

In the meantime my job inspecting the gas masks came to an end as well and I had to take part in our group's combat training again.

We chased across the harvested fields like rabbits, burrowed into the ground like moles and heaved the heavy parts of the mortar from one firing position to the other. And a really horrible wind blew across the unprotected hills. The coming winter was announcing itself. And Wieser was tireless in his enthusiasm, he drilled us as if the destiny of the entire German Wehrmacht rested on our squad alone. He kept his head shaved bald despite the slowly approaching winter. Itter wasn't completely wrong when he often said: "The man looks like a Russian!" Itter liked Wieser by no means, this dislike had already been noticeable during the campaign in Poland and was thoroughly mutual.

But Mertloch had its advantages too. If you had friends or relatives close by you could get a holiday weekend from Saturday midday until the call to get up on Monday.
That was a fine thing which I and our Rhinelanders made extensive use of.

And so I took the very first opportunity for a trip to Hagen. Since Mertloch didn't have a train station, we had to march as far as past Polch each time in order to be able to travel. But what did that matter? You put up with it for the opportunity to go see the relatives for the weekend.

With the precious holiday pass in my pocket, I went off with Huhn, Philips and Odental. From Polch we went to Coblenz with a slow train, but from there with the express train onward through the Ruhr area. Mimi was more than a little surprised when I turned up unexpectedly for the first time to spend a weekend in Hagen. The surprise was entire as I had deliberately not given notice beforehand. We hadn't seen each other since the early summer and the joy at seeing each other again was understandable. Due to the war Hagen didn't have much to offer in the form of entertainments either of course, but that's not what it was about. It was enough for us to go for the odd visit to the cinema, most of the time we spent comfortably at home.

We spoke of getting engaged for the first time in those days. We had known each other long enough now that these considerations couldn't be ignored. And so we agreed, as long as I could take the holidays, to officially celebrate getting engaged before Christmas.

In the endeavour to make as much use of the hours in Hagen as possible, I stayed there until Sunday evening, and only left for Koblenz as late as possible and got there before midnight. At this time of course there wasn't a connection to Mayen anymore and I had to do the rest of the night in the waiting room. I went to Polch with the first early train. Of course the Rhinelanders weren't any different and so in a small group we ran for all our worth to Mertloch. We often only arrived once the company was already standing on the village road for morning roll-call. We smuggled ourselves as inconspicuously as possible onto the tail end of the company with which we were mostly successful. As disagreeable as Wieser could otherwise be in his position, to this matter he turned a blind eye.

There was a change in the company in the middle of November. Hauptmann Hofbauer was transferred to division's officer reserve, in his place came Hauptmann Röhr as the new head of the division. Hofbauer later fell on the Eastern Front.

Hauptmann Röhr became a real father to the company. In him every soldier found an understanding superior to whom he could come with every matter of concern, even those of a private nature.
In the middle of November I submitted a holiday application in the silent hope of receiving an approval soon.

In the meantime the exercises in the field were constantly intensified, exercises in ever larger formations took place. The 3rd G.D. under General Dietl also took place alongside ours in the area around the Eifel. During an exercise as a whole corps our division was inspected by General Beyer of the XVIIIth army corps, as well as Generaloberst List, the commander in chief of the 14th army which we were also part of.

My holiday application was approved surprisingly quickly and on the 29th November I travelled to Hagen for a few days where the official engagement took place and afterwards to Marienfeld in Ostfriesland with Mimi to see my mother and stepfather Malzer.
We spent the rest of our holidays in total seclusion in Marienfeld, a small, isolated town. Because of the purely rural countryside around us there was even better and more plentiful food than in the city.

On the 9th of December I went back to my division in the Eifel. Winter had fully arrived here in the meantime. It had become bitterly cold and the ground frozen hard as stone. But the field exercises were carried on without disruption.

In those days, characterised by a particularly hard frost, I was posted with several comrades to a special mortar class in Münstermaifeld. The course tutor was Hauptmann Hofbauer our former head of company.

I shared my quarters together with Karl Huhn in the attic room of an elderly widow. The one small window barely afforded any light, during the day it was adorned with the most enduring frost patterns, patterns that you couldn't have painted any prettier. The beds were damp and clammy, every morning there was a thick sheet of ice over the water in the metal washbowls. The daily exercises in the countryside became a very frosty affair. The training was ordered into two main parts: practical exercises in the field including shooting exercises and theory lessons.

Every evening I swotted the lessons for the next class with Karl in the cold room. Once we thought we had learned enough, we went into our moist, clammy beds and saw to getting our feet warm.

By then our thoughts were already with the end of the course and the possibility of getting a weekend's holiday again.

At the end of the training each participant was accompanied by a company evaluation, whose contents we alas never learned of. It was one of the many secrets that I never got to know about.

Once we were back in Mertloch we went through some hard, unabated training. Every day we headed out into the field, which was now covered deep with snow, stood and froze, ran and sweated completely at the whim and fancy of our superiors.

Christmas was around the corner. Our first wartime Christmas, would it perhaps be the only one as well? At most we hoped so.

Since we didn't find room in Mertloch to accommodate the whole company for a Christmas celebration, we held it in a hall in Polch. I spent many days putting a comic newspaper together, this occupation spared me again from some of the training in the cold countryside. Ernst Scharf strongly supported me in my work and the orderly room gave me the opportunity to make duplicates of my intellectual outpourings so that every comrade could get a copy.

On Christmas Eve, the air was bitingly cold and the snow crunching beneath our mountain boots, we marched to Polch. Our drinking canteens were filled with Glühwein and two horses carried the rest of our provisions that we'd prepared for the evening in carrier baskets. The party went off real cheerfully as the Glühwein kept us proper warm.

Every winter, no matter how harsh, will come to an end, why should it be any different up here in the Voreifel? The first mild winds stroked across the hills, slowly the ground, frozen hard as stone, began to thaw, it took the last of the rest of the snow with it, soon you couldn't fail to notice it anymore, the winter was preparing to leave. Some sleet still came down on us, but still the sun was slowly taking the upper hand. The thawed ground dried up and the first green slowly came out. For sure, down there in the Rheingau the spring had already arrived, the pussy willows were already blooming there and the little almond trees were glowing pink, we saw it as we looked out of the train window on one of our trips home over the weekend.

One day during this spring... in the course of a field exercise, we came to the edge of a forest far from Mertloch that we'd not known of until then... we pushed deeper into the forest... the still leafless beech trees giving us a lot of visibility... the trunks receded somewhat.... and there she was... mysterious and incomprehensible like from a thousand and one nights ... with numerous towers suddenly rising in front of us like out of a fairy tale... the castle ELTZ.... On a raised seat in a section of the valley thickly hemmed in by forest... white water rushing around her the Eltz... the most beautiful and what with her location the most mysterious castle I had ever seen. Fascinating how suddenly her walls presented themselves to our startled eyes... a fairytale castle for sure... we stood and couldn't look away... an experience for the eyes of every man. We would have only too gladly looked behind those mysterious walls, but the exercise continued, soon she disappeared from view again. Nevertheless this wish of mine would yet be fulfilled, many years after the war had ended.

New rumours came with the approaching spring, unrest came into the divisions. You couldn't say for sure what had changed, but you felt it, something was going on, as we used to say.
Our suspicions didn't disappoint us, when March arrived we had to leave our cosy winter quarters, the troop got moving again.
Lots of unnecessary ballast had built up over the long winter, we couldn't sort it all out from one hour to the next.
We had to leave things we didn't need behind. Everything that didn't belong in our rucksack was given away or sent home. We didn't have things as good as the cooks or the support people after all, they packed all sorts of unnecessary rubbish on the train, they had their secure hiding places that barely any of the superiors knew about.

Some of us had to say goodbye to a girl, or of hosts that we'd taken to heart.

On an early, gloomy morning we left Mertloch, the town that had warmed us over so many cold winter nights.
We went across wide plateaus in a long, arduous march northward.
Uphill.. downhill.. we went singing across country roads towards our destination. After hours our first stop, we put our backpacks down exhausted, but apparently we were still a long way from our destination.

A refreshment from the field kitchen, we started up again.
We put one foot in front of the other, the path seemed endless....
our singing had long grown silent.. our rucksacks weighed
heavily on our shoulders and chafed at our still sensitive skin.
Finally, towards the end of the day, in long winding turns we
climbed down the hills into a sheltered valley.
Here too there were vineyards, the air seemed to be unexpectedly
mild and fragrant, we went down into the Ahr valley. Here
between the protective vineyards, which blocked the way of the
rough Eifel air, the spring had long arrived.

We took up accommodation in the small town of Lantershofen,
not far from Neuenahr.
We settled in as well as we could in the few old houses. Here too
there were kind, friendly hosts, they had long obeyed the
inevitable without grumbling, they ceded their rooms to us
wordlessly.

New rumours made the rounds about an imminent attack to the
west. We didn't really want to believe it, we still hoped that the
war would keep slowly dying down. We carried on getting short
holidays over the weekend, would that happen after an imminent
deployment? Certainly not. The way to Hagen had gotten a bit
shorter now and I kept using every opportunity to go there.

Reinforcements from home arrived again, even in Mertloch
comrades from Tyrol and Salzburg had partly closed the gaps
which arose from losses through sickness and postings
elsewhere. Now we were fully fit for action again.

Across the Ahr valley, there where the vineyards stopped, our
exercise field began. Day after day our combat training was
enhanced further. In the meantime we had mastered our hand

movements for our weapons in our sleep, but it never seemed to be enough for our superiors.

I had requested a short holiday again. When many of us appeared in the orderly room to get our sought after holiday passes Goldtooth just said: "I'm sorry gentlemen, the division decreed a ban on leave a few hours ago, the passes which were already approved can't be handed out to you anymore," we were in a pickle then. A ban on leave could only mean being imminently deployed.

A few days later, General Dietl's 3rd G.D. beside us was withdrawn. What did it all mean? The most absurd rumours went around. Were we to be transferred to mountain regions in the East again for instance? But why only just the 3rd G.D, or were we going to follow? They said the 3rd had gone to Döberitz, Döberitz where was that we asked?... It's a big military training area near Berlin they told us. What was Dietl doing with his men there? Questions after questions that nobody could answer or nobody wanted to answer.

Days went by, we expected to be called off any hour, still nothing happened to us, we continued to stay in our quarters, we kept practicing for deployment in the Ardennes.

In our company they paid particular attention to the health of the horses and how prepared they were for being deployed.
The staff vet turned up from time to time to satisfy himself of the animals' condition with his own eyes.
When such an inspection was announced, which mostly took place a few days beforehand, then the support got really busy.
Horse fodderer Feldwebel Lessov and his assistant Obergefreiter Gödde were at their best then.
The farriers had their hands full, all the straps and buckles had to be checked, the damages repaired by company saddler Lebacher,

the small and large, light and heavy steeds had to be dressed up and brushed up spick and span.

When the time for the check up arrived, the horse attendants had to march past the vet with their charges and report with their name and rank as well as the name of their horses.

Lessov stood alongside the staff vet and woe to the poor horse handler if the vet had anything to find fault with in the animal that was taken past him.

Max Rheinisch, who had only arrived in the company a few days ago as a reinforcement, had a grey haired animal named "Berta" as his charge. Rheinisch and his good "Berta" were both members of the signals platoon.
Back then in his first days, good Max wasn't yet in command of the good connections of his later years, he was still missing braids and medals too, things which improved the self confidence of every soldier. Max was a newly arrived, little Gefreiter and the oral talent which later quickly catapulted him upwards hadn't been able to develop yet up to that point, otherwise Berta's personal presentation would have surely been spared him.

When it was Rheinisch's turn to bring forth the mule which had been entrusted to him, he set into a trot with the horse like all the other handlers. Reluctantly, her shaggy head hanging down like a sulking child, Berta followed the caretaker assigned to her. Having arrived at the staff vet, Max reported as instructed:

"Gefreiter Rheinisch with pack horse Berta."

Either Rheinisch had handled Berta poorly beforehand, or the horse was so delicate and couldn't cope with the excitement of the visit, whatever it was, good Berta suddenly collapsed to the ground, like a wet sack, in front of Lessov's horrified eyes, Max's dumb face and the shocked staff vet.

Rheinisch tried fruitlessly, yanking on the bridle, to bring his fallen Berta onto her feet again. The beast stretched her legs into the air and made no efforts to stand up again.

"You bloody prat! What have you done to your horse?" Lessov screamed at the flabbergasted Rheinisch.

Max, an organ builder by profession, knew as much about horses as a butcher does about baking bread and despite his otherwise sharp wit had no plausible answer to give, he just stood next to Berta helplessly and cursed the beast to hell.

Then the vet took the matter in hand and after a short examination his verdict was certain:

"It's a clear-cut case, the horse has heavy bloating."

The vet had barely said these words before good Berta confirmed it with a hefty horsefart into the open air.
But Lessov screamed at the flabbergasted Rheinisch:

"And you didn't notice that you pillock?" with his arms folded behind his back Lessov went flying for poor Max.

"You damned muppet, get out of my sight, Gödde you take care of the horse, and you, you fruit, you report to me in the morning understood?"
"Yes Sir, Feldwebel, Sir, report in the morning."

From that hour onward Rheinisch was no longer considered to be fit to care for the horses and he was banned from the stable.

Although as I've already mentioned we had well over a hundred horses in the company, I barely came into contact with them aside from the occasional time when I was loading gear onto them. If it did happen, then it wasn't for the best as the following story will show.

We were north of Lantershofen on large, open, lightly rolling countryside, busy scouting and setting up firing positions for our mortars. To the side of us there was a large orchard, particular trees had been assigned to us as targets.

Then Armsdorfer turned up on the scene on horseback and rode directly towards our group. He had a middle to large dun as his steed, a beast known for being stubborn.

Armsdorfer climbed off his horse, came to me and said:

"Poschacher, go, take my horse. Ride over to the artillery platoon and ask Leutnant Neuschler to come see Hauptmann Röhr."
"Yes Sir, Leutnant Neuschler to come see Hauptmann Röhr," I repeated the order, but looked at the platoon leader's horse very indecisively.
"Go man," said Armsdorfer, "you're not afraid of the horse are you?"

I wasn't really afraid of the horse itself, but I didn't think that my riding ability was very good and the platoon leader's horse was a "damned nag" as its caretaker had many times assured me.
But what could I do? If I didn't want to make myself a laughing stock, I had to get on the horse whether I liked it or not.
So I took the reins in hand and swung myself into the saddle, which went better than I had dared to hope.

But the beast of a horse noticed my inexperience immediately, I had barely sat in the saddle before it had raced off towards the orchard with me in tow.

Armsdorfer shouted some instructions after me but I couldn't make them out anymore. The horse was pig-headed and a firebrand at the same time, it had absolutely no intention of going where I wanted it to. It reacted neither to me squeezing it desperately with my thighs, nor to my trying to whip it with the reins.

It pulled its head up, raised its tail and raced straight towards the fruit trees which were anything but high.

It went through under the trees with vehemence, it was passable for the horse, but for me the branches hung too low.

The first branches knocked the beret from my head, but the next ones boxed me hard around my ears, sharp twigs hit my nose. And the damned horse raced onward, it didn't give a hoot about the rider on its back.

"Damned nag!" I shouted and pulled on the reins, I certainly wasn't giving off much of an impression as a rider at that moment but I was just happy to not go flying out of the saddle.

Across from us a ditch appeared, now I'm done for I thought and already I was flying in an arc over the horse's head to the other side of the ditch. The horse had suddenly braced its front legs into the soft soil and had stopped. I unfortunately had still found myself in a forward momentum that had carried me swiftly through the air.

Once I'd shaken off the first of my stupor I was looking out for the crazy quadruped, but I just saw its massive backside with its waving tail disappearing back to where it came from.

"You dirty swine, damn it," I swore. I got on my feet again, didn't seem to have anything broken.

Cursing, I made my way on foot to the artillery platoon which had taken up position close to a small wood. Once I had made my report mountlessly, I was able to go back to my group. Even from far away I thought I could see my comrades smirking gleefully.

And they stood there bowled over with laughter, and Wieser stood there too with Armsdorfer next to him and they were grinning from ear to ear as well, and the damned mule stood next to Armsdorfer as if nothing had happened, and may God strike me down if I'm wrong, even the beast was grinning across its long horsey face.

"Well Poschacher," said Armsdorfer, "you don't exactly make that grand a jockey."

"Well it's not that grand of a horse," I replied angrily.

"The horse can't help that," the platoon leader said, "your rotten posture does it, not even a goat would put up with that."

"I'm not trained as a rider either," I answered.

"That's fortunate for the horses," with this gloating observation Armsdorfer swung himself into his saddle and sped across the countryside to another squad. If he'd have heard what I muttered after him he would have no doubt fallen off his horse on the spot.

On the 10th of April, just as we were getting our princely breakfast from Toni's hands, Tiefenthaler came running out of the orderly room.

"Breaking news!" he was calling from far away: "Gebirgsjäger have landed in Norway, General Dietl has landed in Narvik."

We didn't want to believe it, we considered the words of our "Goldtooth" to be the newest toilet gossip.

"Idiots," he said, indignant at our doubt, "just listen to the news."

But this time he didn't lie, we were all in a tizz. Our comrades from the 3rd GD in Narvik? That sounded completely inconceivable. For the next days there was only one subject for us and it was called "Norway."

This land, it promised adventure, new experiences, maps were opened... a real country for us Gebirgsjäger we knowledgeably established.

But the 2nd GD continued to stay in the West, Gebirgsjäger were needed here too, in the mountains, in the Ardennes. We looked at the maps closely...but in disappointment we realised that they were just glorified hills, what they called "mountains" there.

Our exercises continued with us formed as a whole regiment, we couldn't blind ourselves to it.... something was brewing here in the West as well.

We were soon able to gather from the news that the affair in Narvik wasn't going as smoothly as they'd wanted. The battles were dragging on and the enemy was constantly bringing reinforcements into shore from across the sea.
We no longer believed in an early end to the war, what with the landing in Norway things had escalated for the first time.

"Maybe we'll already be sitting out front of a cafe in Paris by the summer," Mehrl dreamed. He said it during a break in one of our field exercises, we were sitting on the edge of a field and enjoying the springtime sun.
"Paris sounds good," I said, "but for that to happen we first need to get there alive, and then us with all our horses and Paris? I don't think you're right in the head, sunshine."
"And you've no sense for nice dreams!"
"For dreams that are completely and utterly impossible to fulfil, no, I've no sense for those."

"Otto you are, and remain, a spoilsport."

"And Otto," Grabner spun the matter even further, "think of the girls, there's supposed to be some nice birds in Paris, really cute, or are you not interested in girls anymore all of a sudden?"

"Leave him alone," laughed Mehrl, "Otto's engaged now, he doesn't know where he stands."

"What a load of crap you speak, you gossips," I got up, our break was finished and Wieser got us moving again.

It was the 23rd of April, and the day began like any other. The Sarge in Chief had finished his morning roll call, the platoon leaders had taken their divisions over for the rest of the training. Even we in the mortar platoon were marching off with Armsdorfer to our designated training grounds.

We had the place maybe a few hundred meters behind us when Hartmann, a man from the orderly room, caught up with us and delivered an apparently important message to the platoon leader since we turned around on the spot and marched back to the drill square.

The other platoons arrived back with us as well and a big guessing game began as to what was actually going on now. After a long wait they suddenly said, "you're dismissed to your quarters, clean your uniforms until further notice."

"Boys," said Itter, "something's going on, but what? That's the question here."

"Sure, we can see that too," grumbled Mehrl, "it won't be anything good, I reckon its goodbye comfy bed, and bright and jolly off to war."

Grabner grabbed his sewing kit from out of his rucksack, "Maybe we're going to Norway after all, Dietl is clearly having difficulties in Narvik."

"Difficulties?" said Itter, "let's just say it like it is, Dietl is in deep shit there."

"I would rather not say that so loud," Mehrl retorted.

"Ach what, poppycock, we're amongst friends amn't I right?"

"Well 'deep shit' is a bit harsh," Mehrl had found another missing button in his trousers, "a bit of difficulty yes, but Itter you're just a pessimist."

"At 10:00 hours report to the orderly room," at that moment a horse handler had called through the door.

"So we've another hour and a half," Gerl looked at his pocket watch, "I'll hit the sack for another hour, sod cleaning my uniform, Armsdorfer can go and get knotted."

The rest of us had no great desire to do much either it was no doubt just a pointless task to keep us busy, we were just not to lapse into the vice of doing nothing.

And so I started writing a letter to Mimi, Mehrl, Grabner and Itter had a go at playing Skat, or it could have been Bauernschnapser, I can't exactly remember anymore and it doesn't matter either.

We stood on the drill square at the time we were told, including everyone that was under command, even the cooks and the office staff.

The Sarge in Chief reported to Hauptmann Röhr, then the Hauptmann turned around to give us a small speech:

"The 2nd GD," began Röhr, "was alerted this morning. We have until tonight to be ready to march off. We have been chosen on the Führer's orders to relieve the strain on General Dietl in his difficult struggle against a more numerous enemy. In the course of the afternoon we will receive winter attire, this attire will be carried with us on support trains until our deployment. At 20:00 hours the platoon leaders will report to me with their divisions ready to march off, and now men to our new assignment with

gusto... tallyho!"
"Tallyho!"

And so Norway after all: A tremendous bustle seized the whole company. The many changes of location in the past weeks had kept us mobile, in just a few hours we stood ready for our big departure to Norway.

The loading up began in the night already and as the morning of a new day dawned, our train was already rolling towards Cologne .. towards new adventures........ "Farewell to the West!" We looked across the lovely acreage along the Rhine, resplendent in the first springtide, one last time.

– . –

Printed in Poland
by Amazon Fulfillment
Poland Sp. z o.o., Wrocław